Start Your Own

SELF-PUBLISHING BUSINESS

Additional titles in *Entrepreneur's* Startup Series

Start Your Own

Arts and Crafts Business

Automobile Detailing Business

Bar and Club

Bed and Breakfast

Blogging Business

Business on eBay

Car Wash

Child-Care Service

Cleaning Service

Clothing Store and More

Coaching Business

Coin-Operated Laundry

Construction and Contracting Business

Consulting Business

Day Spa and More

e-Business

Event Planning Business

Executive Recruiting Business

Fashion Accessories Business

Florist Shop and Other Floral Businesses

Food Truck Business

Freelance Writing Business and More

Freight Brokerage Business

Gift Basket Service

Grant-Writing Business

Graphic Design Business

Green Business

Hair Salon and Day Spa

Home Inspection Service

Import/Export Business

Information Marketing Business

Kid-Focused Business

Lawn Care or Landscaping Business

Mail Order Business

Medical Claims Billing Service

Net Services Business

Online Education Business

Personal Concierge Service

Personal Training Business

Pet Business and More

Pet-Sitting Business and More

Photography Business

Public Relations Business

Restaurant and More

Retail Business and More

Self-Publishing Business

Seminar Production Business

Senior Services Business

Travel Business and More

Tutoring and Test Prep Business

Vending Business

Wedding Consultant Business

Wholesale Distribution Business

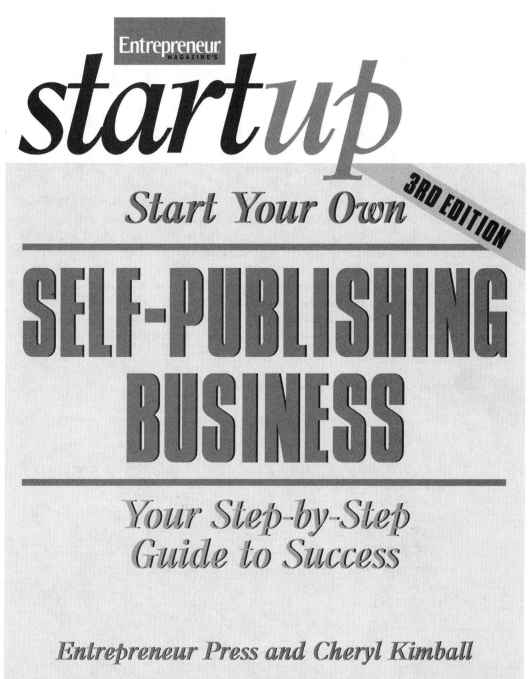

Entrepreneur MAGAZINE'S

start*up*

3RD EDITION

Start Your Own

SELF-PUBLISHING BUSINESS

Your Step-by-Step Guide to Success

Entrepreneur Press and Cheryl Kimball

EP
Entrepreneur.
Press

Entrepreneur Press, Publisher
Cover Design: Beth Hansen-Winter
Production and Composition: Eliot House Productions

This publication is designed to provide accurate and authoritative information in regard
to the subject matter covered. It is sold with the understanding that the publisher is not
engaged in rendering legal, accounting or other professional services. If legal advice or
other expert assistance is required, the services of a competent professional person should
be sought.

Library of Congress Cataloging-in-Publication Data
Kimball, Cheryl.
    Start your own self-publishing business/by Entrepreneur Press and Cheryl
Kimball.—3rd ed.
        p.   cm.
    Rev. ed. of: Start your own self-publishing business/by Entrepreneur Press and
Jennifer Dorsey. 2nd ed. c2007.
    Includes bibliographical references and index.
    ISBN–13: 978-1-59918-437-1 (alk. paper)
    ISBN–10: 1-59918-437-0 (alk. paper)
        1. Self-publishing. 2. New business enterprises—Management. I. Dorsey,
Jennifer. Start your own self-publishing business. II. Entrepreneur Media, Inc. III.
Title.
    Z285.5.A33 2012
    070.5'93—dc23   2012000945

Printed in the United States of America

16 15 14 13 12   10 9 8 7 6 5 4 3 2 1

Contents

▲

Preface

You've chosen this book for a very special reason: You're planning on starting your own business as a self-publisher. You'll be treading ground that most people fantasize about but never actually do. You will be writing your own book and then seeing it through production and promotion to success on bookstore shelves.

You're stepping into exhilarating—and frightening—territory. Owning your own business of any kind means you're the boss; you make the rules and lay down the law. It also means you cannot let somebody else worry about making enough to cover expenses, and you can't pass that intimidating distributor or pesky printer on to a higher authority. You are the higher authority. Add to all these normal new-business anxieties the very natural fear of putting your writing project—your creative heart and soul—out in public where you risk failure and rejection. These are all valid concerns. But concern is not the same as can't, so don't worry. Instead, keep reading.

You're probably contemplating becoming a self-publisher for one or more of the following reasons:

- You've been an author for years and have collected enough rejection slips from conventional publishers to pave the Florida Turnpike.
- You've written books that have been produced by conventional publishers, but now you want to take creative, editorial, and financial control of your own work.
- You want to establish yourself as an authority in your field—be it medicine, law, golf, culinary arts, or whatever—and you believe your own book on the subject will be a smart promotional tool. Maybe you even have your own successful practice, so you already know how to run a business.
- You have a message that's important and can help people, and you believe your own book on the subject will be an effective tool for getting the word out.
- You believe the self-publishing industry is booming, and you're eager to share in the excitement and willing to take a chance on success.

Which did you choose? It doesn't matter, because there is no wrong answer. Any of these responses is entirely correct so long as you realize they all involve a lot of learning and a lot of hard work. They can also involve a heck of a lot of fun, as well as a tremendous amount of personal and professional satisfaction.

Our goal in this book is to tell you everything you need to know to:

- Decide whether self-publishing is the right business for you
- Get your book written and your business started
- Successfully promote your book

We have interviewed many people out there on the front lines of the industry—all around the country—to learn the nitty-gritty, hands-on tasks, tips, and tricks to successful self-publishing. We've set aside places for them to tell their own stories and give their own hard-won advice—a sort of virtual round-table discussion group with you placed right in the thick of things. (For a listing of these successful business owners, see Appendix C at the back of this book.) We've broken our chapters into manageable sections on every aspect of startup, production, and promotion. And we've left some space for your creativity to soar.

We've packed our pages with helpful tips so that you can get up and running as quickly as possible, complete with contacts and sources in the Appendix to jump-start your research. So pour a giant mug of coffee, take a deep breath, turn down the phones, turn off the TV, set your brain to learning mode, and let's go!

Acknowledgments

To Jere—time to write a book!

y great appreciation goes to Rich Mintzer, freelance colleague who provides moral support and a helping hand when I need one, including with the interviews in this book, and Karen Billipp, Eliot House Productions, with whom it is always a pleasure to do a book project.

The
Write Stuff

Self-publishing is a hot industry today and growing hotter all the time. New self-publishers as well as new services for self-publishers and authors are springing up all over the country. Writing stars like Stephen King to publishing powerhouses like Random House are rushing to join the new generation of self-publishers.

▲

Despite the proliferation of movies, TV programs, and videos with which we find ourselves surrounded, Americans read books—a lot of books. According to a report from the National Endowment for the Arts (NEA), adult reading of literature (defined as novels, short stories, plays, and poetry) increased 7 percent from their previous study, the first time the reading rate has risen in the 25 years that the study has been conducted. Book consumers eagerly gobble up everything from nonfiction recipes for improving health, wealth, and spirituality to sci-fi. "We are a nation hungry for information," says Marilyn Ross, an early proponent of self-publishing and co-founder of SPAN, the Small Publishers Association of North America. "People have more leisure time with which they may choose to entertain, educate, or motivate themselves," explains Terry Nathan, executive director of Independent Book Publishers Association (IBPA). "Also, people have developed niche interest areas and want to read all they can on a specific area. Schools have been stressing reading for some time now, not to mention the variety of products available for any age group to read and/or listen to."

An R.R. Bowker report on the state of publishing in 2010, however, shows a dramatically changing complexion of the book-buying market—one that could spell even greater demand for self-published work. With a decrease in brick-and-mortar bookstores comes an increase in online book sales—a self-publisher with a print-on-demand or electronic book sold from an internet storefront is a significant part of the bookselling game in today's world.

This changing market, ironically, has also opened some doors for self-published works to get noticed by the traditional publishers—instead of taking on the risk of a new author, they are letting authors take the risk of publishing a first book and then, if all goes well, the traditional publisher may come knocking on your door.

Tradition, Tradition

So, just what is a self-publisher? As you have probably figured out, it's a person who writes a book, sees it through each step of production—from the artwork for the front cover to typesetting and design to printing—and then goes out and sells and markets it on his or her own.

In the traditional world of book publishing, an author pens a work (in the case of fiction and poetry collections) or an

> **Fun Fact**
> Self-publishing isn't new. Famous self-published authors include Mark Twain, Walt Whitman, D.H. Lawrence of the infamous *Lady Chatterley's Lover*, and Edgar Rice Burroughs, creator of the original jungle hunk *Tarzan*.

in-depth proposal (typically for nonfiction, which relies as much if not more on the information provided than the quality of the writing) and then goes out shopping for a publisher. Usually this is on par with trying for a million-dollar home loan with bad credit, no job, and no fixed address. In other words, it's not easy.

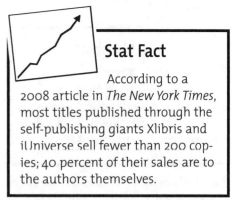

Stat Fact

According to a 2008 article in *The New York Times*, most titles published through the self-publishing giants Xlibris and iUniverse sell fewer than 200 copies; 40 percent of their sales are to the authors themselves.

The major publishing houses (as well as many of the midsize houses) have become more fixated than ever on the bottom line to the point where they cannot and will not take a chance on any project that does not come with as close to an automatic guarantee of success as possible. Tell-all biographies of fallen royalty and rock stars, and ghostwritten autobiographies of movie stars and megafinanciers are shoe-ins. So, too, are novels by proven winners like Suzanne Collins (*The Hunger Games* series) and James Patterson, or business, finance, and self-help books by professional speakers who already command thousands of dollars per engagement. The unknown writer with a new story to tell or a new idea to present faces an uphill battle.

This is not to say it can't be done. New voices are heard all the time. J.K. Rowling, author of the celebrated *Harry Potter* series, for instance, was a first-time writer and welfare mum when her first book was bought by a British publisher, Bloomsbury Children's Books. But like the thousands of aspiring actors who haunt Hollywood hoping for a break, there are far more hopeful authors than published ones.

Travails of a Novice

The novice author's travails don't end when the sale is made. Let's say you're clever as well as lucky—you've written a top-notch book, and you've managed to sell it to a publishing house. Your work is done, you think. You can sit back and wait for the money and the fame to pour in. Well, not quite.

True, you don't need to worry about the cost of the production of the book, but you don't get much input either. Although typically you will get to look at a couple possible cover designs for your opinion, the publisher, who is fronting all the money, will get the final say—sometimes just for the simple fact that decisions need to be made and you are not in the room. Publishers with good author care will do the best they can to include you in the key decisions about your book, you will get to review—and veto—editing, but ultimately, the publisher gets to make decisions without you if need be—unless you are a key author and can negotiate checks and balances in your contract.

Then, after all the blood, sweat, and tears you (and presumably the publisher) have poured into its birth, your book may be released and then abandoned. Most publishing houses spend little time, effort, or money on promoting new books from unknown writers. The vast majority of published authors discover, to their dismay, that the publisher makes no promotional efforts whatsoever. All those autograph parties, book signings, media appearances, author tours, bookstore displays, print advertisements, and newspaper and magazine articles turn out to exist only in the writers' fantasies. And with no promotions to help pave the way to bestsellerdom, all those published books die a quick and untimely death. They don't even have time to languish on the shelves. If they don't somehow sell themselves in a matter of four months to a year, they're yanked out of the stores and the distributor's warehouses, and consigned to book limbo for the rest of eternity.

The Star-Maker

If all this sounds like unrelenting doom and gloom, take heart. There is an upside alternative—you can take the self-publishing route! As a self-publisher, you maintain total creative control of your work. You get to choose how it will look—everything from the size and style of the type to the size of the margins to the dimensions of the book itself. You choose the graphics, line art, or photos that decorate it inside and out. You decide on hardcover, softcover, e-book—all or some of the three. You choose the layout—whether you'll have sidebars (those mini-articles that fit beside the running text), tip boxes, or pull quotes (oversized quotes pulled from the text). You decide on the cover price, which is a major factor in how well the book will sell. You also decide on how you'll sell it: through distributors, by direct mail, through specialty retailers, through catalogs, online.

Perhaps most important of all, you handle the sales and promotions. You become a star-maker. You conceive and carry out a campaign of press releases, media appearances, author tours, internet exposure, media articles—whatever you decide it will take and whatever you want to do—to make your written baby a success.

The Reasons Why

Like just about everything in life, there are some cons that go with the pros of becoming a self-publisher. One is expense. You, not the New York (or New Jersey or wherever) publisher, pay all the costs of production and printing. Another is effort. You have to be willing to expend the energy to plan and then carry out a marketing campaign, for which you will incur more costs. A third potential negative is that you have to have moxie. You must be ready, willing, and able to blow your own horn. This is true for any small-business owner, but even more so for the self-publisher. If you are a shrinking violet, you won't get far. Despite these cons, there are a host of good reasons that lead bright, creative people down the self-publishing lane.

No One Else Will

Some writers take the self-publisher route because no one else will publish their work. Traditional publishers send rejection slips for many reasons other than bad prose. Often manuscripts don't fit the publisher's mold because they're too long or too short, the target market is too narrow, the subject matter is too obscure, the characters or setting don't fit a predetermined matrix, or they "don't quite fit our current guidelines" for any of a dozen elusive factors.

Once upon a time, editors who detected a spark of genius (or just plain mass-market saleability) worked with writers, nurturing and guiding them to the development of a terrific book. Now, with the fierce concentration on the bottom line, editors have become minions of the marketing department instead of shepherds of creativity. So even when they spot a new writer with budding talent, they can't offer a contract unless the book fits the marketing department's "blockbuster" mold to a tee.

A main ingredient that publishers (and literary agents, who sell projects to publishers) are looking for is an author with an established "platform." If you are a professional (lawyer, doctor, psychologist, accountant) who already has a speaking circuit drawing sell-out crowds to your lectures and workshops, you have a ready-made "platform" from which to sell a book you've written. A large percentage of your audience will want to buy your book. If your audiences are comprised of 1,000 people at a whack, a publisher will find your platform to be a strong one from which to sell a book—if you do two speaking engagements a month that draw 1,000 each, you can do the math. Twenty-four such engagements a year can sell several thousand books and produce enough word-of-mouth promotion (people who went to the lecture and bought the book will tell their friends and colleagues, some of whom will buy the book without having gone to a lecture)—well, the upshot is, these days especially, these are the figures that publishers want to be guaranteed.

Why, you may be thinking, should you give that business to the publisher? If you are drawing the crowds to begin with, why not produce the book yourself knowing that you are likely going to make your investment back? Why not, indeed!

> ### Smart Tip
>
> **Tip...**
>
> What's the difference between a self-publisher, an independent publisher, and a small press? A self-publisher produces her own work, while the latter two may publish their own work but also publish the works of other authors.

Control Issue

Authors who have been published by traditional houses, only to find their work hopelessly mangled, sometimes turn self-publisher for their next books to maintain creative control. We have already talked about some of the ways publishers can tamper with the integrity of your book. And there are more. With the proper (often standard) contract, they can obtain the rights to your book but fail to publish it. There should be a clause in your contract that limits the amount of time the publisher can sit on the project without getting it out to the market—but then, if you choose to publish it yourself, you have lost all that time. Some contracts are written so that your publisher gets first-refusal options on your next book or two—which can be great for all concerned or not, especially if you feel they ill-treated the previous book. As a self-publisher, you don't have any of these worries.

Money, Honey

Writers often become self-publishers to keep the lion's share of the profits. In traditional publishing, the author is paid on a royalty basis. This has nothing to do with being crowned king or princess, or even being handed a minor dukedom, but instead refers to the percentage of profits from the book. It can get as complex as quantum physics, but basically it works like this: The writer is paid an advance against royalties, or a sum of money that often represents the minimum royalties the publisher expects the book to earn. Authors usually get half the advance when they sign the contract and begin writing the book, and the other half when the book is completed to the publisher's satisfaction. After the book hits the stores, the writer generally receives between 3 and 7.5 percent of the book's net sales (more on "net" in a minute). These are the royalties. If the book never earns more than the advance, the author never sees another dime, which is what happens in most cases. And advances can be shockingly small: As little as $3,000 for a 50,000-word book is not uncommon.

Notice we said the royalties are paid on net sales, not gross. A book that retails for $14.95 on the bookstore shelf is not bought by the bookstore for $14.95; they have to make some profit. So the publisher discounts the book as much as 60 percent to the end seller, which pays only $8.97 to the publisher. The author's 7.5 percent royalty from this tallies in at 67 cents. Kind of scary, huh?

This means the publisher, which isn't exactly knocking itself out to promote the book, must sell a fraction over 4,477 books for the author to earn back that $3,000 advance on her royalties. When you factor in that many publishers only print 5,000 books on an initial (and probably final) run, you can see that the author is not going to get rich, or even keep body and soul together, on the books' proceeds.

As a self-publisher, you get to keep everything your book earns over and above the actual expenses involved with production and promotion. Instead of cents on the dollar, you'll earn the dollars themselves. Self-publishing is not a get-rich-quick operation by any stretch, but it can definitely be more financially rewarding than going the traditional route. However, you also need to do the sales and marketing to sell enough copies of your book to cover the cost of creating it—and more, if you want to make a profit.

Career Springboard

Sometimes making a direct profit on your book isn't the main goal for publishing the book. Many self-publishers use their books as career jump-starters. If you're planning to segue from your current position into a new life as a professional speaker or consultant, a book can open a lot of doors. It gives you instant credibility. People think that since you're a published author who's written a book on website marketing or financial planning (or whatever your subject is), then you must be an expert. It never occurs to them that you and your publisher are one and the same entity—and they don't need to know.

It goes without saying, of course, that you do need to know your stuff when you write nonfiction. If you offer people information, it's up to you to deliver the real thing. But it is also true that a book—whether traditionally or self-published—is the sort of validation you can't get from anything else.

Make a Difference

Still other authors self-publish to make a difference in the lives of the people around them. They see a need and a way to fill it through their writing, and they feel compelled to put the two together. Anna Jaworski of Temple, Texas, wrote and published her first book after her infant son was diagnosed with a serious heart defect in 1994.

"I immediately asked for information about the heart defect," Anna says. "When the doctors wouldn't give me anything, I started to seek information myself. The only information I could find was dated and very discouraging. I wanted something inspirational and informative. I decided to put together a booklet of helpful information because I was afraid I would not be able to remember everything I needed to know. I wanted a 'reference' book—something I could refer back to when we were having surgery or complications."

> ## Fun Fact
> Self-published success stories aren't limited to those that happened a century or two ago. Two hits are *The Celestine Prophecy* by James Redfield and *The Christmas Box* by Richard Paul Evans. These titles were self-published, then picked up by major publishers—Warner Books and Simon & Schuster, respectively.

Anna soon began sharing her research and inspiration with the parents of other children with the same problem. "I had started a rudimentary support group when my son was in the hospital," she explains. "Even though our children had the fourth most common heart defect (and heart defects are the number-one birth defect in the country), we couldn't find anything in print. In 1996, I decided to publish the booklet I had started writing. I called or sent letters to the parents I had shared information with and asked them for feedback. They requested more information on certain topics that I researched and wrote up. Then I added my son's story at the beginning of the book. My booklet grew to the size of a book!"

Anna knew she had a product that could help people who desperately wanted information. But convincing a publisher was another story. "I queried every appropriate publisher I could find, and all of them sent me back nice rejection letters stating that my intended audience was too small," she recalls. "My husband and I decided that even if we only sold one book, and it helped one family, it would be worth our time and trouble." Anna's Baby Hearts Press now has four books in print, two that she wrote and two collections of essays she edited. Anna also saw the opportunities in e-book publishing and offers her books in electronic editions as well.

Do It for Love

A final—but oh-so-important—reason for becoming a self-publisher is for the sheer joy of it. This is a business that is going to take up a great deal of your time, effort, energy, creativity, and the contents of your wallet. So if you're going to do it, you must love doing it. That's how the majority of self-publishers feel. They love writing, reading, and publishing. They have a story inside themselves that's bursting to be told, and they feel they have to get it down on paper and out in print. There's no choice. Even when the actual writing process seems painful (as it does to just about every author at times), they wouldn't have it any other way. Answering the call of the creative muse is fulfilling, addictive, and just plain fun.

Profits from Pages

How much can you expect to earn as a self-publisher? It really depends on how hard you choose to work at it, what your vision is for your company and your products, and your books' market appeal. You may pen the definitive tome on the mating habits of the earthworm, featuring breathless prose and four-color photos, but you're unlikely to find yourself with a runaway mass-market bestseller on your hands. If, on the other hand, you plan and produce books that appeal to a significant market, you have the potential to do well. (We'll explore market research secrets later on in Chapter 3.)

Industry experts are loath to quote potential annual earnings because they can vary radically from publisher to publisher. Gross annual incomes among the publishers we interviewed for this book ranged from under $10,000 for a newbie to an anticipated $500,000 for a 15-year veteran. "Marketing is the key," says Ross of SPAN. "You can make a living, you can make a comfortable living, or you can starve on the vine." Self-publishing is a business venture and not just an artistic one.

Mary Embree, founder of and now a consultant for SPAWN (Small Publishers, Artists, and Writers Network) and a literary consultant, agrees with this line of thought. "I know one author who wrote and self-published a book aimed at the home-schooling industry and sold 5,000 copies the first year," Embree says. "I know a lot of self-publishers who ordered a printing of 1,000 books and still have 950 gathering dust in the garage after three or four years. That's the norm. Self-publishing may be disappointing unless the author has a workable plan to sell the books."

The financial picture doesn't have to reflect doom and gloom. "Books are fairly inexpensive to produce, and the markup is high," advises Dan Poynter, a self-publishing guru and author of best-selling titles on the subject. "You can produce one for $2 and sell it for $20." There are many expenses that will bridge the gap between these two figures considerably. But, according to Poynter, your gross does

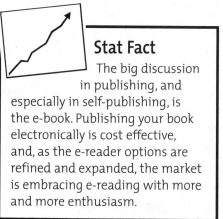

Stat Fact
The big discussion in publishing, and especially in self-publishing, is the e-book. Publishing your book electronically is cost effective, and, as the e-reader options are refined and expanded, the market is embracing e-reading with more and more enthusiasm.

▲

not have to be as high as in other industries because with lower overhead costs, your net is higher.

Poynter makes another positive point for entering into self-publishing: "You do not have to make a lot of money as a self-publisher if your book contributes to your ability to sell other goods and services." If you're a chiropractor, for example, and you write and promote a book on back care, you position yourself to become a sought-after expert in your field—one with a higher earning potential.

Starter Fuel

As the old adage goes, "You need money to make money." In other words, you need startup funds. As a self-publisher, you've got it better than many new business owners, like those who decide to open a coffee house or hardware store. You can start out homebased, which means you won't need to worry about leasing office space. You won't need employees right off the bat—if at all—and you don't need to plunk down funds for specialized equipment and inventory.

All you really need is a computer, software, a printer, a fax machine and/or scanner, and internet access—and you may already have some of these items. Your other major expenses will be for book printing and for sales and promotions.

So what's the bottom line? "It can be minimal: a DBA ["doing business as"] license, letterhead, phone, answering service, fax, and email access," says Nathan of IBPA. "You can work out of your home to start and grow into a company, as many successful self-publishers have. However, many of these publishers have moved from self-publishers to niche publishers, who publish other people's works in a specific genre. These are the successful ones."

"Startup costs are another question for which there is no clear answer," advises Embree of SPAWN. "It depends on how many copies you are going to order from the printer, how it is printed (hardcover or paperback), how much you can do for yourself, and how much you will have to hire out (such as editing and typesetting)."

Startup costs are also extremely dependent on the size of your book—page count as well as outside dimensions—how much artwork is involved, how much equipment (such as computer and printer) you'll need to buy, how elaborate that equipment needs to be, and how creative you'll get with your promotional budget. As a ballpark figure, you can expect to spend $10,000 to $29,000 to get up and running, including printing and starting to promote your first book.

"Our first book cost us about $11,000 to print the first 5,000 copies," says Steve Carlson, a self-publisher in Hinesburg, Vermont, who now also offers consulting

The Risk Factor

Besides earnings and startup costs, two other important aspects to consider are risk and stability. There's no point in throwing yourself and your money into a new business only to discover that it's about as risk-free as a first-class ticket on the original Titanic, or that it's a fad whose time has already passed. You want a business that has staying power.

Self-publishing is likely to be around for the long haul. We live in the Information Age, and people are interested in getting "content" from all sources, including printed books, about how to lead smarter, happier, healthier, and wealthier lives.

Readers are also always in the market for entertainment—from mysteries to romances. If you can produce a book that fulfills this need, and follow it up with another volume geared toward the same interested readers, you've got a winning ticket to a successful business.

The self-publisher's risk factor is moderate. You can't guarantee the success of a book unless you're adept with a crystal ball. But if you choose your market wisely, target it closely, and work diligently at sales and promotions, you've got a fair chance at success.

services and publishes books by other writers. "Fortunately, they sold out quite quickly and we went on to a second printing. The business has always paid for itself, although there were lean times in the early years when we didn't make enough to give ourselves decent paychecks."

Personality Plus

Besides earnings, startup costs, and risk and stability factors, there's one more important element to consider when deciding if self-publishing is the business for you: personality. Not everybody has the makings of a self-publishing pro. This is a career that calls for lots of time spent one-on-one with your computer and nobody else. If you're the type who thrives in the hustle and bustle corporate world, with lots of other bodies and brains sharing your work space, then you may want to think twice.

Stat Fact

Despite the rapid rise in the age of electronic content, don't for a minute dismiss the demise of the printed book. Christopher Kimball, founder of America's Test Kitchen, said in a recent edition of *Publishers Weekly* that the *Cook's Illustrated* publisher had their best year ever in books. Their *From Our Grandmothers' Kitchens* sold 22,000 copies in three eight-minute QVC airings!

Self-publishing also requires that you have a strong sense of what your target market wants to read. You don't have to have your finger on the pulse of the entire nation, but you do—like Anna J. in Temple, Texas, who had intimate knowledge of the experience of a child with a heart condition—need an unerring instinct for the topics that will strike a chord in your particular audience.

You will also need megadoses of talent and creativity. You can get all sorts of assistance with grammar, punctuation, and spelling, but if you can't tell a riveting story that will keep your reader spellbound (and this counts for nonfiction as well!), you definitely need to reconsider. This doesn't mean that only Pulitzer Prize winners or those who won every creative writing contest in high school need apply. One of the most important aspects of writing is that you know your subject, that you're passionate about it, and that your passion shines through. The rest you can learn.

To Boldly Go

To accompany the talent and creativity, you must have follow-through. If you're a dabbler, who thinks writing and then publishing a book might be fun, but you have a penchant for dropping projects before they're half-finished, you won't get far as a self-publisher. Lots of people would like to write a book, but they never get past the wishful thinking stage. As a self-publisher, you'll have to be able to write that book in a timely manner and then see it through all the stages of publishing.

As a final, but terrifically important character trait, you'll need the chutzpah to get out there and promote your books. You can boldly go on TV and radio, or stay discreetly behind the scenes sending out press releases and news articles, but if you really want to succeed, you'll do both. Sales and promotions are the lifeblood of the self-published book, so you'll have to be gutsy at selling a product you truly believe in—your own books.

All Walks of Life

Self-publishers come from all walks of life. The ones we interviewed for this book had a variety of alternate careers including educator, congressional assistant, and

Stat Fact

According to foner.com, bookstore sales were up by around $1 billion, from approximately $13.5 billion to $14.5 billion, in 2010 compared to 2009.

branch manager of a state environmental protection agency.

The tip here is that all these entrepreneurs figured out how to make their interests and their backgrounds work for them in their new careers. They have taken the skills and enthusiasm they had already acquired and applied them to the self-publishing business.

Caring for Your Own

Steve C. in Hinesburg, Vermont, has been a successful independent publisher for 15 years, with more than 20 titles under his belt. "We describe our niche as nonfiction to improve the quality of life," Steve says. "That's a much broader niche than most small presses take on. However, I'd rather publish any book I like than stay with a specific narrow niche. Several of our titles have been on death and dying, but there's no way I'd want to spend full time on those issues." That's a personal enjoyment decision, not a sound business decision. Although their company has expanded into consulting services and publishing books by other people, Steve and his wife started in self-publishing.

"I started in 1986," Steve recalls. "I had left my job as a congressional assistant at that time to care for my mother, who was dying of AIDS. My wife, Lisa, was also tiring of her job as a teacher. She had researched how to care for one's own dead without the help of a funeral director and was eager to write a book on the subject. Her book was the first we published."

Since then, Lisa has left publishing to become executive director of a national nonprofit organization to protect the rights of consumers in their dealings with the funerary industry. Steve has developed other businesses for small presses, including a fulfillment, or order-filling, company that he's since sold and a business software program called Publishers' Assistant.

"Publishers' Assistant is used by hundreds of publishers, mostly relatively small presses," Steve says. "However, that has now become a partnership with my programmer's company, so my involvement is reduced. As a result, my publishing house is now a full-time, one-person company, and I am devoting almost all of my working hours to publishing books."

Fun Fact

Good writing transcends age, gender, and time. The eternally popular tale of mankind's botched attempts at creation, *Frankenstein*, was written by Mary Wollstonecraft Shelley when she was just 21 years old.

▲

Machine Guns and Memoirs

Gary S. in Panama City Beach, Florida, is a state environmental protection agent by day and self-publisher by night. Gary's niche is the biographies of World War II veterans—not the celebrated captains and generals, but average soldiers with their own exciting stories to tell from the front lines. "I started to self-publish in 1999, after I wrote my father's World War II account, and soon realized there was a need for this type of product for veterans," Gary says. "Self-publishing worked best because the men for whom I was writing wanted their stories out as soon as possible, and this was the quickest way to accomplish this goal."

Branching Out

Anna J., who self-published a book about children with heart defects to help other parents through her own experience, also published an inspirational title and branched out to publish the works of other authors who write on similar health-related topics. She transformed her one-woman sole proprietorship into a nonprofit organization with a staff to help with the workload.

SPAWNing a Successful Startup

An Interview with SPAWN Executive Director Patricia Fry

Patricia Fry has contributed hundreds of articles to about 260 different magazines, such as *Writer's Digest, Writers' Journal, Cat Fancy, PMA Independent, Entrepreneur, Mature Outlook, The World and I, Your Health*, and many others. She is also the author of more than two dozen books, many related to writing and publishing, such as the 300-page *The Right Way to Write, Publish and Sell Your Book* (Matilija Press, 2006). She established Matilija Press in 1983 and has produced several of her books through this company. She also has books with traditional royalty publishers.

SPAWNing a Successful Startup, continued

Currently the Executive Director of SPAWN, Patricia was in on the ground floor of SPAWN 11 years ago working alongside founder Mary Embree as she established this networking organization.

Today, the articles she writes pertain mainly to writing and publishing. She also works with other authors and freelance writers on their projects and speaks at several writers conferences throughout the United States each year.

1. What are the hot trends in small publishing?

For inexperienced, hopeful authors, the fee-based . . . publishing service is big. Typically, when someone finishes his or her first book manuscript, they will immediately start searching for a publisher. A Google search takes them promptly to iUniverse, AuthorHouse, PublishAmerica, or other such companies. The author sends his manuscript as requested, it is accepted on the spot, and, in his exuberance, he signs any contract that is put in front of him.

For the slightly savvy author, the trend I see most often is an attempt to get representation by a literary agent and/or land a contract with a major publisher. This author typically quits too soon and either self-publishes or gives up altogether.

For established small publishers, the trend seems to be toward much greater involvement, more industry savvy through research, more creativity in the way they promote their books—more enthusiasm, more hands-on, more success.

2. Are there any categories that stand out sales-wise? Is nonfiction still tops?

I see more memoirs produced by small publishers and one-title authors than practically any other category. These are military memoirs as well as stories of abuse, illness, death of a loved one, overcoming mental illness, spiritual encounters, ancestor history, and even a journal of a Little League parent. Fiction e-books are overwhelmingly outselling nonfiction and children's e-books. Memoirs had their day, but I understand that they are not popular with publishers now unless the author is a celebrated person.

Overall, in the industry, religious/spiritual/inspirational topics are always high on the list of bestselling books. Young adult and juvenile books are on the rise. But, yes, it looks as though nonfiction does sell in greater numbers than does fiction.

SPAWNing a Successful Startup, continued

3. What are your thoughts on e-books? Is it a viable market for small/self-publishers?

With the advent of sophisticated e-book readers and easier access to services and programs that convert manuscripts to the various e-book formats, e-books have definitely come of age. Some independent publishers today are opting for e-books—many are publishing both a print and an e-book version.

4. Would you recommend fee-based publishing? Why or why not?

I rarely recommend them to authors, but I don't bad-mouth them, either. We here at SPAWN strongly recommend that any author who is contemplating a relationship with a fee-based publishing service take two important steps first. Study the publishing industry so that you know your publishing options and the consequences of your decisions. And write a book proposal so that you are acutely aware of the validity of your book, your target audience, and how you will reach this audience. In other words, don't rush blindly into publishing. Do your homework.

Once armed with enough knowledge to make an intelligent decision on your book's behalf, no matter which publishing option you choose, make sure that everything you discuss with the sales rep or publisher is in writing and have an intellectual properties attorney look over the contract.

5. Where should a prospective new small/self-publisher start in regard to market research?

With regard to searching for a publisher, I suggest my book, *Publish Your Book, Proven Strategies and Resources for the Enterprising Author* (Allworth Press), as well as market directories such as *Literary Marketplace* and *Writer's Market*. Also, look at books similar to the one you are writing in local mega-bookstores and see who published them. Contact those publishers.

In regard to book promotion, start by writing a book proposal. Your book proposal will reveal your target audience. Where are they? Where do they shop? What websites do they visit? What magazines do they read? What conferences do they attend? Answering these questions is your first step toward creating your book promotion plan. And then read *Promote Your Book: Over 250 Proven, Low-Cost Tips and Techniques for the Enterprising Author* by Patricia Fry (Allworth Press).

SPAWNing a Successful Startup, continued

6. What's your best advice for someone considering their own publishing business?

In most cases, I would rather see an author self-publish (establish his/her own publishing company) instead of going with a fee-based POD publishing service. I believe that a self-published author is generally more committed to his book—has a more intimate relationship with it—than one who turns the responsibilities over to a publishing service. In most cases, a self-published author generates more sales and more profit than does one who goes with a fee-based POD publishing service.

My hallmark presentation at writers and publishers conferences revolves around the book proposal. And I strongly recommend that any author of any type of book write a detailed book proposal. This is especially important when you decide to self-publish. Publishing is a business, and a book proposal is your business plan.

7. Are there any organizations (besides yours) that you think are valuable for a small publisher?

I would recommend Independent Book Publishers Association (IBPA) and Small Publishers Association of North America (SPAN).

8. Tell us a bit about your organization.

Mary Embree founded SPAWN (Small Publishers, Artists, and Writers Network) in 1996 in Ventura County, California, as a face-to-face networking organization for anyone interested in publishing. She envisioned having meetings where authors could connect with illustrators, where graphic artists could connect with freelance writers who needed brochures designed, etc., and where writers could meet publishers, for example. Within a few months, there were three chapters meeting once a month each in three different counties. Authors were sharing information and resources with one another, working relationships were formed, and everyone was learning from the various expert speakers at every meeting.

About ten years ago, we ceased the face-to-face meetings and turned to the internet where we continue to provide information, resources, and networking opportunities. We have a free monthly newsletter. Sign up for SPAWNews at www.spawn.org. Members receive the newsletter, plus a Market Update that is absolutely brimming with opportunities and information for anyone interested in or involved in the publishing field. We have an online discussion group, plus

▲

SPAWNing a Successful Startup, continued

we offer members the opportunity to include their books and services in the SPAWN Catalog of Members' Books and Services and display and sell their books at various book festivals throughout the year.

Check out Patricia's websites at www.matilijapress.com and www.patriciafry.com and her blog site at www.matilijapress.com/publishingblog. She welcomes dialogue with other writers and publishers, so drop her a line at Plfry620@yahoo.com.

Seeing into the Future

One final issue to consider is the industry prognosis: Will self-publishing be around well into the future, or will it go the way of the cassette tape and pet rock in a matter of months?

Self-publishing has slowly and progressively become "legitimate" over the course of the last two or three decades, but has really come into its own in the past four to five years. And with new outlets for self-publishers, from dotcom bookstores to print-on-demand and e-publishing service providers, the path is wide open for the self-publisher to compete on a far more even footing with the big guys than ever before.

Technology has made it possible for small independent publishers to succeed. With home desktop computers and publishing programs, self-publishers can do much of the work that once had to be farmed out to somebody else at considerable expense. This, coupled with the demise of many of the major publishers, has forced wholesalers and distributors to take self-publishers seriously. It has also forced major publishers to take small presses seriously.

Since many major publishers no longer have the go-ahead to nurture new talent and take creative chances in their own corporate worlds, they leave it to self-publishers to be the incubators of new talent, and then negotiate lucrative deals for successful new titles. This is a win-win situation that isn't likely to change in the near future. In short, the self-publishing trend has taken off in a very positive way.

Self-Publishing
101

OK, you've read through Chapter 1 and decided

that self-publishing is the business for you. Terrific! But before you

can produce that bestseller, you have to know what you're doing.

So don your virtual school jacket and step into the hallowed halls

of Self-Publishing 101.

Ah, Vanity

We've already explored the differences between traditional publishing houses and the self-publisher. You know that the self-publisher not only pens that great novel or nonfiction book, but also sees it through every step of production and printing, and then nurtures its sales and promotion. As a self-publisher, you can keep your books in print for as long as you can make sales—even if those sales are as few as five or ten per month. In contrast, traditional publishing houses may not keep your book alive for more than a year or two, despite the fact that a considerable untapped market may still exist.

Self-publishing isn't new. It's been practiced for hundreds of years. Writers we now consider literary luminaries—including Edgar Allan Poe, Virginia Woolf, and James Joyce—went the do-it-yourself route with great success.

But until fairly recently—within probably the last 20 years—self-publishing was basically the jurisdiction of the eccentric few. The literary world turned up its collective nose at writers who were self-published. It generally meant that your work was so awful that no one else in his or her right mind would print it, and that you had turned to a vanity publisher—always a bad move.

Subsidy publishers are a separate breed of publisher. They are distinct from traditional publishers in that a subsidy publisher does not take on any of the financial risk. You not only hand over your manuscript to them but you hand them the money needed to do all the tasks required to get your manuscript into print, publicized, and sold to the world. The prices charged by subsidy publishers are typically considerably higher than the going rates to have this kind of work done if you were to contract it à la carte to the various outside contractors that you need—copyeditor, proofreader, designer, printer, publicist, distribution house, etc.

As a budding self-publisher, don't let anyone confuse your own legitimate publishing business with a subsidy publisher.

The Three Graces

One really favorable aspect of self-publishing is that it forms a perfect bond with two other complementary businesses—seminar promotions and mail order, which lend themselves ideally to

Smart Tip

New titles that a publisher has just released are called its frontlist. Old standbys, the books that are no longer new but are steady sellers, are called the backlist.

one another and to the business of self-publishing. Together, these businesses make the ultimate trio.

All Fired Up

One of the best ways to promote your books and encourage sales is by giving seminars, workshops, and lectures. People who listen to your presentations get fired up. They are excited about the subject and want to take immediate action. And what better action than to buy your books, conveniently displayed at the back of the room? Seminar professionals have long understood this concept, which is known as making BOR or back-of-the-room sales.

You might think that giving talks is not your style, but think again. As an author/publisher, you'll be promoting your products at everything from miniworkshops at your local library and bookstore to media appearances on local TV. Chances are, you've written a book on a topic you know quite a lot about. Seminars are a logical extension, and they can be fun!

Books by Mail

Another top-notch way to sell your books is through direct mail, which is another term for mail order—where you are promoting directly from your business to the end consumer. Traditionally, publishers have sold their products to their readers indirectly—through special book distributors who sell the products to bookstores (that sell them to consumers). This method isn't always the best one for the new self-publisher, and indeed it should not be the only one.

Distributors typically demand a discount of anywhere between 40 and 60 percent off the cover price of a book, which effectively skims the cream off the publisher's profits before he or she has even considered other costs, like shipping and promotions. In addition, book distributors frequently don't work as hard to sell for small presses as they do for the giants like Random House.

As a self-publisher, you don't have to go solely with the distributor route. You'll have targeted a special market niche that's already interested in your particular topics even before you print your first book. It makes sense to sell directly to those readers via mail order. This gives you a portion of your sales that you don't have to cough up heavy discounts for —and your readers even pay the shipping costs.

We'll come back to seminars and mail order in Chapter 10. For now, keep these options in mind, since they can work wonders for the self-publisher.

Stat Fact

Do men really read more nonfiction than their female counterparts do? According to a recent report from the National Endowment for the Arts (NEA), yes. Just over 62 percent of men who read choose non-fiction. Women choose literary works a little more than half the time, at a rate of about 55 percent.

Anatomy of a Bestseller

Now that we've investigated who will publish your book and how you'll sell it, let's talk about its anatomy. Take a stroll through any bookstore and you'll see that there are dozens, if not hundreds, of variations on a theme. True, they all have a front and back cover with text and occasionally some graphics in between. But they come in all sizes, shapes, and subject matters.

Fib or Fact

Perhaps the biggest difference in the types of books that are commonly sold is whether they're fiction or nonfiction. People are often confused about which is which, but it's simple, really: Fiction is make-believe, a story the author invents for the purpose of entertaining his readers. Nonfiction, on the other hand, is fact—it can be entertaining to readers, but it relays true information rather than an invented tale.

A romance novel is fiction—an invented story about a make-believe hero and heroine. A biography can be romantic, for instance the love story of Princess Grace and Prince Rainier of Monaco, but since it's about real people, it's nonfiction.

Mysteries like those written by Agatha Christie are fiction. The "who" in whodunit, as well as the "what" of what was done, is pure invention. However, a book dealing with a real-life mystery, like who killed the woman known as the *Black Dahlia* in 1940s Los Angeles, is nonfiction, so it's classified as "true crime."

The Nonfiction Edge

Which should you write? Industry experts tend to agree that nonfiction is a far wiser choice for the self-publisher than fiction. If you've been scribbling away at a heart-pounding mystery, a heart-wrenching romance, or some other invented tale, this may seem like exactly what you did not want to hear. But take heart—there are new options, especially in the e-book world, that have only recently become available, making self-publishing fiction a whole new ballgame. Before we get to that, let's explore why nonfiction is generally a better bet for the self-publisher.

First of all, Americans read far more nonfiction than fiction. In a Gallup survey, 46 percent of respondents said they have nonfiction books on their nightstands, while only 35 percent have their noses stuck in novels or other works of fiction.

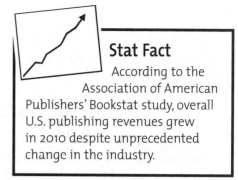

Stat Fact

According to the Association of American Publishers' Bookstat study, overall U.S. publishing revenues grew in 2010 despite unprecedented change in the industry.

Nonfiction categories are experiencing strong gains in both production and sales. You don't have to be a "name" to sell nonfiction. When readers head to the bookstore on the prowl for a good story, they look first for a name they already recognize, like Stephen King, Jackie Collins, or John Grisham. So if you have penned a tale of horror, lust among the monied classes, or a legal whodunit, you've got stiff competition. However, when readers go to the bookstore to find a book on cooking hors d'oeuvres or creating healthy relationships, they look for content rather than celebrity authors.

Hold the Autobiography

The more time you spend in the publishing business, the more you'll hear people proclaim that their life story would make a great book. And while most people's lives—due to the very nature of life itself—contain lots of drama, trials, and tribulations, they're not necessarily the stuff of great prose.

If you harbor this thought yourself, think carefully before committing fingers to keyboard. Have you lived through some great natural disaster or historical trauma? Do you have a truly dramatic story, like having survived frostbite, gangrene, and/or cannibalism on a snowy mountain peak; sailing around the world single-handedly; or being dead for four hours and coming back to tell about it? Have you overcome a terrible physical or mental handicap? Do you have a really interesting and extraordinary job or hobby, like bounty hunter, movie star, Mafia hit-person, CIA spy, or ghostbuster?

These are not all requirements for autobiographical success: People have written winning tomes based simply on growing up a child of the Depression in the 1930s or a Beaver Cleaver-clone kid in the 1950s. But as with fiction, unless you're a stellar writer with an excellent hook on which to base your tale, you're facing an uphill road to self-publishing success.

Sure it helps if you're Martha Stewart or Dr. John Gray, but it's not everything. If your book gives readers information they can use, chances are they'll probably buy it.

Constants with Clout

Nonfiction comes in all subjects, everything from connecting with your computer to communicating with your dog to conducting electricity—and lots more. Some genres, however, have more clout with readers than others. Take a look at these constants of the bookstore shelves:

- *Cookbooks*. Cookery books, as the British call them, were an "acceptable" self-publishing avenue long before any other genre. Today they are even considered collectibles in some circles. Think back to all those spiral-bound volumes you have seen through the years that were put together as fund-raisers by countless junior leagues, church groups, and chambers of commerce. They sell! But you do not have to be a nonprofit organization to write a cookbook. If you've got a flair for food, you might consider this genre, especially if you can target a special niche, like heart-healthy, diabetic, vegetarian, vegan, picky-kid/spouse, or harried working parent.

- *Self-help*. This is a perennial favorite on the nonfiction shelves. Americans are always looking to improve their own self-esteem or their children's self-confidence, to strengthen good relationships or cut off bad ones—in short, to build psychological well-being. If you are a psychologist, psychiatrist, minister, social worker, or other mental health professional with a theory to propound, self-help can be a good nonfiction base for you.

- *How-to*. Another enduring favorite, the how-to guide runs the gamut of topics. You can write—and probably sell—a book on anything from woodworking to quilting, car repair to computer repair, flea market decorating to scuba diving. If you're either a schooled or self-styled expert in just about any hands-on activity, chances are you can turn it into a book.

- *Inspirational/motivational*. Also perennially popular, inspirational and motivational books can be mega-sellers. Just look at all those *Chicken Soup for the Soul* (Health Communications) books—of which there are now an astounding 100-plus volumes and counting! Peruse the scores of minibooks displayed on and around bookstore checkout counters (where they make terrific impulse buys), and you'll see that most of them are inspirational: *A Sister Is a Kindred Soul*, *Love Notes of the Great Poets*, *Grandbabies Are for Spoiling*. The list goes on and on. If you can come up with inspirational or motivational material that strikes a chord in readers, you might do well with this genre.

- *Regional.* This is a relatively unsung genre in which the self-publisher can often excel. If you live in a big city or a heavily toured area, consider writing a restaurant or attraction guide. Or how about a volume featuring local history, local lore, or even area ghost stories? You might target the book toward families with young children, seniors, or the physically challenged. Use your imagination!

The Format

Nonfiction doesn't necessarily mean a 400-page volume of closely spaced text. It can encompass books—or perhaps more accurately, documents—of all lengths and sizes. You can format and sell your text as any one of the following:

- *Full-length books.* We'll explore book sizes and page counts in depth in Chapter 7. For now, let's say that a book by traditional definition is a collection of bound material that contains 48 or more pages, not including its front and back covers.

- *Pamphlets and reports.* These are smaller than books (unless they're produced by an office of the federal government) and focus on a single narrow topic. Bookstores won't buy reports, but some intrepid self-publishers do very well selling them via mail order or on the internet as e-publications. Self-publishing guru Dan Poynter, for instance, sells 51 specialized reports on different aspects of the business at his website, plus offers quite a bit of free information (see Appendix under "Consultants" for contact information). You might publish reports on aspects of foreign or domestic travel, the how-tos of clearing up your credit or obtaining college scholarships, producing various handcrafts, designing a website, or grooming different breeds of dogs—or anything else that's short, informative, and will interest a specific audience.

- *Minibooks.* These are generally of the inspirational/motivational variety we talked about earlier and are impulse buy and/or gift-oriented: *10 Cool Things About Cats, Daughters Are Perfect People*, or *The Fairies' Flower Language*, etc.

Back to the Fiction

Now let's take another look at fiction. As we have explained, fiction has traditionally been a harder sell for the self-publisher. This doesn't mean it can't be successful. What it does mean is that you'll need to double up on your marketing smarts.

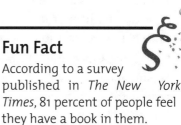

Fun Fact

According to a survey published in *The New York Times*, 81 percent of people feel they have a book in them.

▲

You need to consider how to make a novel commercially viable, advises Marilyn Ross of SPAN. How? Make it regional so it will sell regionally. Give your protagonist an interesting job, like spelunking, that other cave-explorers will want to read about. Really project what the important topics of the day will be when your book comes out so you can serve as an authority on those subjects. "You need to be calculating," Ross says. "You need a hook and you need publicity."

> ### Fun Fact
> In the 19th century, penny dreadfuls were inexpensive, sensational novels of crime and adventure, so called because you could buy them for mere pennies. They didn't have a reputation as literature, but they sold like mad!

Terry Nathan of IBPA agrees. "I think it's much easier with nonfiction, but specialized fiction [e.g., gay/lesbian, mystery, western, and sci-fi] can stand a chance of success as an independent. But general mainstream fiction still needs lots of dollars invested, in most cases, to tell the world about the book and to make a star of its author."

With the recent advent of e-publishing—which we will explore later in this chapter as well as in Chapter 6—the fiction-writer's handicap has begun to fade. As with just about every other kind of business, the internet seems to be leveling the playing field for writers. E-publishing is making fiction a more viable proposition by opening up new avenues of distribution. However, keep in mind that for most self-publishers it's still not anywhere near as profitable as nonfiction.

Fictional Formats

OK, so what kinds of fiction should you publish? There are many formats to choose from, but some are more popular among readers than others.

- *Novel.* This is the one everybody recognizes as a "book," a full-length tale by the likes of Danielle Steele, Dean Koontz, or J.K. Rowling. Novels come in genres like mystery, thriller, romance, horror, sci-fi, or "general fiction," which loosely includes any story that doesn't fit neatly into any of the traditional categories. And being the most recognizable, as well as the most popular type of fiction, novels are also the easiest to sell.

- *Short story.* Once upon a time, short stories were the lifeblood of many a successful author. Then this fiction format fell on hard times: A scant few were published in magazines, and even fewer found their way into books. Recently, however, the short story has bounded back to life due perhaps to the trendiness of 1950s art and artifacts, and traditional publishing houses are pumping out the collected short stories of various writers with zeal. Keep in mind, however, that the general public isn't nearly as interested in short fiction as in novels—if this is what you want to publish, you'll have to market assertively.

- *Novella*. A novella is shorter than a novel but longer than a short story. It's often grouped with two or three other tales of the same length by the same author, into a full-length book. Again, unless you're Stephen King or Nora Roberts, this format is going to be a tougher sell than a novel, but with e-publishing it is more of an option than ever before.

- *Serial*. Long, long ago in a century far away (the 19th, to be exact), serials were very popular. They were actually novels divided into several installments and printed in successive issues of magazines or newspapers. Eagerly devoured by legions of devoted readers, serials were a sort of pre-electronic version of the TV miniseries. Today, after a very long hiatus, the serial has been resurrected, thanks in no small part to e-publishing.

- *Poetry*. Let's face it: Most folks consider poetry to be "arty" and basically unreadable, except as high school or college penance. Even with e-publishing, this is not going to be a major seller. If you're a poet at heart, do it for enjoyment but don't plan on it as a source of sufficient income.

- *Children's picture book*. People often have the misconception that writing a children's book is easy. It's not! A successful picture book is a carefully designed mélange of artwork and words that creates a verbal as well as a visual world. It has to speak to kids, as well as to parents on several levels, who will have to read it over and over and over again. But this doesn't mean you should give up before you start. Children's books can be timeless bestsellers, and there is always room for one more. If you're not an illustrator yourself, find one whose vision matches your own. Plan each scene on each page with care and with its own message, just as Anna J., the self-publisher in Temple, Texas, did with her children's book.

Outsourcing Options

If you're reading this book, you're probably a writer already—or you've at least got a pretty fair idea of the topic(s) you plan to write about. However, if you love the idea of publishing but are not sure you can pen an entire book on your own that people will actually want to read, fear not. There are several other sources from which to choose that will still give you the creative power of the press, while letting someone else do the brunt of the writing:

- *Out-of-copyright books.* Haunt garage sales, flea markets, and used book stores, and you can turn up terrific old books that are now in the public domain. When exactly a work is out of copyright can be complicated. Go to the Library of Congress website at www.loc.gov/copyright for more information and always check with your attorney. With a little imagination and a catchy introduction, you can turn all sorts of dated material into a charming or clever outing. How about a 1890s *Boys Own Paper* book on camping skills, or a sweet foray into Victorian manners with an antique wedding planner?

> **Fun Fact**
>
> Charles Dickens' immortal tale of lost boys and larceny among the lower classes, *Oliver Twist*, was originally published as a serial.

- *Anthologies or collections.* Take a noodle from the bowl of the prolific *Chicken Soup for the Soul* publishers and put together an anthology of tales by various authors. Each story should have a common theme, like Victorian ghost tales, yarns for sailors, or gems for gardeners. Alternatively, you could take a more factual approach and put together a collection of articles on a particular topic—anything from dyslexia to the business of jewelry design to the truth about UFOs. You might commission new material, or reprint stories or articles that have already appeared elsewhere. If you take the latter approach, make sure the rights to the story are actually available before you include it (see the section on subsidiary rights in Chapter 13).

- *Other writers' books.* Once you hang out your publishing shingle, you'll discover that authors will flock to you. You may already know several writers who would love to have you publish their books. If you don't, join a few writers' groups, which you can find in your hometown or in the global village of the internet. You'll probably find an author in one of these groups whose work is worth nurturing and then publishing.

The Potential of e-Publishing

We've made enticing allusions to e-publishing throughout this chapter. So now, without further ado, let's delve into e-publishing and find out what it involves.

e Is for Internet

The "e" stands for "electronic," but what it means to you is "internet." When you publish a book the traditional way, you have it printed on paper and bound between cardboard covers. Then you take your dead tree, paper-and-ink books and distribute them to bookstores, libraries, specialty stores, and direct mail customers.

When you e-publish a book, you place your text on an internet website where it can be purchased directly by readers. This neatly eliminates two of the self-publisher's biggest costs: printing and distribution. Most e-publishers offer consumers several options for transforming their work from electronic bytes to readable book. Consumers can:

> **Fun Fact**
> The website www.self-publishingresources.com points out that e.e. cummings' first book, *The Enormous Room*, was self-published. He dedicated it to the 15 publishers who rejected it. The book is now considered a master-piece.

- Download material onto their computer's hard drive and then read the text on the computer's monitor, or print a hard copy using their own printer
- Purchase the material in CD form so they can read it using their computer or print a copy
- Purchase the material as a printed dead tree or p-book that will be mailed to them (an option not offered by most e-publishers)
- Download the material onto an e-book reader (a hardware device about the size of a paperback book, which allows material to be read on screen)

The e-Advantage

As a self-publisher, you can put up your own site, or you can upload your book on one of the dozens of e-book sites that are springing up all over the internet. There are numerous advantages to the latter:

1. You let somebody else do all the work of converting your text to a PDF file, a language computers use to translate your text into a downloadable format and then back again to plain English.
2. Some e-book sites provide "cover" art for your book, which saves you the expense of finding and then paying an illustrator.
3. The site acts as a virtual bookstore where readers will hopefully choose your title from among all the others offered, thus providing you with "shelf space" without having to go through traditional avenues of distribution.
4. E-book sites offer generous royalty schedules—generally from 30 to 70 percent of the list price of each title. Keep in mind, however, that e-books often sell for less than conventional p-books. The norm is anywhere from $5 to $8.95,

although prices can soar to $19.95. Or they can "sink" to $2.99 but perhaps sell exponentially more copies to reach higher earnings in the long run than a higher price might.

5. Some sites have editorial guidelines and don't accept every author and every title, while others are happy to let anybody upload anything.

6. Most e-book sites are more than happy to accept fiction!

Too Good

If all this sounds too good to be true, it's not. E-publishing is phenomenally exciting. The dawn of the e-book came and went without the earth-shattering sales many industry spectators were anticipating. However, some of the early resistance and issues have started to iron themselves out. The market is becoming much more accepting of the e-book format. According to www.selfpublishingebooks.com, sales figures are encouraging, with a 2.4 percent increase in e-book sales in 2010, accounting for 19 percent of HarperCollins' overall sales in that year. The market has responded with improvements in e-book readers and greater accessibility (i.e., lower costs for the readers) than ever before.

However, like any other form of publishing, e-publishing demands scads of promotional time, effort, and talent to achieve true success. If you're not willing to make that commitment, your title will probably languish on the virtual shelf of the e-book site just as it would languish on the racks of a brick-and-mortar bookstore.

> **Fun Fact**
> Stephen King's writing career almost ended up in the wastepaper basket. After suffering the rejection of two earlier novels, King tossed a work-in-progress into the trash. His wife, Tabitha, dug it out and convinced him to forge ahead. In 1974, Doubleday bought that manuscript—called *Carrie*—providing the King of horror with enough money to quit his day job as a schoolteacher and write full time.

3

Plotting Your
Bestseller
Market Research

Authors often believe that they should write a book first, then find an audience later. This is a fine approach for fiction. And it may be a viable proposition for the nonfiction writer who's a dabbler or hobbyist—but it's not necessarily profitable. As a self-publisher, you're writing and producing a book with a specific goal in mind: to make money. You may have other goals in mind as well, like Anna J., in Temple, Texas, whose primary goal is to help the families of critically ill children. But if a goal of your publishing venture is to make money, or at least for it to pay for itself, you can't be successful without understanding your book's potential market first.

So your first mission in becoming a self-publisher is to conduct market research. This will help you determine whether there is in fact an audience, or market, for your book. Your research should tell you how large that market is and even narrow down what specific elements your target market wants to read about in your book.

The First Task

The first task you will have is to decide what exactly your book will be about. You may already have made this decision, down to the tiniest detail, or you may still have a wide-open field in front of you. Either approach is fine, so long as you keep in mind the following guidelines:

- *Be a cheerleader.* Enthusiasm sells books. You can't write a winning book on a subject you think is dead boring. Cast your mind back to the agony of all those fatally dull high school and college term papers. It's no fun to write about something you're completely uninterested in, and it will show in your text. But if you write about something you feel truly passionate about, you stand a better chance of excelling at it.

- *Be in the know.* You must have a thorough knowledge of your subject. Knowledge gives your words confidence and credibility—the first steps to bestsellerdom. If you do not know everything about your subject, get out there and research, research, and research some more and build some credentials for yourself.

- *Fixate on your focus.* Make sure your book has a well-defined subject. A cookbook called *Good Food* won't attract anybody in particular—it isn't focused on any specific interest, need, or goal. But a cookbook called *Festive Parties for Frazzled Folks*, or *Brain-Booster Cookery*, or even *Cooking Lean* will attract a legion of readers with their promises of stress-free party giving, boosted brain power, or slim and trim tummies.

- *Quench a thirst.* Remember that readers buy books based on their wants and needs, thirsts that you as a self-publisher can slake. These can run the gamut: a desire to retire rich at age 40 or a need to find a better-paying job; a desire to find a husband or a need to save a marriage; a desire to grow bigger flowers or a need to feed a family on home-grown vegetables. Besides hard-core nonfiction topics, readers of all ages, genders, and walks of life have an unquenchable thirst for entertainment and inspiration in the form of fiction, biographies, autobiographies, and humor.

Your Target Market

Now that you've decided what you'll write about, you've probably already figured out—at least in part—who you're writing it for. This is your target market. And it's very important. You would not write a book called *Home Driveway Auto Repair* with the goal of selling it to urban New Yorkers who do not have driveways, or to people who think Makita is a furniture style and not a power tool.

If your target market is too small, your book is unlikely to be lucrative. If you write a genealogical history of your immediate family, for instance, you'll have eliminated your entire market once your parents, your siblings, and Aunt Ethel and Uncle Bill buy copies. (And they probably won't actually buy those books anyway. They'll insist that as family they should get complimentary copies.) But if you write a history of the Celtic families of California (with yours just one among them), you may find you have thousands of readers to sell to.

Nudging into Your Niche

As you target your market, start thinking market niche. This is your special corner of the market, the area of expertise and interest that makes your book, and what you have to say in it, stand out from any competition you may have. There are lots of books on the shelves, for instance, on crafts. But if yours is specifically for busy working people who don't have the time to fashion Christmas tree decorations or Independence Day doodads (until you show them how), then that's your niche: crafts for the constantly hectic.

If you write a self-help guide on the power of positive thinking, you'll have to compete with the scads of similar volumes already out there. So you will want to

> **Tip...**
>
> **Smart Tip**
>
> If you are serious about finding the most accurate, up-to-date sales and market information, consider purchasing a membership to Nielsen Bookscan. Yep, this is the same group responsible for the Nielsen TV rating system. They extended their reach to books, music, and even software. You can harness the power of Nielsen research and search for sales information by title, author, category ... you name it. Though pricey, the information is worth its weight in iPads! Check out bookscan.com to find out more.

consider a market niche that makes yours special. Is it positive thinking for the hopelessly pessimistic? Is it positive thinking for families to practice together? Or is it positive thinking for teachers?

Spend time online and in bookstores finding out more about what's already out there on the shelves and find a totally new spin on the subject. See what sells well and what doesn't, and consider the customer comments of your competitors. Many times, those comments provide clues on what worked in a similar title and what didn't, giving you a roadmap of where to take your unique approach.

Gary S., the self-publisher in Panama City Beach, Florida, found his market niche in books that deal with the experiences of World War II veterans. His books are oral histories, personal stories told directly by participants in the action—which sets his works apart from the tomes written by historians who hadn't "been there and done that" themselves. Anna J.'s market niche is that her books are written for families that have a child with a heart defect—a special group for whom no other books exist.

Clarity Sells

Once you decide on a subject for your book, you'll want to narrow its focus. The clearer you are about your topic and who you're writing it for, the easier it will be both to write and sell. If you're an avid gardener, for instance, you could choose any one of several intriguing directions to focus on:

○ A guide for the after-work gardener

○ A children's book for the young beginning gardener

○ A manual on gardening in your specific region of the country

○ An anthology of inspirational stories by gardeners of all ages and walks of life

○ A gardener's cookbook

○ A book on gardening as therapy for the elderly

○ And lots more! Use your imagination!

Researching Your Reader Base

Once you target your market and develop your special niche, you'll want to research it to make sure it's large enough to support your publishing efforts. There are all sorts of ways to go about this, from gathering statistics to taking informal surveys.

Send Me a Letter

One sure-fire way to ascertain the size and interest level of your target market is via direct-mail surveys. You won't blanket the entire state of Mississippi or the San Francisco Bay area (or wherever you live) with questionnaires; this would be extremely expensive, as well as unproductive. Instead, you'll narrow your focus to the very potential readers you want to attract.

If you're writing an alternative therapy book for people suffering from arthritis, for instance, you would send surveys to members of local, regional, and national arthritis support groups. If you are penning a book on closing techniques for real-estate agents, you'll send your surveys out to the members of various real-estate boards.

If you belong to an association, organization, or listserv (an electronic mailing list), and it just happens to be affiliated with your target market, you have it made. You may already have a directory packed with names and phone numbers at hand. If not, you may be able to beg, borrow, or buy a directory from the organization's main office. If your market niche is something more general, like a volume of inspirational thoughts for each month of the year, you might still start off with the members of your club or group. Your common membership will act as your proverbial foot in the door. If you don't belong to any groups, how about a church roster or neighborhood association? Use your imagination!

What should you ask? Check out the "Market Research Survey" on page 36. Your queries will relate to your own target market and written product, but you can use this as a starting point for what and how to ask.

Stat Fact
According to ezinearticles.com, the main topic people buy e-books on is how to make money. Second in line is how to save money, while third is how to save time.

Hello Central

Another way to reach potential customers is through telephone surveys, which are basically the same as direct-mail or listserv surveys—with one important difference. People don't always react kindly

Market Research Survey

This sample survey is designed for market research for a book on affordable housing for seniors.

1. If you're a senior citizen, what is your age? _____

2. Are you living on a fixed income? _____

3. Have you experienced difficulties finding affordable housing? _____

4. If yes, what avenues have you explored and what were the results? _____

   _____

5. Where are you living now (i.e. apartment, house, condominium, etc.)? _____

   _____

6. What do you pay for rent per month?
   ❑ $200 to $700   ❑ $701 to $1,400   ❑ $1,401 and up

7. Is your rent subsidized by the government or another agency? _____

8. Do your children or other relatives help to pay your rent?_____

9. Would you be interested in a book that would guide you to find affordable housing? _____

10. How much would you be willing to pay for such a book? _____

11. What specific information or problems would you like to see addressed in relation to this topic? _____

    _____

    _____

12. Have you read a book or pamphlet of this type in the past? _____

13. If so, did you find it helpful? Why or why not?_____

    _____

Market Research Survey, continued

14. Please comment on the title *Affordable Housing on a Fixed Income* (love, like, dislike, or detest, and why): _____

_____

_____

15. Please comment on the title *Home Alone: Affordable Housing for Seniors* (love, like, dislike, or detest, and why): _____

_____

_____

to unsolicited calls these days when telemarketers are striving mightily to drive us all around the bend with their poorly timed appeals. Unless you've got thick skin, it can be difficult to make cold calls to people you don't know and pick their brains.

However, if you use a membership list from an organization you belong to, you may have a foot in the door. Your call won't seem quite as unsolicited if you can say that you (or your sibling, spouse, or child) belong to the Upper Peninsula Chapter of the Antique Car Restoration Society or the Michigan Educators Society, etc.

Tip...

Smart Tip

Anna J., the self-publisher in Temple, Texas, used listservs (email message-sharing groups) to help determine her market. Since she belonged to several listservs for parents of kids with heart defects, she was able to judge the number of families who needed her books.

Statistics on Tap

Besides going directly to your prospective readers for your market research, you'll also want cool, calculated statistics. For that book on alternative therapies, you will want to know facts like the number of arthritis sufferers there are in the United States. For a regional title on coastal home design, you may need to know how many people

An Added Bonus

There's a secret bonus to taking market research surveys: Your respondents help you write your book! When you ask what specific elements prospective readers would like to see addressed, you know what to include in your book.

Of course, you have to be selective about the results. If one person out of a hundred claims to want to read about growing deadly nightshade in a garden text, you can safely leave that topic aside. But if 95 people out of the same 100 ask for information on growing tomatoes in a shade garden, you can assume this is a subject most readers will genuinely be interested in.

You can also use this survey information in your back-of-the-book blurb—the sales material you print on your back cover. How? Write up something like, "*Shade Tree Gardening* answers the questions America's home gardeners want to know!" Or, "*Shade Tree Gardening* is the book America's home gardeners helped design!"

build second homes on the Florida Gulf Coast.

The answers to questions like these will help you determine just how many prospective readers you can expect and if that number is large enough to be lucrative. Where do you get all this statistical stuff? Try the following sources.

Library Look-Up

Ask your local reference librarian, a person well worth making friends with. Pay her a visit and explain what you need to know and why. Librarians live for books, so the fact that you're writing one gives you extra brownie points. Tell your librarian that you need to know how many florists, bed-and-breakfast inns, or adults with Alzheimer's there are in the United States. She

Tip...

Smart Tip

It's long been a known fact that people are unlikely to return a mail survey unless you offer them an incentive. Email surveys are no different, so get creative! Give your recipients a coupon for 10 percent off your book when it comes out. This gives you a head start on advance sales and also helps spread the word about your book. Provide your incentive in the subject line of your email or they may never open the survey to get to the discount offer.

will provide you with stacks of demographic statistics; more facts and figures than you might imagine could possibly exist.

Get on the Net

You'll find the answers to all sorts of fascinating questions on the internet. For starters, check in with the U.S. Department of Commerce (www.doc.gov) and the U.S. Census Bureau (www.census.gov). Click on any number of general and specialized search engines, from Yahoo!, to Google, to InfoJump, and get the scoop from millions of articles, publications, and websites that relate to your area of interest.

Try the Target

Sometimes the best place to go for information on a target market is the target itself. If your market is crafters, for instance, you'd contact the National Craft Association and the Association of Crafts and Creative Industries for counts of their members. To find out the number of dog breeders, you'd talk to the folks at state and regional breeding societies. You get the idea.

Check Out the Competition

While you're doing your market research, don't forget to check out what sort of competition your book will face. Ask any literary agent, and they'll tell you that's one of the first things they consider. Specifically, you want to look at these key questions:

- How many books are already out there on your subject?
- What are their strengths and weaknesses compared with the one you plan?
- What sets your book apart from the crowd?

This part of your market research is fun—it means that, darn it, you'll have to abandon doing the laundry, mowing the lawn, or preparing your income tax return, and spend time in the bookstore. Peruse the shelves.

Beware!
Those up-to-the-minute rankings on Amazon.com are great, but keep in mind that they don't tell the whole story of a competitive book's sales. They provide snapshots of how a particular book is performing on a particular day. Complete the sales picture with comprehensive sales information from Nielsen Bookscan.

Look at any book that could conceivably match yours and see how it stacks up in respect to the key questions above.

Keep in mind that the bookstore is where you want to be. The library is not the best place to do this kind of research because most of its volumes will be several—or several dozen—years old. You want to know what readers will see today or tomorrow that will compete with your volume, not what was popular 5, 10, or even 20 years ago. You want to know what other publishers' market research has shown to be worthy of stacking on those bookstore shelves today. And that is what bookstore crawling will tell you.

Smart Tip

Tip...

The fact that there are no books the least like yours on the shelves can be a plus—or a minus. If you find a dozen titles on financial investments, it doesn't necessarily mean the market is saturated; it means people are eager readers on the topic. If you can't find even one volume about cockroach farming, this can be a valuable clue that there's no market for the subject.

4

Your Publishing House
Office and Business Structure

Every publisher, from the mighty Time Warner

Publishing to the smallest small press, has a "house," or office.

As a self-publisher, you'll need one, too. You'll also need a sound

business structure that will take you from novice book producer

to seasoned publisher. In this chapter, we'll investigate the issues

involved in getting established, including your legal business structure, company image, and domain name, as well as dealing with zoning regulations and Uncle Sam. It's not all drudgery, and it is crucial for getting your business off to a good start. So let's get to it!

Creating an Image

Even though self-publishing has come out of the closet and is now a respected segment of the industry, it can still easily carry a stigma of amateurism. So the image your company will have is important. You'll want to craft one that will tell readers, reviewers, distributors, bookstores, and everybody else you'll deal with on a business basis that you're a professional.

The Name Game

The first element of your image is your company name. It's going to reflect not only your first book but also all the others to come, so plan it carefully. You might choose a name based on the types of books you'll publish, like "Gardeners Press" for a publisher of gardening guides, or "Cookbook Nook Publishing" for a cookbook publisher. The upside of this technique is that readers know exactly what to expect from you—and that's a plus. The downside is that if you decide later on to add to your repertoire by publishing quilting books in addition to cookbooks, your name will be misleading.

You might try naming your company after a local or regional feature, perhaps "Three Trees Press," "Seaside Publishing," or "Moonlight & Magnolias Press." Instead, you might decide on something quirky like "Glitterbug Press" or "Three Jakes Publishing," which is perfectly fine—just make sure that your name properly reflects your products. For example, if you plan to publish serious works like surgical manuals for physicians, a name like "All Thumbs Press" won't give you much credibility.

Beware!
If you name your company after yourself, as in Joe Doaks Publishing or Doaks Press, book reviewers and other industry movers-and-shakers will likely brand you an amateur self-publisher and refuse to take your book seriously. And if you ever decide to sell your press, your name on it won't be a valuable feature.

Name Fiction

Once you've decided on a company name, you'll need to register it with your local authorities. In doing so, you need to make sure that no one else in your area is already using that name. You also need to ensure that no one else in your area can legally take on your business name at a later date, and you give your company its first legal status. This is important: Banks will not give you a business account without a fictitious business name statement, also called a DBA, which stands for "doing business as." And without a business account, many vendors will not deal with you.

Smart Tip

Don't panic if your most obvious domain name has already been taken; there's usually a way around it. If your company is called "Bell Book Press," for instance, and there's already a www.bellbook.com, try something like www.bbpress.com or www.bellbookxpress.com. Get creative!

Tip...

Obtaining a DBA is easy, although the process varies a bit in different regions of the country.

In many states, this process has become electronic, at least in part. In both Florida and New Hampshire, for example, you can do a quick name search online (although your name choice is not officially yours until the paperwork is filed and approved). The appropriate form for applying for your trade name is also available online but you must print out the form, fill it out, and either hand deliver it or send it in by mail. When approved, you will receive an official letter or certificate and you can now legally begin using your DBA.

Your Domain

While you're registering your company name, you should also consider registering your business website name, or domain name, which is the www.whatever.com thing people type in to access your virtual office. There can be only one company per domain name, so you'll have to think up several versions of the name you want in case one has already been taken.

Here's what you need to do: Go into your web browser and type in www.networksolutions.com. Once you're at the Network Solutions website, which is very user-friendly, follow the easy directions and check to see if the domain name you've chosen has been taken. If it has, keep choosing alternatives until you find a permutation that's available; then register it online. The cost—if you already have a web host for your site—is $35 for a one-year registration. There are other domain registrars as well, such as GoDaddy.com.

Business Name Brainstorming

List three ideas for a business name based on the type of books you plan to publish (paranormal, romance, children's fantasy, auto repair, etc.).

1. _____

2. _____

3. _____

List three ideas for a name combining a favorite theme with your planned products (i.e., New Age, eco-awareness, empowering women, etc.).

1. _____

2. _____

3. _____

After you've decided which name you like best, have you:

❏ Tried it aloud to make sure it's easily understood and pronounced? (Has it passed muster with your family? Have you had a friend call to see how it sounds to say it, and hear it, over the phone?)

❏ Checked your local Yellow Pages and/or searched the internet to make sure the same or similar name is not already listed?

❏ Checked with your local business name authority to make sure it's available?

Of Logos and Letterhead

There's more to image than a name. Your visual image—the colors, graphics, typefaces, and paper stocks you choose for everything from stationery to brochures—also plays a starring role in how people perceive your company.

If you'll publish books for the home handyperson, for instance, design a logo that says home repair with saws, wrenches, or hammers embellishing your company name. If you'll publish travel books, splash your materials with travel stickers, suitcases, or a stylized cruise liner. And if you publish sci-fi tales, how about a logo featuring a UFO or an extraterrestrial? You can play with designing your logo yourself or search the internet for appropriate clip art, but this can often smack of amateurism—something to avoid in an industry that has just crawled out from under the amateur rock in a big way.

> **Smart Tip** _Tip..._
>
> If you choose to have your stationery professionally printed instead of going with your own desktop publishing, check prices with a variety of vendors: local printers, quick-copy centers like FedEx Office, and also office supply supercenters like Staples and Office Depot.

You expect people to pay you for what you do best—write books—so why not plan to pay someone whose craft is graphic design to design a knockout logo for you? After all, your logo is something that you will use forever and represents you and your company. Ask the designer to provide it to you digitally so you can do things like create online letterhead and email it to book cover designers.

You can design and print everything from letterhead and envelopes to business cards using your own computer system. Since the process does not have to be expensive, use papers with oomph—those with weight, class, and distinction:

- Letterhead paper weight should be about 24 pounds—not the copier-grade see-through stuff that's 20 pounds. You might try a style that's specially textured for added interest.
- Business cards that you print off your computer come in sheets with each card perforated so you can tear them out easily. Go for stock with fine perforations so they look professionally printed; avoid the sheets with raggedy "punched" edges.
- Envelopes should match your letterhead and your business cards.

Laying Your Foundation

Your publishing house will need more of a foundation than a business name and a domain name. You'll need to decide on a legal structure, check into sales tax, get insurance coverage, and line up an attorney and an accountant—all the nitty-gritty stuff that will give your company a solid base on which to grow.

The Soul of Your Proprietorship

To appease those hard-working IRS employees, your business must have a structure. You can operate it as a sole proprietorship, a partnership, or a corporation, with variations thereof. Many self-publishing newbies go with the simplest and easiest version, which is the sole proprietorship. If you'll be starting out on your own, you may choose the same option. It's the least complicated and the least expensive.

You can always switch to another format later on, if and when you take on partners and employees. Anna J., the self-publisher in Temple, Texas, for example, has chosen to reformat her company as a nonprofit corporation after four years as a sole proprietor. This is time-consuming and expensive, and it's not a do-it-yourself option—you need the assistance of an attorney. But Anna decided to go for it because the money she saves on taxes will enable her to help many more families with sick children.

A Taxing Affair

If you plan to sell books by mail order (which includes internet sales) or in person at seminars and workshops, you will need to register to collect sales tax by applying for a state sales license or permit. Sales taxes vary by state and are imposed at the retail level. This can all get a bit complex. You only charge sales tax to mail order customers who live in your state—when you ship out of state you don't charge tax. The best way to handle the situation is to check with your accountant when you get to that point. He or she can advise you on where to get your license and who to charge for what.

Expert Advice

Attorneys are like plumbers: You don't want to think about them until you need one, but as a business owner, you should have a good attorney on call—one that knows the intellectual property business. You will want her to check over any contracts you write with wholesalers, distributors, book clubs, printers, and other authors or publishers. You'll also need your lawyer to advise you

Mission Style

While you're setting up the elements of your publishing house, you'll want to design a mission statement. This is a short and sweet summary of your company's products, philosophy, market niche, and goals. The mission statement is the business version of the positive-thinking "sticky" notes you put on your bathroom mirror. It gives your company a plan—and a style—which are easily referred to and easily remembered.

A mission statement for a self-publisher of parenting books might look something like this:

> Parent City Press is devoted to helping parents raise a new generation of caring kids. Our mission is to foster a feeling of community among parents and children around the world with a series of books by and for parents of smart, happy young people. Our goal is steady and incremental growth and annually increased profits that will fund us in teaching the global village to raise its children wisely.

on the fine points of general small-business law. You won't need to call her every week, or even every month, but there's no point in waiting until you have a problem to establish a relationship.

Along with that on-call attorney, you'll want to look into hiring an accountant to fill out your tax returns and advise you of any special ways you can save money with your business structure.

And don't forget your insurance agent! He can be an invaluable source of information and expertise. If you'll be homebased, you'll need to find out if your homeowners' package covers your business assets, inventory, and equipment, or if you need additional coverage. If you're based outside the home, you need coverage for these same items, as well as your physical location.

On Location

One of the great perks of being a self-publisher by trade is that you can work at home. You don't need a high-traffic or high-visibility location, so you don't need to set up shop in a trendy part of town. Because all your business is virtual, you won't need an executive office with client seating or a Lucite-and-chrome conference room. The only space requirement is an area large enough for your desk, your chair, filing cabinets, and a bookcase.

The home office is convenient: It cuts commuting time and expense down to zero. It's also economical—you don't need to spend money on leased space, extra utilities, or lunches in the building cafeteria.

Working at home is not compulsory for the self-publisher, but it's a definite plus, and one that you should not ignore. Unless you've got a boisterous family or a roommate who's an aspiring rock-and-roll drummer, wait until your company has outgrown your home work space to shop around for something else.

The Home Office

The self-publishers we interviewed for this book have home offices. If you go the same route, you can locate your office work space anywhere in the house that's convenient; but ideally, you should have a dedicated office, a room that's reserved just for the business. You can locate this room in a den, a FROG (finished room over garage), the garage itself, or a spare bedroom. Keep in mind that whatever space you choose will be your work station and command center.

If a dedicated office is not an option for you, you can also station yourself in a corner of the kitchen, or at the dining room table. If you've got a noisy family, however, a cubbyhole in your bedroom is liable to be much more conducive to quiet, clear thinking than a nook in the family room with the TV blaring at all hours.

The Big Write-Off

A big advantage to the home office is the ability to wear two hats—to be at home with your family and be at work at the same time. Another advantage is the ability to count your home business as a tax write-off. The IRS will graciously allow you to deduct money from your income taxes if you're using a portion of your home as your income-producing work space. You can deduct a percentage of expenses equivalent to the percentage of space your home office occupies. If, for example, you're using one

> **Tip...**
>
> **Smart Tip**
> If you plan to work from home, you'll want to check into zoning regulations. Find out from your city government whether any permits are necessary. If you need a zoning variance, apply for that, too.

room in an eight-room house, you can deduct one-eighth of your rent or mortgage, plus you can deduct one-eighth of your utility bills.

There is an "if" involved here. You can only use this deduction if you're using a space in your home that serves solely as your office. If you have turned your spare bedroom into your office, and you don't use it for anything but conducting your business, then you qualify. If, however, your office is tucked into a corner of the kitchen, and you're still feeding people in there, you don't qualify for the home office deduction (unless you can convince the IRS that the microwave oven is actually some sort of quick-dry printing device).

Organized and Efficient

Even though you will be working at home, it's important to remember that you are still a professional. Your work quarters, like yourself, should be organized and efficient. If at all possible, designate a separate room with four walls and a door. Aim for pleasant, quiet, well-lit surroundings. You're going to be spending a lot of time in this space, so you want it to be comfortable.

Find a desk or a table large enough to hold your computer, keyboard, phone, pencil holder, stapler, etc., and that will be big enough to have room to spread out your working papers.

Make sure you have enough space to neatly file bids from printers, distributors, and other vendors. You'll also need a place to file manuscript pages in various stages of revision, artwork, and order forms from customers. You'll probably need a separate room or storage area to stash your company brochures, catalogs, and other direct-mail materials, as well as industry magazines you'll subscribe to and copies of your own books!

Whether you use the fanciest hanging file folders in mahogany drawers, or simple manila ones in cardboard boxes, you must be able to access this information quickly and easily. It's no fun digging through the back of the clothes closet or running out to the garage every time somebody calls with a question.

The Storage Space

You'll need storage space for your books after you get them from the printer. We'll

Smart Tip

Tip...

You'll need enough space for your company "shipping department," an area you'll use to package your products for shipping. It doesn't matter if it's the kitchen table or a special workstation in your office, so long as there's adequate room to spread out your materials and wrap that package professionally.

▲

The Home Office

Use this handy worksheet to locate and design your home office.

Start by listing three possible locations in your home for your office, which should include a work area for you and enough space for your desk, computer, and telephone.

1. _____

2. _____

3. _____

Make a physical survey of each location.

❑ Are phone and electrical outlets placed close enough to your equipment so that they can be accessed easily? Or will you be faced with unsightly, unsafe cords snaking across the carpet?

❑ Measure your space. Will your current desk or table (or the one you have your eye on) fit?

❑ Do you have adequate lighting? If not, can you create or import it?

❑ What is the noise factor?

❑ Is there room to spread out your work?

❑ Optional: How close is it to the kitchen? (This can be either a plus or minus, depending on your current waistline.)

Take a survey of possible home storage spaces for books.

❑ Is there adequate lighting, ventilation, and space for you to easily access books?

❑ What is the humidity factor?

❑ Will you need to construct special shelving or add other storage space? If so, make notes here: _____

_____

explore this issue further in Chapter 8. For now, consider having to store a print run that's anywhere from 150 to 5,000 books. Do you have a garage or spare room where you can store them in clean, dry, low-humidity splendor?

If not, you'll have to look into renting a space, as Anna J. in Texas does. "I used to have all my books in my house, but since I printed 5,000 copies of each of my last two books, I have had to rent a climate-controlled storage facility," she says.

For Steve C. in Hinesburg, Vermont, storage is not a problem. "I live in the country on a big piece of land, and my favorite hobby is building and remodeling," Steve says. "So I've built whatever storage facilities I need. If I lived in a city apartment, that obviously wouldn't be an option. More and more publishers are signing up with the kinds of fulfillment services that store large quantities—companies like Publishers' Shipping and Storage, Rayve, and Pathway. When they get an order from Ingram [a book wholesaler] for 90 cases of books, they just call the storage company and have the books shipped from there. Of course, there are still lots of self-publishers with one or two titles who find their garages adequate for storage—as long as they don't mind parking in the driveway."

The Commercial Office

If you decide to go for an office outside your home, you can choose just about any spot, so long as it's clean, dry (books don't like dampness), quiet, and accessible to the UPS courier for those book deliveries.

You could go with a downtown loft, a space in a light industrial park, or an older house in a quaint historic district. Since you won't need visibility, you could even start out by subleasing space from another aspiring businessperson who could use help with the rent.

Outfitting Your Space

Whether your office is in an historic building, a modest office plaza, a downtown office, or a barn by the river, you'll need the same basic setup as in a home office. You'll need plenty of room for your files, plus your desk, chair, a few pieces of visitors' furniture, and desks and chairs for any employees you may hire.

Whether in a home or commercial office, your computer should occupy a place of honor, away from dirt, drafts, and blinding sunlight. The same applies to your printer and fax machine. And don't forget to outfit your office space with every worker's favorite piece of equipment—the coffee maker!

Take into consideration, too, book storage and shipping issues. If you go with a light industrial site, it will likely include a warehouse or work space in the back that

▲

The Commercial Office

This worksheet will help you plan your commercial office.

Start by listing three possible locations for your office based on proximity to your home, rental price, and storage space for your books:

1. _____

2. _____

3. _____

Make a physical survey of the interior office space of potential locations.

❑ Is there enough room for desks, computers, and telephones for you and for employees who may need their own units?

❑ Can phone and electrical outlets be accessed easily at potential workstations?

❑ Is there adequate lighting and proper ventilation?

❑ Is there adequate storage space?

❑ Optional: Where will you place a coffee maker? A refrigerator?

can serve as an ideal storage and packaging space. But if you'll take on a quirkier alternative, like a room in somebody else's office, you might need to go with an off-site, climate-controlled storage unit to hold all your books.

Keep in mind that the book publishing biz entails a lot of time sitting at a work station in front of a computer. Consider the ergonomics of your work station—chair height, monitor distance, keyboard style—and be sure to have lots of task lighting in all the right places. Your comfort and your health depend on making good choices in these areas.

5

Your Startup Finances

As you know, one of the really grand things about self-publishing is that your costs can be relatively low. You won't need a commercial space, workroom, or equipment for scads of employees, and, if you publish electronically or on-demand, you won't need thousands of dollars of inventory to put on store shelves. But self-publishing isn't cost-free, either. Your expenses will fall into three basic categories:

1. *Company expenses.* These are the expenses like a computer, software, telephone, and membership fees to various organizations that you'll incur whether you produce one book or a hundred.

2. *Book production expenses.* These costs will be different for each title you publish; they include things like printing, illustration, and copy editing fees (see Chapter 6).

3. *Sales and promotion expenses.* The costs associated with sales and promotion will be covered in Chapters 9 and 10. Distributors' fees and shipping costs will also fall under this category (see Chapter 8).

In this chapter, we'll explore the costs involved in starting your self-publishing company. We'll return to the costs associated with book production and selling and promoting your books in later chapters.

Computer Caveats

Perhaps the most important item on your startup list is a computer system—a hard drive, monitor, mouse, modem, and printer, plus whatever peripherals you choose to tack on. A good system will allow you to shine as a self-publisher by taking on all these tasks on your own:

- Writing and editing your manuscript.
- Writing and editing promotional materials like press releases and reviews. (Yes, you will sometimes create your own for reviewers to print!)
- Creating your own brochures, display ads, and other direct-mail pieces.
- Generating stationery, invoices, and order forms.
- Tracking royalties (your own from e-publishing sites and/or those you pay to other authors).
- Performing accounting functions and generating financial reports.
- Maintaining customer databases.
- Accessing research materials and other resources online.
- Creating a website and selling via an online or "virtual" brochure or catalog.
- Communicating with repeat and potential customers, suppliers, vendors, and distributors via email.

For those readers young enough to remember when calculators first made it beyond scientists and to the general public, they cost well over $100 and up. Now you can buy a calculator that does the most complex scientific calculations that is smaller than your cell phone (in fact, most cell phones contain a calculator) and costs $2.95 at the big box store checkout counter. Computers have gone a similar trajectory, with operating systems that supply a calculator as an "accessory" program.

Your new computer should be Pentium-class with the latest version of the Windows operating system, since this is what the majority of software packages are geared toward. Computer specs change almost weekly, but for not much more than $1,000, if not less, you can get a desktop computer with almost unbelieveable amounts of short-term and long-term memory that will run almost any software you might want, store photos, etc. Although CD/DVD drives are almost a thing of the past, they haven't quite reached that status so be sure to get a computer with a drive. That same $1,000 can cover a package that includes the CPU, keyboard, and a 20- or 21-inch monitor with built-in webcam and speakers. Packages may include even a basic printer, but you will want to have a reasonably sophisticated printer that can spit out a paper copy of a your manuscript in a short amount of time. Even if you plan to do most of your editing electronically, there is still a place for having a "hard copy" in your hands.

Soft on Software

As beneficial as your computer is, it can't help you unless you give it software to make it sing. A stunning array of software lines the shelves of most office supply stores, ready to help you perform every business task—design and print your own checks, develop professional-quality marketing materials, make mailing lists and labels, even act as your own attorney and accountant.

Most new computers come pre-loaded with all the software you'll need for basic office procedures, although the preloaded basic software may not be complex enough for your needs and you may outgrow it pretty fast. Like the specs of the hardware, you can often buy packages with software upgrades preloaded per your specifications (and increased cost accordingly). You'll also need to look into the following programs:

- *Word processing*. A good basic program such as Microsoft Word or Corel WordPerfect Office can be had

Smart Tip
You can get all your computer components separately, which is an OK way to do it if you have very specific things you want. However, many times it can be less expensive to purchase a package but upgrade one individual component.

55

for around $100. With this software, you can write your book, as well as correspondence, contracts, press releases, articles, and whatever else strikes your fancy. Microsoft Word can be bought as a package within Microsoft Office, which also includes some configuration of the database program Access; the spreadsheet program Excel; the design program Publisher; and the presentation program PowerPoint, depending on what version—Home and Office, Small Business, etc.—you choose to purchase.

- *Accounting.* These software programs are a sort of checkbook on a CD, and they make record-keeping a breeze. You assign categories such as office supplies and business travel to the checks you write, and at tax time you print out a report showing how much you spent for what. Your accountant not only thanks you but also gives you a discount for not having to wade through all your receipts. You can expect to pay $30 to $180 for a program like Intuit Quicken for Home and Business, Intuit QuickBooks, or Peachtree Accounting to track your business finances.

- *Desktop publishing.* This type of program will help you transform the manuscript you generate with word processing software into a format that book printers will accept. You can also use this software for creating sales and promotional materials. The two true publishing programs available are pricey and often considered challenging to use. So be prepared to work at it, and eventually you will learn to love them. Choose Adobe InDesign or Quark Xpress, which both dent your wallet for around $700.

- *Mailing list management.* For those mailing lists you're developing of past and potential participants, you'll also want to purchase a list management program like My Mail List and AddressBook from Avanquest for around $30. You can organize mail lists, create and import databases, and design a variety of mail pieces.

- *Software designed for publishers.* Instead of going amateur with a mailing list program and a general-purpose accounting program, you might opt to start off with the real thing: software designed especially for publishers. Publishers' Assistant by Upper Access Inc. gives you everything you need to track invoices, royalties, and inventory; handle billing and order entry; and manage your mailing lists. Pencil in about $495 for the "Sonnet" version, or be ready to shell out big bucks to the tune of $2,245 for the "Epic"

Dollar Stretcher

When you purchase your new computer, you can often buy it preloaded with word processing and accounting programs that will suit your needs. If you negotiate wisely, you might save valuable software dollars.

edition. You can download a free trial of any version of the program, but you are limited to 24 uses (see the Appendix for contact information). Other popular publisher software programs include Publishing Solutions from Quality Solutions Inc. and Publishing Manager from Trilogy.

Go ISP!

As a self-publisher, you must have a safe and reliable ISP, or internet service provider, such as America Online, AT&T, People PC, Net Zero, or countless others. With the power of the World Wide Web at your command, you can go anywhere on the globe instantly, all from the comfort of your own desktop. You can research, promote, and sell books, as well as communicate with customers and vendors. And it's cheap! Most internet service providers, or ISPs, charge about $20 to $25 per month and give you unlimited web and email access.

Web Weaving

As a self-publisher, you should have your own website. If you plan to sell by mail order (which includes internet sales), a company site can be a boon. And even if you don't go this route, a website can help promote your books.

The cost of putting up and maintaining a business site can vary considerably. If you're lucky enough to have a computer brain in the family, or if you take the time to become your own computer expert, you can pencil in a zero under website design and construction costs. There's a definite learning curve, but once you have it, you can make all the changes you like whenever you like, without having to rely on an outside source.

Many entrepreneurs opt for outsourcing this task instead. What can you expect to pay if you outsource website construction? You can pencil in about $300 to $500 for hands-on help from a website designer. As a third option, you may be lucky enough to have a qualified friend or relative who'll put up your site in exchange for lawn mowing, baby-sitting, or a steady supply of home-baked cookies. Don't forget that you'll also need a web host (see Chapter 11 for more information). For now, plan on spending anywhere from $10 to $75, and more, depending how much

Smart Tip

Website design and hosting fees may be higher in large urban areas. Shop around. It doesn't matter if you're in Atlanta, Chicago, or Los Angeles; you can hire a webmaster in Pipsqueak, South Dakota, and work with the designer as easily as if he or she were next door.

you want to update the site per month for basic web hosting. See Chapter 11 for more on websites.

Doing It Digitally

If you plan on producing your own website or your own advertising materials (or both), you might want to spring for a digital camera. With one of these gadgets, you simply snap photos of, say, the slim-and-trim participants in your aerobics book, or the crafts projects in your candle-making title. Then you connect the camera to your computer, move your mouse around a bit—and presto! You've got the picture right in your desktop publishing program. Expect to pay from $200 to $500 for a good-quality digital camera.

You may also want to consider a scanner—a nifty gadget that digitizes graphics from just about any printed medium—books, photographs, brochures, original art, or postcards, for example. You can pick up a basic scanner for about $100 to $200; look for one with resolution of 4,800 x 9,600 dpi (dots per square inch) or better.

Photo Finish

Once the photo is in your computer, you can manipulate it in all sorts of interesting ways, acting as your own photofinishing expert. You can crop it; expand it; zoom in or out on various features; blur the edges for that shot-through-gauze look; make it look like a watercolor, pastel, or oil painting—ad infinitum, depending on the kind of photo-manipulating software you have. This stuff is not only great for business purposes, it's a heck of a lot of fun! Some digital cameras, like Kodak, come complete with this software. Or you can purchase any number of programs, from Corel's Paint Shop Pro Photo, priced at about $100, to Adobe's Photoshop, which costs about $600.

Printer Mania

A good printer is a must. Not for your manuscript—which your printer or e-publishing site will want sent by email, internet, or on a portable drive and of

Dollar Stretcher

If you like Adobe Photoshop but can't justify the price, try Photoshop Elements for around $100. If you can live without all the bells and whistles, you'll find it performs many of the same functions as the standard version.

which you may likely print but one hard copy—but for all the other materials you'll produce. You'll have promotional materials, order forms, mailing labels, contracts, statements, and sundry other materials that will need to look polished and professional. The materials you produce will be a direct reflection of your company.

Take a Number

You'll also want to figure in the cost of buying ISBNs (International Standard Book Numbers) as part of your company setup expenses. The ISBN is a number that is used to identify a book by edition, binding, and publisher. There's a price tag attached to the ISBN.

A single ISBN costs $125. If you are pretty certain you are only going to publish one book, then go for it. But if you are likely to publish just one more book, go for the group of 10 ISBNs purchase—that's like getting eight for free. You can purchase them in bigger bulks as well: 100, 1,000, or even 10,000 at a gulp. You will pay extra for expedited processing.

Where do you get your ISBN numbers? You can purchase them only through one source, R.R. Bowker in New Providence, New Jersey, which acts as the ISBN databank, as well as the purveyor. Go to www.isbn.org to order your numbers online or download a snail mail order form. You can order one ISBN at a time, and you can order an ISBN for your e-book. If your book is available in hardback, softcover, and as an e-book, you need to order three ISBNs, one for each version. At isbn.org, you will find MyIdentifiers.com, where you can purchase ISBNs and bar codes for your books. ISBNs are assigned instantly upon paying for your order.

To make your publishing life sans souci, or carefree, you may want to spring for a SAN, or Standard Address Number. This is a number used by publishers, libraries, bookstores, and other industry buyers, vendors, and suppliers to give them instant computerized billing and shipping information. With a SAN on your letterhead and invoices, any library or bookstore that purchases from you can immediately plug your address into their system and pay you ASAP.

SANs cost $150 per address. If you have separate payment and shipping addresses, you'll need two SANs. Go to www.isbn.org and then click on the SAN button to order your number(s).

You'll want sharp, bold graphics and high print quality to give your business an aura of confidence and success. You'll also want a printer that's fast. There's nothing quite like the frustration of waiting for material to trickle out of a slow-going printer: One page per minute can seem like one page per hour.

Fortunately, the really hot-stuff printers are much less expensive now than ever before. You can purchase an inkjet, many of which can produce all the wonderful colors of commercial artwork. Color-capable models print more slowly than black-and-white models do, but if you'll be printing lots of marketing materials, like brochures and newsletters, then color should be a consideration. You can expect to pay from $150 to $300 for a color inkjet printer, and from $200 to $1,000 or more for a basic laser printer.

Fax Facts

Now that just about everybody communicates by email, a fax machine is not a hard-and-fast necessity, but it's a nice touch. Customers who can't—or won't—order products on the internet can fax their book orders to you. And you can fax RFQs (request for quote) to printers, who usually have pre-printed forms on which you check the services you want.

You can purchase a basic plain-paper fax for as little as $50 to $150, or a fancy multifunctional machine incorporating fax/copier/scanner/printer from $250 to $800.

Phone Fanatic

We assume that you already have a telephone, in which case you already know all about phone bills. And as a businessperson, you can't let phone calls go unanswered—it's unprofessional and results in lost orders. If customers can't reach you, they give up and don't order books. The phone company's line installation fee should run you in the range of $40 to $60. Check with your local phone company to determine exactly what these costs are in your area.

If you're working from a home office (or even from a commercial one), you'll want a two-line phone so you can put one line on hold while you are answering the other. A speaker is also a nice feature, especially for all those on-hold-forever calls to your banker, attorney, insurance company, or whoever. Your hands are free to work on financial data or your latest advertising materials, your shoulder remains unhunched, and there's no earring jabbing you in the side of the head while you listen to Muzak and wait your turn.

You can expect to pay about $70 to $150 for a two-line speakerphone with auto redial, memory dial, flashing lights, mute button, and other assorted goodies. Add another $20 to $100 for an answering machine, or $6 to $12 per month for voice mail service.

You also probably already have a cell phone. If you don't want a dedicated cell phone line for your business (many use it instead of having a landline at all), then you can still have your business landline number forwarded to your cell phone when you are away from your desk but still want to get business calls. Cell phone packages run the gamut for costs, particularly as more and more features are added. "Smart" phones are handy for businesses—you can check and respond to emails and search the internet from just about anywhere.

> **Beware!**
> Don't "enhance" your voice mail message with background music or a cutesy script. It's just not professional. And don't use an electronic message—potential customers want to be sure they have reached the business they thought they called. Create a personal message but keep it simple. Give your business name—spoken clearly and carefully—and ask callers to leave a short message and a phone number. Thank them for calling and assure them that someone from your office will return their call as soon as possible.

Misery

If you've read Stephen King's *Misery*—or seen the movie—you know how really traumatic it can be to lose that book you have been working on so diligently. (If you aren't up on your King, take our word for it. You do not want to chance losing a manuscript. It's every writer's worst nightmare.)

Why are we suddenly discussing the subject? To convince you to invest in an uninterruptible power supply, or UPS (not to be confused with UPS—United Parcel Service), for your computer system. This is especially important if you live in an area where lightning or power surges are frequent phenomena. (Or if you have a pet or small child who thinks disconnecting the power is kind of fun.)

If you're a computer newbie, you may not realize that even a flicker of power loss can shut down your computer, causing it to forget all the data you have carefully entered during your current work session, or—the ultimate horror—fry your computer's brains entirely. With a UPS in your arsenal, you won't lose power to your system when the house power fails or flickers. Instead, the unit flashes red and sounds a warning, giving you ample time to safely shut down your computer.

If you'll be spending a large amount of time on the internet, which accesses the World Wide Web through the telephone, you want to be sure that your UPS includes phone line protection. You can expect to pay between $70 and $200 or up for one of these indispensable units.

A surge protector safeguards your electronic equipment from power spikes during storms or outages. Your battery backup will double as a surge protector for your computer's hard drive (or CPU) and monitor, but you'll want protection for other valuable office equipment, like your printer, fax machine, and copier. They do not need a battery backup because no data will be lost if the power goes out, so a surge protector will do the job for a lot less money (expect to pay in the range of $15 to $60). If you've got a fax machine, be sure the surge protector also defends its phone line.

> **Tip...**
>
> ### Smart Tip
>
> Although an uninterrupted power supply/surge protector and battery backup are a must, to really cover your backup needs, be sure to sign on to an online backup system, known as "cloud storage," like Mozy or MobileMe from Apple. Once or twice a day, the cloud backup system updates its memory with anything that you have stored on your computer since the last time it backed up. Costs can be as little as $5 a month.

Electronic Money

An electronic credit card terminal can be a major boon to your business. Remember that you'll likely be selling your books on the internet, by direct mail, or to specialty stores, as well as through a book distributor. So you'll need a method of accepting payments, and credit cards are the method of choice. They make payment easier and faster for customers and for you because you can take credit card information over the phone, on the web, or by fax, and send out the order immediately.

More and more merchant card service firms are springing up that cater specifically to the SOHO, or small office/home office, and to the internet entrepreneur. Shop around (especially on the web), and you'll find a variety to choose from.

What can you expect to pay for an electronic terminal? Fees depend on several factors, including the company you go with and your personal credit history. Take a look at the Electronic Card Terminal Fees on page 63 for an idea, but also keep in mind that this is an industry that's growing rapidly with better deals all the time. You can lease or purchase the terminal itself from the merchant bank, or you can go the bargain hunter route and buy a used (but still serviceable) machine from a company that's gone out of business or has upgraded its unit.

Electronic Card Terminal Fees

Item	Fees (Swiped*)	Fees (Mail, Phone, or Internet Order)
Discount rate *(Multiply each transaction by this rate, i.e., $200 ticket fee x 1.59% = $3.18 that the bank charges you to process the transaction.)*	1.18% to 1.89%	2.09% to 2.50%
Transaction fee *(another fee the bank adds on for each transaction processed)*	20 cents	25 to 30 cents
Monthly statement fee	$5 to $10	$5 to $15
Monthly minimum *(If your monthly sales are less than the minimum amount, you pay this amount.)*	$10 to $20	$10 to $20
Application fee	$0 to $75	$0 to $75
Programming fee	usually free with equipment lease or purchase	usually free with equipment lease or purchase
Electronic card terminal	$300 to $600 purchase or $19 to $72 per month lease option	$300 to $600 purchase or $19 to $62 per month lease option

*Merchant card services charge higher discount rates for orders taken by mail, internet, or phone than for those handled in person, or swiped, through the credit card terminal. Why? Because if a customer signs for your product or service while he's standing there, you and the merchant service run less risk of a charge-back.

In addition to the fees shown here, you may be charged an *address verification* fee per transaction, a *daily batchout* fee to send charges from the electronic terminal to the merchant service in batches or chunks, and an annual membership fee. Be sure to ask and negotiate before you sign up!

You can also simply use PayPal, the online payment service owned by eBay. Go to PayPal and set up an account. Depending on the level of service you choose, customers can pay for your books with several different types of credit cards or directly from their PayPal account to yours. You get an email notice from PayPal that someone put money in your account and for what. When you go to your PayPal account, you get the address for shipping (if applicable), and if you are shipping a physical book, you can click a couple buttons to create a pre-paid mailing label, print it out on your printer, attach it to the package, and put it in the USPS mailbox

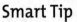

Smart Tip

The copier is an optional item, but as you grow you may find it a necessary luxury for running off forms, brochures, fliers, and other goodies. It's far easier to run off a few copies in your own office than having to run down to the copy center every time the need arises. Copiers range from $200 to $2,000 and up. If you feel the need to collate to your heart's content, consider leasing a higher-end model.

at the end of your driveway (or nearest post office). Fulfillment of orders can take minutes! You can also opt for UPS or FedEx shipping; drop it at the closest drop box.

Domain Décor

Office furniture for your publishing domain is another optional item. It's important that your work environment is comfortable and ergonomic, but if you are homebased

Not Going Postal

If you plan on selling via direct mail, a postage meter may keep you from "going postal." Depending on how snazzy a model you choose, you can fold, staple, insert, seal, label, weigh, sort, stack, wrap, and stamp your mail. Phew! And, it used to be that you'd have to lug your postage meter down to the post office and stand in line to get it reset, but you don't have to anymore! Now you simply reset it via phone or computer.

The fancier and faster the machine, the more expensive it will be to rent, lease, or purchase. As a ballpark figure, you can expect to rent a combination postage meter/electronic scale for about $18 to $100 per month. Check PitneyWorks.com for information about Pitney Bowes authorized digital postage meters.

it's perfectly acceptable to start off with an old door set on cinder blocks for a desk and an egg crate for your files. When you're ready to go the big step toward real office furniture for that oh-so-professional look, you've got a stunning array of possibilities to choose from.

The big office supply warehouse stores typically offer midrange desks from $200 to $300, computer work centers for around $200, printer stands from $50 to $75, two-drawer letter-size file cabinets (which can double as your printer stand) from $25 to $100, and bookcases for $25 to $70.

Chairs are a very personal matter. Some people like the dainty secretary's chair for its economy of space; others want the tonier, high-back executive model. There are chairs with everything from kangaroo pockets to pneumatic height adjustments. Prices range from $60 to $250 and up.

Pen and Paper

Don't forget that you'll also need paper—lots of it—to print various drafts of your book as well as press releases and correspondence. Plan on allocating about $45 for a box of good-quality printer/copier paper. This will give you ten reams of 500 sheets each. (It might sound like a lot of paper, but it goes quickly!)

You'll also need envelopes, business cards, pens, pencils, and all those miscellaneous office supplies like paper clips, cellophane tape, and staples. And if you'll do any sort

Spawn of Publishers

While you're investigating professional associations, check out SPAWN, which is the acronym for Small Publishers, Artists and Writers Network. This group has a slightly different mission, as its name implies. SPAWN seeks to give authors, illustrators, graphic designers, and photographers, as well as editors and self-publishers, a place to share information and ideas.

SPAWN's $45 annual membership fee includes a newsletter, a member directory, chapter meetings, discounts on seminars and workshops, discount supplemental health benefits service, an online bookstore for small publishers, discounts on web services, and your very own web page. Plus—as an added bonus—SPAWN members get a discount on their Publishers Marketing Association membership.

of mail order (which includes internet sales), you'll want shipping materials in which to send off your products. You'll spend in the range of $100 to $150 for a starter collection of shipping supplies, including sturdy bubble-lined envelopes, sealing tape, and a gun-style tape dispenser.

Get Professional

We've now given you a shopping list of every office gizmo you'll need to get up and running as a self-publisher—including two take-along checklists to have in hand when you hit the office and computer superstores. You will find "The Self-Publisher's Office Equipment Checklist" on page 68, and "The Office Supplies Mini-Shopping List" on page 67.

But there's still more to come! You should also budget for membership in professional organizations and subscriptions to industry publications. Taking these steps gives you up-to-the-nanosecond information on news, reviews, and issues in the publishing world. You'll also have access to industry gurus who can answer pressing questions, as well as a support team of other publishers who are actively "being there and doing that."

"It's good to belong to as many organizations and networking opportunities as you can spare time for," advises Steve C. in Vermont. "They provide opportunities to keep abreast of the constant changes in the book businesses and to share insights and ideas that will help you sell books.

"I belong to Independent Book Publishers Association (IBPA), Small Publishers Association of North America (SPAN), National Association of Independent Publishers (NAIP), the Vermont Book Publishers Association (VBPA), and Independent Publishers of New England (IPNE)," Steve says. "I'm also an associate member of American Booksellers Association (ABA) and an active member/participant in the pub-forum listserv [a forum for independent book publishers offered through eGroups, a free service that lets you create or join email lists (www.egroups.com/group/pub-forum)].

"Among the magazines I take (other than those associated with the organizations I belong to) are *ForeWord* and *Publishers Weekly*," says Steve. Another group I belong to that is not specific to a book business is Vermont Businesses for Social Responsibility. If that didn't exist I'd probably join the Chamber of Commerce

Dollar Stretcher

Membership in professional associations often qualifies you for discounts on a variety of services, from insurance to shipping.

The Office Supplies Mini-Shopping List

Items

❑ Computer/copier/fax paper	$
❑ Blank business cards	
❑ Blank letterhead stationery	
❑ Matching envelopes	

❑ Shipping materials (for mail orders):
    ❑ Bubble-lined envelopes
    ❑ Sealing tape
    ❑ Tape dispenser	

❑ File folders	
❑ Return address stamp or stickers	
❑ Extra printer cartridge	
❑ Extra fax cartridge	
❑ CD-ROM discs	
❑ Flash drive for backup	
❑ Mouse pad	
❑ Miscellaneous office supplies (pencils, paper clips, etc.)	
Total Office Supplies Expenditures	$

and Better Business Bureau, but being a member of a BSR group establishes to the public that you are a highly ethical business."

Spanning the Industry

The Small Publishers Association of North America (SPAN—spannet.org) is a terrific place to start your professional hobnobbing. With more than 1,100 members, this group offers all sorts of membership perks including:

The Self-Publisher's Office Equipment Checklist

Use this handy list as a shopping guide for equipping your office. It has been designed with the one-person home office in mind. If you've got partners, employees, or you just inherited a million dollars with the stipulation that you spend at least half on office equipment, you may want to make modifications.

After you've decided what you want to buy, fill in the purchase price next to each item, add up the total, and use this figure in the "Your Company Startup Costs" worksheet on page 74!

❏ Windows-based Pentium-class PC with SVGA monitor, modem, and CD-ROM	$
❏ Laser or inkjet printer	
❏ Fax machine	
❏ Software:	
❏ Word processing	
❏ Desktop publishing	
❏ Specialty software	
❏ Mailing list management	
❏ Phone(s), two to three lines	
❏ Answering machine (or voice mail)	
❏ Uninterruptible power supply	
❏ Flash drive	
❏ Surge protector	
❏ Calculator	
❏ Electronic credit card terminal (cost to lease or buy)	
❏ Postage meter (cost to lease)	
Not on the critical list	
❏ Digital camera	
❏ Scanner	
❏ Copier	
❏ Desk	
❏ Desk chair	
❏ Filing cabinet	
❏ Bookcase	
Total Office Equipment/Furniture Expenditures	$

- Access to the SPAN blog, IndyPub, about all-things-publishing
- Discounts on industry publications
- Participation in book expos, fairs, and other exhibitions
- Royalty-free sales of your books on SPAN's online bookstore (i.e., you do not have to pay them royalties for being listed on their site)
- Discounts on book freight and shipping, including FedEx
- Co-op advertising program
- Waiver of book wholesaler fee
- Access to library distribution services

What does it cost to join SPAN? At this writing, annual membership tallies in at $89 per year, which isn't a bad investment!

IBPA

Another handy organization to be affiliated with is the Independent Book Publishers Association, or IBPA. With more than 4,000 members, IBPA advances the efforts of book, audio, video, and CD publishers worldwide. Like SPAN, it also offers many perks for its members, including:

- Various discounts on publishing/advertising/marketing services
- Dispute resolution program
- Exhibit opportunities at book trade shows
- Discounted freight and mailing services
- Health insurance
- Liability insurance
- Merchant credit card acceptance program
- Discounted rate for Nielsen Bookscan
- Monthly newsletter

The cost for all these member services depends on the number of employees in your company. For a publisher with one to nine employees (which will more than likely describe you at this point), the annual membership fee is $95.

Read All About It

There's no dearth of reading material in the publishing industry—in fact, there's so much that you could easily spend all your time perusing other people's texts instead of producing your own. But as a savvy self-publisher, you will want to stay up to speed in the field. We recommend you start with subscriptions to the following three publications. (You can check out many more that are listed in the Appendix at the back of this book.)

1. *ForeWord*. Who couldn't like a publication with world headquarters over a chocolate shop? Besides understanding one of the truly important food groups, *ForeWord* does a wonderful job of providing news and reviews specifically about small and independent presses. A must-read, so budget $40 for 12 annual issues.

2. *Writer's Digest*. This venerable publication is as the name implies written more for writers than publishers, but since self-publishers are both, it is always full of helpful tips and hints. An annual subscription of 13 issues costs about $20.

3. *Publishers Weekly*. The name says it all—news, reviews, and lots more for the publishing trade. It's pricey at $240 per year, but read by everybody who's anybody in the field.

Are You Insured?

Don't forget insurance. Since your office will most likely be in your home, you'll need to find out if your homeowner's package covers your business assets, inventory, and equipment, or if you need additional coverage. As a ballpark figure, allow from $100 to $500 annually over your existing homeowner's policy. Then you'll want to add special publisher's liability coverage to cover you for horrors including errors and omissions or defective advice. Budget $1,200 to $2,500 per year; costs vary depending on your gross annual revenues.

Tally It Up

OK, now it's time to don your bookkeeping cap and tally up the company setup expenses we've investigated in this chapter. Besides the ones we've already checked into, you will want to add other expenses like business licenses, business insurance, legal advice, and all the other costs intrinsic to any company's birth. To give you an idea of how much you can expect to budget, check out the "Equipment Expenses" and "Self-Publisher Company Startup Expenses" charts for two hypothetical self-publishers, Glowworm Press and Bell & Candle Publishing (see pages 71 and 72).

As you peruse these publishers' setup costs, you will see that Bell & Candle is spending significantly more than her colleague, even though both companies will be

Equipment Expenses

Furniture, Equipment & Supplies	Glowworm Press	Bell & Candle Publishing
Computer system (including printer)	0	$2,500
Fax machine	$150	$250
Software	0	$995
Phone system	$70	$90
Uninterruptible power supply	0	$125
Surge protector	0	$34
Calculator	$25	$75
Postage meter	$24	$117
Copier	0	$500
Electronic credit card terminal	$300	$450
Desk	0	$300
Desk chair	0	$100
Printer stand	0	$70
File cabinet	0	$50
Bookcase	0	$70
Printer/copier paper	$25	$50
Blank business cards	$6	$12
Letterhead paper	$30	$30
Matching envelopes	$35	$35
No. 10 blank envelopes	$3	$6
Shipping materials (for mail orders)	$117	$150
Address stamp or stickers	$10	$10
Extra printer cartridges	$70	$70
Extra fax cartridge	$80	$80
Mouse pad	0	$10
Rewritable CDs	$7	$12
Flash drive	$25	$50
Miscellaneous office supplies	$50	$100
Total Expenditures	**$1,027**	**$6,341**

Self-Publisher Company Startup Expenses

Costs	Glowworm Press	Bell & Candle Publishing
Professional associations	$190	$235
Equipment and office supplies (see chart on page 71)	$1,027	$6,341
Licenses	$100	$100
Phone (installation/line charges)	$90	$90
Subscriptions	$50	$219
Legal services	$375	$375
Miscellaneous postage	$50	$50
Internet service provider (six months)	$120	$120
Website design and marketing	0	$500
Web hosting (six months)	$180	$300
Insurance (six months)	$850	$1,150
ISBN (set of 10)	$205	$205
SAN	0	$100
Subtotal	**$3,237**	**$9,785**
Miscellaneous expenses (add roughly 10 percent of total)	$324	$979
Total Startup Costs	**$3,561**	**$10,764**

homebased with the owner as the only employee. The biggest cost differences can be attributed to computer and website-related items. Bell & Candle, for instance, will go with an all-new, top-of-the-line computer system and software, while Glowworm will use the owner's existing system and software. And Glowworm's computer-savvy owner will also design and put up the company's website, while Bell & Candle's owner will outsource these functions.

You can use the worksheet "Your Company Startup Costs" on page 74 to list the expenses you will have for setting up your own company. If you make a few copies of this sheet, you can work up several options, compare them all, and decide which will be the best one for you.

Romancing the Bank

Now that you've done all the arithmetic, you can determine just how much capital you'll need to start your company. If you find that your bank account falls short of the necessary funds, you can show all these beautifully executed figures to prospective lenders. This will help you convince them that your business is a good risk and that you'll be able to repay a loan without difficulty.

You might want to consider financing through your bank or credit union. In this case, your projected startup costs will be extremely important. The bank will want to see all of this information neatly laid out and carefully calculated. You'll also want to show them all the statistics you can gather about the bright future of the self-publishing industry.

Friends and Family

Most entrepreneurs use a very exclusive source to finance their startup expenses—family and friends. You may choose to go this route yourself, especially because bankers are generally not very gung-ho about so-called nontraditional businesses like self-publishing.

If you go with someone from your own inner circle, you'll have less paperwork to fill out, and you can let your financier share in the excitement as your company takes off. But remember that you'll still need to figure the repayment of borrowed funds into your costs, and that you should treat your repayment agreement as seriously as you would any bank loan.

Going Plastic

Another route many entrepreneurs take to obtain financing is through an entity as close as your back pocket—the credit card. Before you choose this option, take a look

Your Company Startup Costs

Professional associations	$
Office equipment (insert total from "The Self-Publisher's Office Equipment Checklist" on page 68)	
Licenses	
Phone (installation/line charges)	
Subscriptions	
Legal services	
Internet service provider	
Website design and marketing	
Web hosting	
Office supplies (insert total from "The Office Supplies Mini-Shopping List" on page 67)	
Miscellaneous postage	
Insurance	
SAN	
ISBN	
Subtotal	$
Miscellaneous expenses (add roughly 10 percent of total)	
Your Total Startup Costs	$

at your available credit balance and at the annual percentage rate. Card companies frequently offer low, low rates as an incentive to sign up or to use their service; they usually raise these interest rates after a certain period of time. Go with the one that offers the best rate for the longest period.

6

More Bookkeeping
Production Costs

In the last chapter, we explored the costs involved in setting up your business office, including everything from computer equipment to memberships in professional organizations. But there's much more to the excitement—and the expense—of self-publishing. There are also the actual costs involved in producing a book, from proofreading, to illustrations, to printing, if that's the route you decide to take. We'll investigate all of that in this chapter.

Pre-Production Basics

Prospective self-publishers always want to know: How much does it cost to print a book? This is a very good question, but printing is only one aspect of getting a book from your imagination into a bound group of pages. A better question to ask might be: How much does it cost to produce a book? A lot of elements go into a book's production long before it's ready for the printer, things like cover and interior design, copyediting, and proofreading. These are important elements that you do not want to skimp on. If your book's artwork is clumsy, the layout is awkward, and the text is riddled with typos and grammatical glitches, it smacks of amateurism and nobody is going to buy it. Distributors, booksellers, and librarians will perceive your book as the worst form of self-publishing, and prospective readers won't buy it—if it's nonfiction, they will not feel that the information looks reliable. If you're a professional who can competently perform some of these services yourself, terrific! If not, it's worth it to pay someone else to do them for you.

Look at the chart called "Book Production Costs" on page 92 as you read through this chapter. You can use the costs incurred by our hypothetical publishers, Glowworm Press and Bell & Candle Publishing, as a guide for what your costs may be. Glowworm Press is going with a 6-by-9 softcover (or trade paperback) that will be 192 pages, with a four-color cover and no interior artwork. Bell & Candle is going for a snazzier presentation, with a 6-by-9 hardcover (or case bound book) that will be 288 pages, with a four-color dust jacket, and no interior artwork. We've also provided a worksheet for determining your own book production costs on page 97.

A Book by Its Cover

The old adage that you can't tell a book by its cover doesn't hold true in the publishing world—at least not as far as readers are concerned. The average consumer spends an astonishing eight seconds perusing a book's cover before moving on to the next selection on the shelf. That means your book has eight seconds to make a positive impact—eight seconds to communicate its value as a source

Smart Tip

Tip...

When discussing graphics, four-color actually refers to all the colors in the rainbow. It's called four-color because every hue and shade is derived from a specific mix of four basic colors: blue, red, yellow, and black, which you will see abbreviated as CMYK: cyan, magenta, yellow, and black.

of information or entertainment. That is not much time. And it's the reason that many savvy publishers turn to professional book designers to produce their covers. Even e-books need a "cover."

"A designer who specializes in book covers knows about the appropriate positioning of text and graphics, the power of the spine and back, the 'rules' for bar codes, how to prepare artwork for specific book manufacturing methods, how to speak the book printer's language, and understands the critical scheduling and positioning of your book cover design in the marketing process," explains Kathi Dunn of Dunn & Associates Design (dunn-design.com) in Hayward, Wisconsin. "If you choose to hire a graphic designer who is not experienced in book cover design, be sure you have time to invest in supervision and are willing to take responsibility for the results."

Dunn & Associates is one of the savvy book design firms who have embraced the burgeoning self-publishing world. Their website offers tips for self-publishers that will help make the design process go more smoothly. And for those that want to be led through the process of creating their book, they have created a Bestseller System™ which, while a considerable expense, may pay for itself in the long run. If you plan to do more than one book, you won't be stumbling along learning the process on the fly.

How much does it cost to have a cover professionally designed? Prices vary with the type of cover, colors, images, graphics, and effects. A one-color softcover book will be far less expensive than a fancy four-color dust jacket with multiple images or graphics embossed with foil lettering. As a ballpark, pencil in a minimum of $1,000 to $2,500 for a "full-service" design. There are many design companies offering cover design for as low as $300, but do your homework. They may not offer original designs or might make liberal use of stock photography that you are likely to see pop up on other covers. Be sure you know what you are getting for your money.

Designer Search

Since the cover design of your book is so critical to its success, how do you find a designer that will do your project justice? Choose one with whom you can forge a healthy relationship, counsels Pam Terry, owner and senior designer at Opus 1 Design in Beverly Hills, California. "Feel that she's enthusiastic about your work. See if you like her style. Make sure she's open for comments, suggestions, and critiques.

"Don't expect free work beforehand to see if she understands your idea," Pam adds. "Pay to see roughs only—maybe $200 for some very rough sketches to see if she's on the right track. If you have an idea about how you want your book to look and there's another book that looks similar, bring it along or let the designer know the title. She can look it up on Amazon.com."

Don't think just because you are publishing an e-book that you won't need a cover. Creating a cover for your e-book gives your book an identifier that can be the same for all versions of the book, from hardcover to paperback, to e-book to print-on-demand versions.

Drawing the Line

If you plan to produce a children's book, or other title that includes drawings and other artwork, you will have yet another reason to think about hiring a professional. If you're an artist or have one in your family, you're home free. If not, you'll need to hire an illustrator.

"I hire a graphic artist to do my covers and have hired other artists for interior illustrations," says Steve C. in Vermont. "If you're not good at packaging, you should hire a professional. The biggest mistake many new publishers make is producing a book that looks like amateurs threw it together. It doesn't matter how good a book it is—if it doesn't look professional and attractive, bookstores and distributors won't carry it, and it won't get reviews. You'll die with a garage full of copies."

Prices for professional illustrators are all over the map and depend on whether you'll need a few black-and-white line drawings or dozens of pages of four-color, full-page splendor. The only real way to pencil this expense into your book budget is to get quotes based on your particular needs. Shop for an illustrator by going to the Society of Children's Book Writers and Illustrators or the Graphic Artists Guild. (See contact information in the Appendix.) You can find names of illustrators by checking the cover and interior illustrator

Smart Tip

"Don't take any changes by the copyeditor personally," counsels Laura Poole of Archer Editorial Services in Durham, North Carolina. "We don't mean to hurt your feelings or slight your writing skills. We want you to sound good on paper!"

credit (usually cited on the copyright page) on books you like whose covers and/or illustrations are in the same style as you envision for your book.

Copy Quality

The copyeditor, also called a content editor, is another professional you should turn to. This behind-the-scenes expert will read your text or copy to make sure that your material isn't garbled, inconsistent, or otherwise confused.

Copyeditors look for all sorts of manuscript problems, like the fact that you change tense from present to past and back again throughout your text, or the fact that your character's mom is named Thelma in Chapter 2 and Nonie in Chapter 6. (Hey, it happens. You change the name in mid-manuscript for whatever reason and forget to go back and correct earlier pages.) They can catch errors like the fact that you said cold cereal is unhealthy in Chapter 3, but that granola is good for you in Chapter 4. Copyeditors also look for style glitches. Say you put tip boxes in every chapter except Chapter 8, or that you start each story with

> ### Smart Tip
> *Tip...*
>
> Text in a finished book should be single-spaced. But when you submit your manuscript to a copyeditor or proofreader to be worked on, send it double-spaced. This gives them room between the lines to make corrections and also marks you as a professional.

a quote but stop doing so halfway through the book. In other words, they nitpick—but in the best way. When you're writing a manuscript, it's hard to see the forest for the trees, but a good copyeditor can do just that.

"I was a professional editor before I started this business, but even so, when I'm editing a book I become too close to it to see all the mistakes, the awkward phrases, the gaps in information, etc.," says Steve C. in Hinesburg, Vermont. "I usually do the heavy editing, then send it out to two or three freelancers. Some of the freelancers are professionals, others are English majors who love books and offer their services for cheap. The more literate people who go through a book to make corrections and suggestions, the better book it will be."

Anna J. in Texas agrees. "I hired an editor and proofreader for my third book, which had a lot of text," she says. "I'm glad I did. She has a degree in English, and she was wonderful. Hiring her was good for a number of reasons. She was a stickler for perfection and looked things up when she wasn't sure if something was 'stylistic' or just plain wrong. She worked with me throughout the process and asked me what kind of editing/proofreading I wanted and adhered to what I said. But most importantly, she was unfamiliar with the jargon and experiences of the authors, and her fresh perspective brought to the forefront any passages that to a layman were a bit unclear."

How much should you pencil in for a copyeditor? Ink in $2 to $3 per manuscript page—which is double-spaced with one-inch margins and standard 10-point to 12-point font (see Chapter 7), advises Laura Poole of Archer Editorial Services in Durham, North Carolina. You may also see prices quoted by the hour; a ballpark range is $25 to $50 per hour, a lot of which depends on the level of editing your particular book needs.

How do you know whom to choose? "Find someone who has experience editing the type of book you've written," says Laura Poole. "Use someone with whom you are comfortable. Be willing to submit a sample (from two pages to a whole chapter) for an editor to do, and be willing to pay for their time."

Proof Positive

Copyeditors typically also serve as proofreaders—at the manuscript stage. Once your book is "set in type," you will want to have it proofread again by someone who is concentrating just on that. It's extremely difficult to detect these sorts of glitches in your own work—you're so close to it that you can be completely blind to a blatant typo even when it has stared you in the face through ten revisions. The proofreader also is able to catch mistakes that are made in the copyediting process, as text is revised and rearranged. Rates for a good proofreader range from $1 to $2.50 per page.

By the Numbers

Every book, like every good secret agent, has to have a number to go along with its name. For books, this number is the ISBN, or International Standard Book Number. Every book has its own individual 13-digit ISBN printed on the back cover or dust jacket as well as somewhere in the front matter or first few pages.

The ISBN is like a fingerprint—it identifies you as the publisher and also identifies each of your products as a specific version of a specific title. The classic hardcover first edition of *Raising Radishes for Fun & Profit* will have a different ISBN than the revised second edition. The paperback edition will carry its own ISBN. The Japanese-language version will have a different ISBN than the English one. And the audiobook of *Raising Radishes* will have its own separate ISBN, different from both the book and DVD versions.

We placed basic ISBN costs under your company setup expenses since you will need to purchase these numbers in groups of at least ten at a time, regardless of when you intend to use the numbers. They must be purchased through R.R. Bowker in New Providence, New Jersey (www.isbn.org).

Lucky Number 13

In 2007, the book industry converted its 10-digit ISBN system to 13 digits. Why? In short, there was a number shortage. So many books are being published, the amount of 10-digit numbers was running low. The new 13-digit system will allow the ISBN system to grow its numbering capacity and allow for more numbers that can be assigned. In addition, the new system will make the book numbering system complement the global EAN.UCC ID system that most other consumer goods use for identification purposes.

Two new prefixes were added to the system—978 and 979. The 978 prefix will be added to the front of current ISBNs and one new digit will be added at the end. Voila! The 979 prefix will only be used once all of the 978s are gone and cannot be used to convert back to a 10-digit ISBN.

If you have already purchased a boatload of ISBN-10 numbers, you can convert them to ISBN-13 by visiting www.isbn.org and clicking on the "ISBN-13 Support" link. There, you will find a handy-dandy converter tool that's a snap to use.

Another facet of the change is that all publishers will cease using the UPC barcode on the back of books and will instead use the EAN barcode. Since some consumers will continue to reference old ISBN-10 numbers when ordering books, be prepared to transact with that number, but discourage its use and spread the word about the new system.

For more information, you can download a PDF of *ISBN-13 For Dummies* on the ISBN website.

Name, Rank, and Serial Number

If you plan to publish serials—which include magazines, newspapers, annuals, frequently revised directories, and other ongoing publications—you'll need an ISSN or International Standard Serial Number. ISSNs are basically just like ISBNs except that:

- Their eight digits don't mean anything in particular (see "Anatomy of an ISBN Number" on page 85 for comparison).
- They describe the whole of a series, like *The Butterfly Breeder's Home Companion* magazine, issues 1 through 25, instead of one specific issue. They also describe "continuing resources" that most publications make available online. There are specific restrictions on what internet-based content does and does not require an ISSN, so check the ISSN website for more information. (For example, different language versions and media outlets get different ISSNs.)

There's no charge for an ISSN. For more information, check out the ISSN International Centre website at www.issn.org.

Bar Codes in Bookland

In addition to your ISBN (or ISSN), you'll need a bar code for each book title that you publish in hard copy. This is simply the book's ISBN and its price, rendered in store-scanner format and called the Bookland EAN number with price code. Unless you absolutely, positively plan to sell only to passersby at flea markets or at your annual church bazaar, you must have a Bookland bar code. Bookstores and their wholesalers insist on them so they can ring up books at their registers equipped with scanners.

You buy one digital file of the Bookland bar code for your book, and then you have it printed on the back cover of each copy. The cost is reasonable, and you can get them from a variety of sources. Check out the Appendix at the back of this book for contact information.

Advanced Information

Once you've received your ISBNs, you'll need to fill out an ABI, which is an Advanced Book Information form. This step is critically important because the ABI form gets your book into the bible of the publishing industry, R.R. Bowker's *Books in Print*. Booksellers and librarians, as well as everybody else in the trade, use *Books in Print* as the source for information about titles in print and their publishers. If your book is not listed here, it might as well be lost in the ether.

You can fill out an ABI form on the internet for free, so there's no reason not to do so. Go to the R.R. Bowker website for

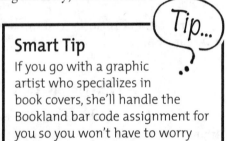

Smart Tip

If you go with a graphic artist who specializes in book covers, she'll handle the Bookland bar code assignment for you so you won't have to worry about it.

publisher services, www.bowkerlink.com, and click on the "Books In Print" link at the left of the screen. Make sure you apply about six months before your book rolls off the printing press. You must have an ISBN before you can fill out your ABI, so don't procrastinate on that, either.

Getting Carded

Yet another alphabet item to tackle is applying for your book's LCCN or Library of Congress Catalog Card Number. This is like an ISBN for the library trade. It's assigned by the Library of Congress and allows librarians all over the country to order books by the numbers from the Library's catalog. Since the majority of public and private libraries subscribe to this catalog and order freely from it, your book will lose out if it's not listed.

The Library of Congress is a bit picky about what types of publications it chooses to assign LCCNs to. Among the materials that get the thumbs down are: books under 50 pages in length, except for picture books; religious school materials; workbooks; mass market paperbacks (which are the kind of novels found on supermarket and drugstore racks); and e-books.

Anatomy of an ISBN Number

As of January 1, 2007, the entire book publishing world converted to using a 13-digit ISBN. Each ISBN is divided into five sets of numbers of various lengths, separated by hyphens. Here's an example of the difference between the 10- and 13-digit ISBN.

ISBN-10 looks like:

ISBN 1-891984-06-3

Group or country identifier

Specific title or edition of title

Identifies the publisher

The "check digit"; validates or ends the ISBN; occasionally an X

ISBN-13 looks like:

ISBN 978-1-891984-06-8

New prefix
Group or country identifier

Specific title or edition of title

Identifies the publisher

New different "check digit" that validates the ISBN-13

You can find a complete list of unacceptable materials on the Library of Congress LCCN website at http://pcn.loc.gov/pcn005.html. (Don't be misled by the fact that, in true government-speak, the LCCN is called the PCN here. It means Pre-assigned Card Number because the number is assigned before the book is printed.) You can also apply for your number on this site. It's free—all the Library asks is that you send a complimentary copy after publication. This means your book will be on the shelf at the nation's library in Washington, DC!

Newly Revised

Plan ahead when you write that nonfiction book. If it contains material that should be updated every few years, you can make the necessary changes and reprint it as a revised edition. The beauty here is that it will be a brand-new book (with a brand-new ISBN), and you can start your pre-publication marketing campaign all over again. You'll have new reviews from book industry publications, niche industry publications, and other opinion molders.

Don't get confused about the difference between reprints and revised editions. A reprint is another printing of a book with no changes made to it (except perhaps to fix a few previously unspotted typos). A revision is a book in which a significant amount of material has been changed—because new information has been added, new research has been done, contact information (like addresses and phone numbers) has changed, or any combination thereof.

This is another task that you'll need to complete well before your book goes to the printer. If you wait until after printing, you can't list your LCCN on the copyright page where it belongs.

The CIP on Your Shoulder

One more item to concern yourself with before your book goes to print is the CIP or Cataloging in Publication record, which is also issued by the Library of Congress free of charge. This is the block of text you find on the copyright page of LCCN-registered books that gives all the technical stuff librarians love, including Library of Congress subject headings, Dewey decimal numbers, and Library of Congress classification numbers.

The CIP is important for any book that has an LCCN—but there's a catch. Even though the Library of Congress hands out LCCNs to books from even the newest of publishers, it won't give out CIP records until you already have three previous titles under your belt. And the Library of Congress will want proof in the form of front matter (the pages that precede the main body of a book) for several forthcoming books from your company, by more than two authors. For more information, check out the CIP website at http://cip.loc.gov/.

But there's hope. You can also develop your own P-CIP, which is a CIP made up by a publisher or its agent. Quality Books, a distributor based in Oregon, Illinois, which specializes in library sales, will provide a P-CIP record for you for around $150. It also provides an excellent explanation of CIP information on its website. (You'll find Quality Books listed in the Appendix of this book under "Distributors".) If you want to go it alone, ask your local librarian for help.

Print Talk

Now that we've explored your book's pre-production costs, it's time for the issue that first-time publishers are most interested in: printing costs. Here again, there's no set cost for all books. Each book is a separate entity and can be radically different from the next. A 32-page children's book, with full-color graphics on each page, will cost a heck of a lot more than a 32-page, text-only pamphlet on opal hunting in Arkansas. And a 192-page softcover book of house plans will carry a different printer's price tag than a 288-page hardcover romance novel that has a glossy, gold-embossed dust jacket.

In addition, printers' bids can vary wildly from one company to the next, or even from one job to the next. It's extremely important to get a variety of bids each time you have a book printed—printing represents a large percentage of book creation costs, so you don't want any big surprises at this stage of production.

There are over 40 book printers in the United States. Get estimates from as many as possible—it's perfectly acceptable to send an RFQ or request for quote to them all. You can send or fax a letter; however, many print shops have "quick quote" forms you can fill out and submit online. This is a great convenience, except that you immediately realize there are an overwhelming number of choices, all of which are set out in terminology only printers (and seasoned publishers) understand.

As we go through this chapter, we'll delve into the most common printing choices that you'll need to make. You'll soon be speaking printer lingo like a pro. For now, though, take a look at the sample "Quick Quote" form on page 88, and then see the response that you would get from the printer in the form on pages 89–90, "Price Quote from a Printer."

Keep in mind that you can't know everything about book printing your first (or even second or third) time out. Book printing companies, on the other hand, do this for a living. They know it all, and they're usually quite willing to help. Find a printer you trust and can communicate with; then explain your project and don't hesitate to ask questions.

Vital Statistics

Before you can get any sort of printing estimate, you must know the vital statistics of your proposed book including:

Quick Quote

Thomson-Shore also has a multipage online RFQ form that walks you through all the details of the quote.

Thomson - Shore, Inc.
phone (734) 426-3939 • fax 800-706-4545

Remit Quotation To:

Company _____

Address _____

City _____ State ___ Zip _____

Contact Name _____

Phone _____ Fax _____

E-mail _____

Book Specifications:

Title_____

Author_____

Page Count_____ Quantity_____

Trim Size_____

Expected date job would arrive at T-S _____
$\overline{\text{Month/Year}}$

TEXT COPY
- ○ Output-Ready PDF
- ○ Bluelines
- ○ Digital Bluelines
- ○ APP/PostScript/PDF
- ○ Halftones #_____
- ○ Camera Ready Copy

TEXT STOCK

Recycled*	○ Yes	○ No	*Available for certain trim sizes
Natural	○ 50 lb	○ 55 lb	○ 60 lb
White	○ 50 lb	n/a	○ 60 lb
○ Other_____			

TEXT INK
- ○ Black Ink Only
- ○ Bleeds
- ○ Black & 1 PMS
- ○ No Bleeds

BINDING
- ○ Perfect Paperback
- ○ Sewn Paperback
- ○ Other_____
- ○ Smyth Sewn Case
- ○ Notch Case
- ○ Cloth Type _____

SHRINKWRAPPING
- ○ Individually
- ○ In Groups

——— *COVER* ———	——— *JACKET* ———
FURNISHED COPY	*FURNISHED COPY*
○ Camera Ready	○ Camera Ready
○ Trouble Free Disk	○ Trouble Free Disk
○ Composite Film	○ Composite Film
○ *T-S* to Separate	○ *T-S* to Separate
STOCK	*STOCK*
○ 10pt C1S	○ 80lb Enamel
○ 12pt C1S	○ 100lb Enamel
○ 65 lb White	○ Other_____
○ Other_____	
PRINTING	*PRINTING*
○ Black ink	○ Black ink
+____ PMS colors	+____ PMS colors
○ 4-color process	○ 4-color process
COATING	*COATING*
○ Gloss Lam Coating	○ Gloss Lam Coating
○ Matte Lam Coating	○ Matte Lam Coating
PROOFS	*PROOFS*
○ Blue	○ Blue
○ Waterproof	○ Waterproof

Provided courtesy of Thomson-Shore Inc.

Price Quote from a Printer

Thomson-Shore, Inc.
7300 West Joy Road Dexter, MI 48130-9701
734.426.3939 Fax 800.706.4545
www.tshore.com

Read carefully and call immediately with any changes or questions!

9999
Glowworm Press
1 Firefly Lane
Luminescent, FL 10000

DATE: 04/06/07
QUOTE NUMBER: 178476
ACCOUNT NUMBER: 9999

Peter Moss
Ph:
Fax: (000)000-0000

TITLE:	THE NIGHT GARDEN
AUTHOR:	MOSS
QUANTITY:	1000, 3000, 5000
TRIM SIZE:	6 x 9
PAGES:	192
COPY:	Text - Customer furnished trouble free postscript or application files.
	Cover - Customer furnished TS supported, trouble free application files with 4 color image in place. Price will be confirmed upon review of disk.
	Proofs - 1 Full text proofs (Digital) and 1 Set(s) Digital Color proof of cover included.
PRESS:	Text - Black ink throughout, without bleeds.
	Covers - 4 color process plus Matte Lamination on outside. Note this coating is subject to scuffing and marking at the slightest pressure.
STOCK:	Text - 60# Natures Natural - (50%PCR), 360 ppi.
	Covers - 10pt. C1S.
BINDING:	Perfect binding in 32's.
PACKING:	Bulk Pack - Single Wall Carton
SHIPPING:	FOB Dexter, MI.
TERMS:	To avoid delays, arrange credit prior to sending job.

PRICING:	1000	3000	5000
PREP/PLATE	628.00	628.00	628.00
COVER	800.00	927.00	1,053.00
PAPER	473.00	1,340.00	2,202.00
PRESS	297.00	507.00	717.00
BINDING	485.00	926.00	1,364.00
	==========	==========	==========
	$ 2,683.00	$ 4,328.00	$ 5,964.00

OVER/UNDERS $ 0.82 each.

For new titles, T-S to archive digital files for an additional one-time fee of $40 per title.

Please Contact:

These prices will be honored for thirty (30) days from the date of this quotation. Signing and returning this quotation or the submission of your Purchase Order within those 30 days will secure the pricing for ninety (90) days from the date of this quotation. Any job received after ninety (90) days will be subject to new pricing. A confirmation, including new prices for any changes, additions, or alterations to the above specifications, will be sent to your after your order is received.

Accepted by:_____ Date:_____

Provided courtesy of Thomson-Shore Inc.

Price Quote from a Printer, continued

TERMS AND CONDITIONS

The following "Production Procedures" constitute a binding agreement between you and Thomson-Shore. By signing the price quotation, submitting a purchase order and/or letter of specifications for work to be performed by Thomson-Shore, you agree to be bound by all terms in this document. In addition, by submitting a job to Thomson-Shore as described on its "Confirmation of Specifications and Price" (CSP) form, you agree to be bound by all our "Production Procedures".

1. When your job is received, we will acknowledge its arrival within one day of receipt. The notification will be emailed/faxed and provides you with the job number, and the name of your customer service representative at Thomson-Shore. When your job is scheduled, your CSP will be emailed/faxed; the CSP provides your projected ship and proof date.

2. If your job has any changes from the specifications on our quotation, the CSP will indicate your revised prices based on the final specifications. If this price change is less than $200.00, we will email/fax the CSP to you. If it is more than $200, we will contact you with details. When the CSP is emailed/faxed, production has started. If you have any questions or concerns at this point, it is important that you call us immediately.

3. If your Thomson-Shore customer service representative has questions regarding your expectations, he/she will call you before proceeding. This will be done before we send you the CSP.

4. If you have not requested a proof, we will print and bind your book without submitting anything for you to check. If you require digital proofs (a proof of the text pages submitted for approval prior to printing) there is a cost for this and it will add a minimum of one week to our production time. If you originally requested a digital proof of the text, it will be included in our quoted price and will show up on our quotation in the category of "prep/plates". The digital proof is meant to show you the margins, order of pages and the location of any strip-ins you might have. It is not meant to be proofread for typos. Our schedule assumes you will approve the digital proof, as well as other proofs, within 24 hours. We send out all proofs for approval via Federal Express, standard overnight, unless otherwise instructed. The cost of this mailing is not included in our quotation.

5. If you prefer, you could request digital proofs of just the first 32 pages instead of the entire book. This would be less expensive than a complete digital proof and it would let you see how we interpreted your margin instructions. T-S also has the capability of providing proofs via email or FTP.

6. To work efficiently and commit to reliable schedules, we need your entire job and final specifications at one time. We will not begin production of your order until the complete job is in our plant.

7. Your schedule could be affected if you require changes during the production process i.e., quantity change, an additional proof, new copy submission. If changes are made and your schedule is a concern, please let us know immediately.

8. When your job is complete and ready for shipment, we will ship it motor freight. Accessorial charges, i.e., inside delivery, residential delivery, lift gate, are additional and will be invoiced accordingly. Shipping time is not included in our production schedule and will usually add from one to five working days to get from Dexter to locations in the continental U.S. Please refer to our online Shipping Terms and Procedures Guideline located on our web site for more detail.

9. When a Thomson-Shore estimator quoted your project it was most likely quoted F.O.B. Origin, freight prepaid and charged back. In simple terms, F.O.B. (Free On Board) refers to the responsibility for freight cost and transit risk. F.O.B. origin means that under the terms of sale the buyer bears all freight and associated charges, owns the goods in transit, and is responsible for any claims that may arise as a result of transit.

10. If we have an email address for you, T-S will email a delivery confirmation the evening of your shipment. If you have other requirements, please let us know.

11. We will ship the quantity you order with a maximum possible overage or shortage of 10%. These will be charged or credited at the over/under price.

12. Thomson-Shore works with several area vendors that can help you with the distribution of your books. The following applies to drop shipments (transportation via UPS, FedEx, USPS). Any job that requires shipment to more than two destinations and requires more than two cartons (if shipped via any method other than motor freight) will incur additional charges as follows: $6 for each additional destination greater than two plus $6 for each carton more than two for shipments other than motor freight (such as UPS, FedEx, USPS, etc). Shipments of advance copies for approval are not included. Please contact your Customer Service Representative for more information regarding distribution vendors or handling charges.

13. Your CSP will include a one-time fee of $40 for the archival of your digital files. The fee includes storing your electronic files in the archive library and providing online reporting; it must be paid at job invoice. If you prefer not to store electronic files at Thomson-Shore, please let your CSR know. Negative storage will continue to be invoiced a yearly storage fee (Jan-Dec) of $30 per title (first two years of storage are gratis).

14. Your agreement with Thomson-Shore is made at Dexter, Washtenaw County, Michigan. The prices in the quotation on the other side of this page shall remain in effect for thirty (30)days; we may, in our discretion extend this period beyond thirty (30) days. You should obtain credit approval prior to sending the job to us; this will eliminate a possible delay. Thomson-Shore reserves the right to reject any order within ten (10) days after receiving complete text copy, digital files, or furnished film; Thomson-Shore may reject the order based on content, or any other issues which, in Thomson-Shore's sole discretion, Thomson-Shore believes justify rejection of the order. These reasons may include, but are not limited to, rejection of content, which Thomson-Shore finds objectionable, illegal, or offensive.

Provided courtesy of Thomson-Shore Inc.

- Trim size, or outside dimensions
- Number of pages
- Cover (hard or soft)
- Type of binding
- Number of ink colors for text
- Number of ink colors for graphics
- How material will be supplied (on disk or camera-ready)
- Paper stock
- Cover stock
- Type of cover finish
- Type of packaging (shrink-wrapped, in cartons, etc.)

Beware!
A local, general-job printer is fine for printing up church newsletters, wedding announcements, and neighborhood garage-sale fliers. However, they don't know much more about book printing than you do, and their prices are astronomical. Go with an established, experienced firm that specializes in printing books and has the presses that allow them to print books cost effectively.

Wow! Where to start? We'll delve into all the details in Chapter 7. For now, let's look at our hypothetical publishers' costs in the "Book Production Costs" chart on page 92.

Glowworm Press, seeking a niche in gardening books, plans to start off with a print run of 3,000, 192-page, perfect-bound (softcover book binding in which the cover is glued onto the page ends), trade paperbacks with four-color covers. Its first title will be *The Night Garden*. Bell & Candle Publishing will ignite its sales with a print run of 5,000 of its inspirational-genre book titled *Soaring on Invisible Wings*. Bell & Candle will go with 288-page hardcover with four-color dust jacket for this inspirational volume.

As with the company setup costs, Bell & Candle will spend significantly more than her colleague will. The greatest cost difference is in the printing—Bell & Candle's print run is 2,000 copies higher and almost 100 pages more per copy than Glowworm's. And while Glowworm is going the inexpensive trade paperback route, Bell & Candle will spring for hardcovers with dust jackets, both of which are pricey options. You'll note that the inspirational publisher is also spending considerably more than her garden-buff colleague for cover art and for copyediting—the latter because she's got more pages to edit.

Front-Line Wisdom

"The biggest mistake many new publishers make is to have a book printed by a local general-purpose printer," advises Steve C. in Vermont. "You need a short-run book printer, because the cost will be half or less, and the quality will be better. Always

Book Production Costs

Costs	Glowworm Press	Bell & Candle Publishing
Bar codes	$20	$20
Copyright	$30	$30
Cover art	$1,500	$2,500
Copyediting	$384	$625
Proofreading	$192	$250
Indexing	$384	0
Printing	$5,032	$15,801
	for 3,000 copies	for 5,000 copies
Total Production Costs	**$7,542**	**$19,226**
Per-Book Cost	**$2.51**	**$3.85**

go for several bids—the one that had the best price last time may not this time. There are some printers every small press learns about, such as Bang, Data Reproductions, McNaughton and Gunn, and Hignell. That's not a comprehensive list, but they are among the small number of printers that would be on anybody's bid list. Another smaller one that I like is Master Printers of New England. There are others that are well-known because they advertise heavily in small-press publications, but which, if you network with other small presses, you'll learn to avoid. The above are regular short-run book printers, good to use if your first printing will be in the 1,000 to 10,000 range or more."

Covering the Spectrum

"Visit your printer," urges Anna J. in Texas. "I haven't done that yet, but I've had three different printers; two worked out beautifully, and one did not. I had to hire a lawyer and in the process have learned that I should have taken the time to travel to the printer to visit with them before sending them my manuscript.

Smart Tip

Tip...

If you have color illustrations, the printer will send match prints, which are like color copies, for you to proof and send back. These are preferable to emailed PDFs because color is not typically "true" when viewed on a screen. Sometimes, the old school is the best school.

"I would also suggest getting a lot of bids and a lot of samples," Anna says. "I was amazed at the differences in bids I got for my projects. The quality of printing and binding also covers the spectrum. I also kept track of how long it took printers to get their bids to me after I sent them an RFQ. If it took them a long time to get a bid to me, that told me something about that company.

Smart Tip

A hickey is not what you get from smooching on the front porch after dark, at least not in the printing world. Here it means a speck or a blotch on a page.

"Join a publishing listserv (online) and ask other publishers for recommendations. That's how I got my second printer (and I would have used them for my third book, but it wasn't cost and time effective because they're an overseas printer).

"Another must for a new publisher is to develop a good working relationship with your printer before you send the manuscript," the mother of two suggests. "I thought I put everything in writing, but my lawyer says that we need to do more than what printers traditionally do. The contracts we sign benefit the people drawing up the contracts—the printers. My lawyer suggested that next time I work with a printer, I have some clauses added which benefit me—just in case mistakes are made during the printing process. It might cost a couple of hundred dollars to hire a lawyer, and you may not even need those clauses; but when you have a problem, you lose a lot more than a couple hundred dollars, not to mention a lot of sleep.

"Along those lines: Keep a phone/communication log. Every time you talk to your printer, write down the date, time, and what was said. This way if you have problems later, you can refer back to your log and say who you talked to and what was agreed upon. You have to have this kind of documentation in case you have problems later," offers Anna.

Proof Is in the Pudding

June H., the horror-story maven, concurs. "Do get at least three bids from printers and look at some of the work they produce," she says. "The packaging of a book can make the difference between whether a prospective customer picks up your book to look at the content. You can't sell a book if no one picks it up off the shelf.

"Once you've made a decision on a printer—and I recommend one as nearby as possible because you'll be working closely with them—make sure to get a contract in writing that covers everything from artwork (including covers), to the size of the book and typesetting.

▲

Get with the Program

An important book-printing issue is the format in which you'll deliver your manuscript to the printer. The more work the printer has to do, the more he'll charge you. If you send your work on CD as a Microsoft Word file, the printer will have to typeset it, import it into Adobe InDesign and then into PDF or portable document format files for you. This is expensive—about an extra $2 to $3 per page.

If you do the work yourself and send the book to the printer on a CD-ROM, flash drive, or via email in a zip file, as an InDesign file, or already formatted in PDF, the printer has to do far less work. It saves him a step and saves you money, as much as 15 percent, says Maria Smith of Thomson-Shore, Inc., a book printing company in Dexter, Michigan.

As an added bonus, when you format your book in InDesign and then generate a PDF from the InDesign file(s), what you see is what you get. There's no guessing about how it will end up looking. You'll be able to see it and make any changes long before you send it off to the printer.

Your printer may also provide you with a password to their FTP (file transfer protocol) site where large files can be transferred electronically.

"You can save yourself a few dollars if you typeset your own work and present it to the printer in camera-ready format," the Michigan resident explains. "This means all they do is reproduce what you give them. This can be accomplished on any computer by setting your margins to the size you want, say 5-by-7, 6-by-9, or whatever you choose."

However, be sure you are giving the printers the same specs for your book and that they are quoting on the same quantities, color treatment, paper quality, etc. You don't want to get three quotes that are essentially comparing apples to oranges to mangoes.

"As a last note, if you do your own typesetting, you are responsible for proofing the galley, or final copy, before the book is bound; so do proof carefully. What you give them is what they print. On important issues such as ISBNs, take along a copy of the correct number when you go to the printer to proof. I once had an incident where the printer had put the wrong ISBN on my book, and since I did not catch it, I had to pay extra for stickers with the correct number and do each book by hand. Your ISBN is your book's identifier; if it's incorrect, bookstores will have a difficult if not impossible time trying to find it for the consumer," says June.

After you submit your book to the printer on Microsoft Word (even better if you can submit it on Adobe InDesign as a PDF file), he goes to work performing the magic that turns it into a real book. What the printer does exactly is mysterious and involves all sorts of cameras, printers, binderies, and other pieces of heavy machinery. Basically, he sends your text to a digital image center, which transforms your pages into signature-size flats of paper. What was formerly known as bluelines, so named because they look exactly like those blurry blue-ink plans architects and engineers are so fond of, are now printed digitally in (usually) black and white. In this case, the proofs look exactly like your book, down to the trim size. These digital prints are your final opportunity to make any changes to the book before it goes into production.

The printer will send these digital prints to you for proofing. Be sure you examine them with X-ray eyes. Make sure no pages are missing, that they're all in the right order, and that they're all properly numbered. Look for missing lines of text, and text or images that are not where they're supposed to be.

If you find errors the printer has made and point them out immediately, they can be corrected free of charge. But if you shrug, pronounce the digital prints as OK without really checking carefully, let the book go to print, and then find errors—it's too late. And if you decide at this point that, hey, maybe you'd like to add two pages or move that sidebar from page 7 to page 12, it will cost you money. So don't get creative at this stage—do it before you submit your manuscript.

Once you send back the digital prints, the book goes to print. When the printing is all done, it's shipped to you. Take a moment out from all the heady excitement to examine not just one book or two, but several boxes of books. It doesn't happen often, but printers do goof. Your books can arrive with the covers glued on upside down or an entire signature missing. It's better to catch these errors in your garage than after books have been shipped to your customers.

Printing Price Tag

We're not done yet. The price tag for each job will change, depending on how many copies you want. Although the overall cost may be more, the more copies you order, the cheaper the per-book cost. So you have to decide how many books you can afford for your initial run, as well as how many you estimate you can sell.

Take another look at the "Price Quote from a Printer" on pages 89–90, and you'll see that the bottom line jumps each time the quantity gets larger. At the same time, however, the per-book cost gets smaller. If Glowworm press has 1,000 books printed, the per-book cost will be $2.68; for 3,000 copies, it will cost $1.44 per book; and for 5,000 copies, the price plummets to $1.19 each. If Glowworm prints even more, say, 6,000, 8,000, or 10,000 copies, the price will go even lower.

But don't get too carried away. Industry experts generally recommend that you go with an initial print run of at least 3,000 books, but no more than 5,000. It takes about 3,000 to get the first good price break, but going with radically more than 5,000 is unwise unless you are so sure of your marketing plan and get a feel for how fast and how well your book sells.

Overs, Unders, and Other Quirks

Print runs never come out to an exact count. If you order 5,000 books, you may end up with 5,106 or 4,923—or some other number entirely. The difference is called overs and unders, and printers are routinely allowed a 10 percent margin either way. If your run comes out over, you'll be charged a flat fee for every extra copy. Look for it on your invoice. Your quote from the printer should tell you how much you would have to pay for overs and unders. The sample quote on pages 89–90 shows that Glowworm will be charged 82 cents each for extra copies.

While you might not particularly want overs, asking for "overruns" is a smart idea. Overruns are extra copies of your cover that you can request, which cost as little as $20 per 100 for the four-color, perfect-bound variety. You can use these overruns as publicity and advertising tools, or to send as tokens of appreciation to people who helped bring your book into the world, like a mentor, editor, designer, or artist—and do not forget Mom and Dad!

The POD Effect

"An option used by a lot of small presses is print on demand or POD," says small-press pro Steve C. Books are printed one at a time, and they look just exactly like conventionally printed books. The per-unit cost is higher, of course, but you run no risk of dying with 5,000 books in your garage; you can just print them as they sell.

"The most popular [POD] printer by far is Lightning Source," Steve explains. "There are probably others that are as good and cheaper. But the advantage of Lightning Source [see Appendix for contact information] is that it's a division of Ingram [a major book-wholesaler]. If you are printing a book that may sell only 300 copies, you may have a hard time getting it listed with Ingram, so it would be hard for people to special-order

Smart Tip

In the printer's RFQ (request for quote), you'll be asked if you want your books shrink-wrapped. Your answer should be "Yes." Shrink-wrapping protects your books from damage in transit. Have them wrapped in bundles of two to four—the staff at the local bookstore will be less inclined to unwrap individually shrink-wrapped books, which means customers won't be able to browse through your book to see if they want to purchase it.

at bookstores. But if it's printed by Lightning Source, it will be automatically listed by Ingram, and bookstores will be able to easily obtain copies."

CreateSpace is Amazon's print-on-demand division. Other companies have similar POD programs.

Print-on-demand providers are proliferating as quickly as e-publishing sites, and POD has been around for well over ten years. They act much like e-publishers—as a virtual bookstore for your title—but with an all-important difference. In addition to "shelf space on their sites," they also print actual perfect-bound paper copies of your

Bright Idea

Instead of filling out a different "quick quote" for each printer with different variables, format your own RFQ (request for quote) as Anna J., the self-publisher from Temple, Texas, does. Send it to all the printers on your list so you get a standard bid for comparison, instead of having to make sense of the jumble of possible choices.

Your Book Production Costs

Use this form to develop your own book production costs. Make several copies and get estimates from several different sources, then choose the best—and least expensive—option.

Bar code	$
Copyright	
Cover art	
Illustrations	
Copyediting	
Proofreading	
Indexing	
Printing	
Your Total Production Costs	$
Divide by number of copies	
Your Per-Book Cost	$

▲

Why POD?

A recent study in *Publishers Weekly*, produced by Vista International, ranks the top reasons for going with print on demand. They are:

○ Generating profitable business

○ Satisfying customer demand that would otherwise go unsatisfied

○ Creating sales from backlist titles that would otherwise be lost

○ Reducing investment in inventory

○ Reducing risk in printing decisions

---

book. Because books are printed with state-of-the-art laser copiers that use regular paper, instead of on web presses that must be fed huge signature-size sheets, POD sites can provide as few—or as many—copies as you like on request. And they look just like traditional p-books.

Like e-publishers, each POD provider has its own pricing and royalty structure. Generally you can expect to pay nothing or up to $1,200 in setup fees, depending on how much you want to spend on add-on services like copyediting, layout, and cover design, and your own web page. Specific costs vary radically, depending on the POD provider and the service program you choose, so you may or may not be saving on the add-on costs as opposed to outsourcing these tasks on your own. The bottom line, however, is the cost for the books themselves. With rising production and printing costs for traditional publishers, the POD option is looking more attractive each day.

The upside of POD is that you don't pay for books until you have orders to fill. The downside is that they're a lot more expensive than traditionally printed books. Trade paperbacks printed POD cost from $6 to $10 each, which is a far cry from the $2 and under costs you get when you go with a conventional run of thousands at a time. Some POD sites, like Xlibris (www.xlibris.com), don't charge printing costs, but their royalties are far less—10 percent to 25 percent of a set list price—as opposed to sites like Trafford (www.trafford.com) that charge for printing but offer up to 60 percent royalties.

So why would you want to go with this method? It's cheaper in the short haul. You might print 100 to 500 copies, send half (or more) of them out for review to opinion molders, and then sit back and wait for orders before committing to a larger print run. This way you get an idea of how many books you'll want to order from the traditional printing press before you invest in a large run.

More Bang for Your Book

You can get even more bang for your book by producing it in a few alternative formats. You can transform those printed words into an audiobook package, a video production, or even create your own merchandising goodies.

Easy Listening

Audiobooks are particularly popular with people who attend seminars and workshops, and they make terrific BOR or back-of-the-room sales products. You sell the CDs immediately after your seminar, while your audience is still hyped up and eager to hear more on your subject. You can make even more profit by offering a downloadable version (like those available on iTunes or Audible.com, for example) that requires less production cost.

Since almost everybody is a commuter these days, audiobooks are in demand as antidotes to highway hypnosis. Audiobooks are also a wonderful way to provide your title to people who have poor vision or who are blind. In addition, they make fun gifts for children when accompanied by simple picture books so kids can "read aloud" to themselves. Even for adults, audiobooks are read-aloud versions of the print version—it's not necessary to fancy them up with actors playing different roles or with expensive sound effects. In fact, the simpler the better, since adding too many special effects tends to muddy the clarity.

Audiobooks are fairly simple to produce—you've already got the ready-made script to follow. Many audiobooks, however, are abridged (or condensed) to keep both costs and retail price down. You can go with either version, but do your market research to determine which your niche market is more likely to purchase. Digital audio files, like those available on iTunes, for example, have allowed more publishers the leeway to record books in their entirety, since there is no CD duplication cost involved. Today, you can find most complete books available in this format, with the abridged versions available on CD.

Keep in mind that you will pay for a full-fledged audio production as well as for having the sound files mastered and duped (duplicated). Recording the program yourself with a home voice recorder at

> **Tip...**
>
> **Smart Tip**
>
> If you're the brave soul who wants to record his own audiobook in a home studio, there are some great computer programs that will help you add professional polish. Try Sony Sound Forge Audio Studio for around $70, or on the higher end, use Adobe Audition for around $350—it's said to be tops for Podcast production.

your kitchen table is not a good idea (the end result will sound dreadfully tinny and amateurish). However, there are many brands of quality voice recording software currently on the market that do a remarkably professional job—if you have the most updated equipment to use with it, including a higher-end computer with CD duplication capability and a studio-quality microphone. Your best bet is to check with your local music or audio solutions store to find the most economic and professional recording equipment.

Spring for a professional in-studio job if you are unsure of your technical skills. You will find audiovisual production services listed in your local Yellow Pages as well as on the internet, or contact a local radio DJ who will have access to professional equipment and will be delighted to take on the job at a discount rate. As with printing and most other services, the more CDs you buy, the cheaper your costs.

Speaking of improving your bottom line, give serious consideration to offering only a downloadable version of your audio book. Listeners simply expect to be able to listen on their iPod or other MP3 device, including their smartphone. The savings for publishers of going exclusively downloadable (in duplication, packaging, and distribution) is passed directly to the consumer in the form of a cheaper, more accessible medium. Take a look at the "Audiobook Production Costs" chart on page 101 to get an idea of price range for both CD and downloadable options.

Lights, Action, Camera!

Unlike audiobooks, video productions won't fit every book format. Since your audience is not likely to be fascinated by watching you sitting in a chair reading your own words, you'll have to carefully consider what—if anything—you can do to make this a viable product.

Fiction is probably out. Unless you already own a full-fledged production company and have (or can get) the budget for actors, sets, location shooting, a director, a cameraperson, cameras, etc., the costs are entirely too prohibitive.

But lots of nonfiction lends itself to fairly inexpensive video. The cheapest of all is the type produced by seminar professionals who hire a videographer to record them during an actual session. The recording is then edited, packaged, and sold as a BOR product.

Audiobook Production Costs

Book on CD or Electronic File

Studio time	$250–300 per finished hour
Sound engineer	$125–200 per finished hour
Producer	$200–1,000 per finished hour, based on experience
Narration talent	$275–400 per finished hour
Editing	$200–300 per finished hour
Post-production	$100–200 per finished hour
Duplication (CD only)	$1–3 per CD, depending on total number of units

DIY Recording

Laptop with CD burning capability	$1,100–2,500
Audio recording/editing software	$70–400
Recording equipment	$100–1,000, depending on make and model
Duplication (CD only)	$1–2 per CD
Design software for creating cover art	$100–700
Jewel cases	$.50–1.00

○ Duplication cost per CD will decrease as total units increase

○ Don't forget that you'll want artwork for your J-cards (CD covers) or album covers. Some studios will handle the printing for you; at others it's up to you.

Cookbooks, exercise manuals, and how-to books can also lend themselves to video productions. People like to see a live person demonstrating how to frost a cake, crunch those abs, build a deck, or make gift wrap with rubber stamps. Because you don't need actors, special sets, or any of the rest for these types of productions, you can keep your costs down. Make sure you keep it interesting, though. Keep things moving, use humor when you can, and talk to your audience as if they're actually in the room with you.

As with audiobooks, you must hire a video production professional. Even if your brother-in-law has a nifty camcorder and does all your family's reunions, he most likely doesn't know enough about sound, lighting, and duping to produce a saleable product.

▲

Merchandise Madness

You can develop all sorts of merchandise to tie in with your book—everything from calendars and note cards, to T-shirts and toys. Again, you will have to take your book's genre and subject matter into account, but you can also get creative.

Anna J. sells heart-shaped pins to readers of her books for and about families that have a child with a heart defect. You might design a simple cloth doll from a character in your children's book. You might sell coffee mugs imprinted with an adage from your motivational or inspirational book, a calendar based on your gardener's diary that

---

Do Right, Copyright

Neophyte writers frequently worry that someone will steal their work if they don't copyright it. This is rarely a problem. In the United States of America, your work is automatically and immediately copyrighted as soon as you've created it. And just about any creative work is copyright-protected, including the following:

- ○ Literary works, which can encompass computer programs
- ○ Songs and other musical works
- ○ Plays and other dramatic works
- ○ Movies and audiovisual works
- ○ Pictorial and graphic works, as well as sculptures
- ○ Sound recordings

However, since you'll be publishing your book, you will want to file a formal registration with the U.S. Copyright Office. All you have to do is fill out a form obtainable on the office's website at www.copyright.gov. Online registration is $35. Your copyright is effective on the date the Copyright Office receives all of the materials, and you should receive a certificate of copyright within about four months. Copyright law is complicated, but as a rule of thumb you can figure that your protection exists until 70 years after your death. To read specifics about copyright, go to: www.copyright.gov/circs/circ1.pdf. For specifics about your particular publication, consult your attorney.

---

shows readers when to perform various garden tasks, or a chef's apron emblazoned with the name of your cookbook.

You can buy all sorts of goodies, from coffee mugs to mouse pads to tote bags, fairly inexpensively and have them imprinted with whatever you like. You can also have products like dolls and other toys made up by specialty manufacturers. Look for suppliers and giftware manufacturers in your local Yellow Pages or on the internet.

Going e!

E-publishing is yet another venue for your book. Although still in its infancy, e-publishing is hot and getting hotter by the nanosecond, with everybody from giant publishers to small independent publishers to stars like Stephen King getting into the act. E-books are exciting for publishers because the cost of printing and binding is eliminated. Readers download titles directly onto their computers and print them out on their own machines. They're exciting for readers because they allow instant gratification: You can browse books and then download and read them immediately. And e-titles are usually cheaper than their paper counterparts. Publishers pass on to their readers the money they save by not using a printing house.

There are three ways to produce your own e-book:

1. Set up your own website and sell online.
2. Sell through an e-publisher like Booklocker.com (www.booklocker.com).
3. Sell through an e-book reader site.

The main thing they all have in common is that you must make your book available in PDF or HTML (hypertext markup language) format so it can be downloaded. In addition, your niche market must be computer-savvy—if they're not, they'll never find your book much less be able to read it. Let's take a look at the advantages and disadvantages of each of these approaches.

The Do-It-Yourself Site

Since you'll probably have a website anyway, you may want to offer your title in downloadable format. You will already have your book in PDF—that's how you delivered it to your printing house—so it's not much more of a step to upload it to your website.

The big advantage here is that since the book is yours and the site is yours, you don't have to share the profits with anybody. The disadvantage is that you'll have to take readers by the e-hand and lead them to your site. Unless you do stellar marketing, they won't find you as easily as they might if you go with a big e-publisher.

e-Book Publishers

You may choose to go with an established e-publishing site (see the Appendix for a listing of several e-publishing providers). The advantage here is that they're like big e-bookstores and thus have the capability of attracting lots of browsers. People who may be surfing the site, not looking for your book in particular, may happen upon it and decide to buy it. Another advantage is that some e-publishers will translate your text into PDF for you. This is a plus if you decide to put up new titles that haven't already been made PDF-ready.

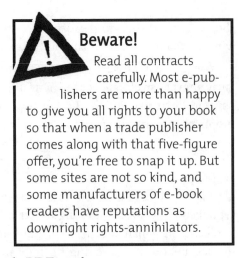

Beware!
Read all contracts carefully. Most e-publishers are more than happy to give you all rights to your book so that when a trade publisher comes along with that five-figure offer, you're free to snap it up. But some sites are not so kind, and some manufacturers of e-book readers have reputations as downright rights-annihilators.

The disadvantage is that you will have to pay royalties for the privilege of being on the site's e-list. Royalty rates vary from 20 to 70 percent, depending on the site. And remember that royalties are based on the book's price, which will be lower than the version found in brick-and-mortar stores. Some sites are free, but with others you'll pay a setup fee of up to $500.

The important thing to remember about e-pub sites is that even though your title is "on the shelf," you must still do just as much promotion as you would for your print version.

e-Book Reader

The technology of "Star Trek: The Next Generation" is already here—at least as far as those nifty little computers-as-books are concerned. Unless you've been living in a cave for five years, you will have heard of the Kindle from Amazon or the Nook from Barnes & Noble. And the iPad is an e-reader and more. You can download a book in seconds and store dozens, if not hundreds, in your e-reader device of choice. You can read a book on-screen, on the go—at the airport, in the supermarket checkout line, or wherever you happen to be. While some e-book readers are set up to accept PDF format, others demand HTML (the language web designers use to set up and edit sites) or OEB, which is open e-book (a language used to produce some e-book content).

Consumers can buy texts specifically formatted for e-book readers online at virtual bookstores. Or they can go directly to the e-book reader manufacturers' sites to purchase texts.

The e-book reader is making the evolution of the e-book move at lightning speed. Upgrades, enhancements, and improvements to existing e-readers are coming on the market practically every week. The e-book and the e-reader have turned the traditional book publishing industry upside down; as a self-publisher, you would be wise to keep as abreast of it as possible.

Writing and Designing Your Book

At this point, you've done your market research—you know what type of book you want to publish and in what genre. You've done the math—you know what efforts and expenses are involved in setting up your office and producing your first title.

If you haven't already, it's now time to actually put pen to paper, or fingers to keyboard. In this chapter we'll explore the facets of book creation and design, from organization to paper stock and cover design.

Exhilaration and Panic

Writing a book is one of the most exhilarating and also one of the most daunting things you can do. If you're a born writer—one of those people who's been scribbling stories and publishing "newspapers" since the age of 8—then you already know all about the joys—and terrors—of authorship. If you've never tackled any written project other than the ones forced upon you by school or your job, you may face the prospect of actually producing a book with the same sort of anxiety you'd feel building your own space station!

Writing 101

The key to any successful writing project, fiction or nonfiction, is organization. The more planning you do before you actually begin writing, the easier and faster it will go. Try these tips for turning your germ of an idea into a completed, savvy manuscript:

- *Give your book a working title*. It's much easier to think of your project in terms of a finished, polished book when it has an identity.

- *Draw up a chapter-by-chapter outline*. Give each chapter a title and a paragraph that describes what information you'll cover.

- *Now go one step further and make a detailed outline of each chapter*. You don't have to write a magnum opus, but list, item by item, the points you intend to cover.

- *If you'll use quotes and statistics, start gathering material*. Make up files for your research and interviews, and stash your materials in folders labeled for each chapter. Carefully note where you got the information from and when.

- *Make a deliberate effort to start writing*. Pour yourself a nice, fresh cup of coffee, sit down at your desk, take a deep breath, and start writing. Starting a brand-new book is usually the hardest part. You haven't found your voice yet, and you and your book have not really gotten to know each other. It will get easier as you go along.

- *Keep in mind that every writer has good days and bad days*. The trick that separates real writers who finish books from dilettantes who do not is that real writers keep slogging ahead, even on days when the task seems hopeless. Set a weekly goal for yourself and stick to it: three pages a day, two hours a night, or six hours every Saturday—whatever you can fit into your schedule.

Ghosts and Other Writers

What if, despite your very best efforts, you can't write your way out of a paper bag? Or you don't have the time to devote to writing an entire book? You've got options. You can hire a ghostwriter or a co-author. You provide the ideas, information, and research, and leave the writing to them.

A ghostwriter is a writer who works behind the scenes to put your material into professional prose worthy of publishing. Your name goes on the book, and you are touted as the author. Celebrities often "write" their autobiographies using the talents of ghostwriters. There's no reason you can't do it too—except the added expense.

Beware!
If you quote copyrighted material in your book, you must get permission first. If you use statistics, you must cite the source where you found them.

A co-author is like a ghostwriter, except that he or she shares writing credit with you on the book's cover and title page. Where the title page of a ghostwritten book might read *Do It Yourself Divorces* by King Henry VIII, the title page of a co-authored book would read, *Do It Yourself Divorces* by King Henry VIII, with Irving Levine.

The cost for a ghostwriter or co-author is entirely dependent on who you hire, how much of the manuscript you may already have written, how much sprucing up and organizing it needs, how much additional research you want done, and what financial arrangements you make. Most ghostwriters or co-authors expect to be paid royalties, or they expect to be paid on a work-for-hire basis (which means you pay a flat fee and no royalties). But as a self-publisher, you can make any arrangement that suits you and your writer. That said, be sure to do a simple written contract that spells out each of your responsibilities, timing, and payment.

You can find a ghostwriter or co-author at the American Society of Journalists and Authors, within the pages of *Literary Marketplace* (R.R. Bowker), or by nosing around in various publishing and writing websites.

Layout and Design Decisions

If you write a book that's published by someone else, you turn in your manuscript, and that's it. The book's design pretty much remains a mystery until your complimentary copies arrive in the mail. But as a publisher, you need to be every bit as concerned with the book's design, layout, and appearance as you are with its message. This is where you see and deal with all those behind-the-scenes things that a publisher would have dealt with for you.

The design will affect your book's production costs and ultimately your profit margin. As you already know, all sorts of factors—from the number of pages and the type of cover, to the amount and style of artwork—play a role in printing expenses. The higher your costs, the smaller your bottom line. Your book's design also plays an important role in whether potential readers perceive it as a title they want to purchase. People judge a book not only by its cover but by whether it is:

- Too long (too much of a reading task to tackle)
- Too skimpy (not enough material for the price)
- Too expensive
- Too cheap (priced significantly lower than other books—may be perceived as not being very good)
- Too amateurish

Your printer can help you with some of these elements. Your graphic designer or cover artist can help with others. But the final decisions—and final appearance—are up to you. So, ready? Here we go!

All books have basically the same layout, which makes it easy to plan yours. You always have lots of room for creativity within your text, of course, but if you deviate from the basic setup, your book will look unprofessional, not to mention strange.

Some sections are standard format: All books have them in roughly the same place, and except for how you design the actual page and what you actually say, there's not a lot of decision-making to do. Other sections are optional—you can leave them out, or you can put them in if you like for information or design purposes, or if your page count demands them. Why would your page count "demand" an optional section or two? Because of signatures.

The Signature

Book pages are not printed one at a time the way you run a page from your computer through your personal printer. Instead, they're printed on signatures, huge sheets of paper on which 16 or 32 book pages are laid out and run through the press at once. After printing, the signatures are neatly sliced into 16 or 32 individual pages and then bound together.

When you lay out your book, you strive for an even signature—i.e., one that's a multiple of 16. That's why our hypothetical publishing companies chose to go with a 192-page book (12 signatures, 16 pages per signature) and a 288-page book (18 signatures, 16 pages per signature). The further away you veer from an even signature, the more expensive your print job will be because the printer has to chop pages from that huge sheet of 16 or 32. And printers don't like to do that.

> **Fun Fact**
>
> Winston Churchill, who wrote 14 books between the end of World War II and his death at age 90, began every day at 8:30 A.M. with a work-in-progress, a glass of whiskey, and his signature cigar—in bed.

You can always add material to the front or back of your book to fill out a signature, like quotations, author or publicity blurbs, and extra order information. You can always leave a couple of blank pages at the front or back if absolutely necessary. And you can go for a partial signature of eight pages—which is not the ideal, but isn't too drastic either.

You won't know exactly what your page count is until you finish writing the book in your word processing program, import it into in a publishing program like Adobe InDesign, and then lay it out. But that's OK. You can add or delete material as you go along.

Use the "Book Layout Checklist" on page 112 to see what goes where and to check off the sections of your book as you complete them. Remember that the standard elements you would include in a fiction book differ from those you would include in a nonfiction book.

Page Primer

Now that we've discussed some of the basics of book design and layout, let's investigate what the inside pages of your book will look like. A lot of this information applies both to printed and e-books.

Front Matter

The pages at the beginning of your book are called the front matter and consist of everything up to the copy that makes up the body of your text. The best way to decide how you want your front matter to look and feel is to peruse books whose style you admire, and see how they're laid out. Then, keeping in mind signatures, page counts,

Book Layout Checklist

Book Section	Fiction Book	Nonfiction Book	Element Completed
Front matter			
Book blurbs	*Optional*	*Optional*	
Half title page	**Standard**	**Standard**	
Title page	**Standard**	**Standard**	
Copyright page	**Standard**	**Standard**	
Dedication	*Optional*	*Optional*	
Acknowledgments	*Optional*	*Optional*	
Quotation(s)	*Optional*	*Optional*	
Table of contents		**Standard**	
Foreword		*Optional*	
Preface		**Standard**	
Body			
Your text	**Standard**	**Standard**	
Back matter			
Afterword		*Optional*	
Appendix/ references section		*Optional*	
Glossary		*Optional*	
Index		**Standard**	
Author bio	*Optional*	*Optional*	
Order form/ contact information	*Optional*	*Optional*	

and standard book layouts, set your own similar style for addressing the elements that go in the front matter of your book:

Bright Idea
You can often get a busy opinion-molder to "pen" your foreword if you offer to write it for her. Then all she has to do is approve it and put her name to it.

- *Book blurbs.* This is optional publicity material and can consist of one page or several pages. Use this section for any pre-publication endorsements from opinion molders—quotes like, "*The Night Garden* should be required reading for anyone who enjoys gardening, entertaining, or just a soul-soothing brush with Mother Nature at the end of the day.—*Horticulture* magazine." You need at least one page and preferably two or more of these blurbs. If you have only a few, save them for the back cover.

- *Half title page.* The half title page is the first standard page of your book. It contains your title and subtitle, and that's all.

- *Title page.* This is your title and subtitle again, with the author's name, as well as the publisher's name, logo, and city/state.

- *Copyright page.* Here's where you put your copyright date, the person who owns the copyright (you as the author, the author whose work you're publishing, or perhaps your family trust, if that's how you've set up your legal organization). You should also add the words "All Rights Reserved" and a statement that your material cannot be reproduced without your permission. You may want to add a disclaimer to the effect that you have not intentionally made any errors or insulted anybody. If you've included excerpts from someone else's work that need to be attributed (like song lyrics or poetry), you say so here. This is also where you put your ISBN, LCCN, and CIP record.

- *Dedication.* Here's your chance to show your appreciation to a mentor for opening your eyes to the joys of gardening or your spouse for encouraging you or your parents for raising you to love fresh vegetables, whatever. A dedication is short, sweet, and to the point—just a few lines on the page.

- *Acknowledgments.* This is where you recognize everybody who helped make your book a reality—the industry experts who shared information, the reference librarian who looked up countless statistics, the editor who caught all those nasty copy goofs, and your spouse who selflessly washed dishes and kept the kids entertained while you wrote. Acknowledgments should also be brief—no more than a page, tops.

- *Quotations.* You may want to set out a topical quotation from a great thinker (or Bart Simpson, depending on the tone of your book) or an excerpt from a poem or song. This can have a very nice effect, so long as it relates to the book as a whole. Don't add something just to fill space, especially if it doesn't really enhance your book.

- *Table of contents.* List each chapter in your book by title, with the page on which it begins. This usually applies only to nonfiction. With the exception of the wonderful *Harry Potter* (Scholastic Inc.) books and some other juvenile works, giving titles to fiction chapters has gone out of fashion.
- *Foreword.* This is a sort of pre-introductory blurb about why your book has merit, and why you as its author are a pro on the subject. A foreword is written by someone else; a preface is written by the author. It's not a must, but if you can coerce a mover and shaker in your target market to write a foreword for your book, you can use it as a terrific PR piece on your front cover. An example would be writing a book about pop music and putting "Foreword by Lady Gaga" on the cover. Forewords are not long (three to four pages).
- *Introduction.* This is a brief section in which you explain why you penned the book and what it will help the reader achieve. Again, it does not have to be long; five pages or so is fine.

The Body

This section contains the meat and potatoes of your book. It should include your chapters, charts, illustrations, and whatever else goes into giving your readers the information and inspiration you've promised.

What you decide to include in the body of your book will largely depend on what your subject matter is and what treatment you have chosen (fiction or nonfiction, poetry or self-help, etc.). Some authors may need more chapters than others to effectively communicate their message. Some authors may want illustrations to accompany their text; others will not. Look at similar books in your topic area or genre to see how other authors have approached putting together the body of their book.

While you're laying out your book, decide if you'll add tip boxes and/or sidebars to the body text. Tip boxes are one-sentence to one-paragraph factoids that you can scatter throughout the text to add extra comments, comic relief, or highlight important points. Sidebars are one-quarter-page to one-half-page mini-articles that complement the text.

Beware!

Publishing programs like Adobe InDesign and Quark Xpress are notoriously not user-friendly. Don't force yourself into a deadline situation where you have only a short span of time to lay out your book. Instead, give yourself time to get acquainted with one of these programs and up to speed on using it. And realize that no one learns this stuff overnight.

In addition to imparting information, tip boxes and sidebars also serve to break up the text and create visually interesting pages. Pull quotes are another element that can serve this purpose. A pull quote is a particularly interesting phrase or sentence from your text that you "pull" and reprint elsewhere on the page in a much larger font, usually in bold face or italics, to draw the reader's interest to that page.

Back Matter

The sections that come after the body of your book are called the back matter. As with the front matter, the best way to decide how you want this material to look is to get ideas from books that have a style you admire already. The back matter of your book may include the following elements:

- *Afterword.* Also called an epilogue, this is the finishing note of your book, the wind-up in which you leave your reader with some final thoughts and messages. Like the foreword and introduction, the afterword should be fairly short. A half-dozen pages is more than adequate.

- *Appendix.* Here's where you give readers resource information so they can go on to tackle their own projects. You might list handy reference materials, organizations and associations, helpful vendors, websites, or pertinent government bureaus. If you have more than one appendix, you call them appendices.

- *Glossary.* This is a minidictionary in which you list the buzzwords specific to the topic you have explored throughout your text.

- *Index.* If you're writing nonfiction, an index is practically a must. Readers will refer to the book often over the course of weeks, months, or even years, and it's nice to give them an easy way to access specific information. If you're extremely detail-oriented, you can put together your own index. If not, it's best to hire a professional. Ask other professionals in your field for referrals or approach publishing organizations/associations that you belong to for suggestions.

- *Author bio.* People always want to know something about the author, so

Smart Tip

Tip...

When you list sources in your appendix, make sure you are as accurate as possible with your contact information. If you get sloppy and neglect to check the information twice before you go to press, your readers will call you—repeatedly—asking why they can't locate your source. Make sure nobody has changed phone numbers or URLs (website addresses), etc., before you declare the appendix ready for print.

▲

give them the groupie-info they crave. Keep it short, though; a few paragraphs is fine. For a hardcover book, the author's bio may be placed on the inside of the dust jacket at the back of the book.

- *Order form/publisher contact information.* Always put an order form at the back of the book so readers can send for an extra copy—this works more often than you might imagine. People who like your book will want to order copies for friends or relatives, or someone who sees your book in an office or shop may want to order one. You might combine your order form with your company contact information, especially if you have other products to sell.

Fit and Trim

The trim size, or outside dimensions of your book, will naturally play a major role in your page count. This is one of the first things your printer will want to know. Some printers may have competitive pricing in one trim size and be horribly expensive in others, so make sure you talk with a printer before you decide what size book to print. The bigger the book, the more text will fit on a page, and the fewer pages you'll need. There are exceptions, of course, such as children's picture books that have minimal text despite a larger trim size.

The most common trim sizes are:

- 5.5 inches by 8.5 inches (most popular)
- 6 inches by 9 inches (also very popular)
- 7 inches by 10 inches
- 8.5 inches by 11 inches

The first two trim sizes are trade paperback sizes, meaning simply that they're standard for books sold to the trade—in other words, to bookstores, libraries, and other publishing industry types.

One other trim size you'll see bandied about is mass market paperback, which refers to all those novels measuring 4.5 inches by 6.75 inches that you see in the supermarket checkout lanes and airport newsstands. Unless you believe your book will sell primarily to these types of markets, it's best to stick to the larger trim sizes.

> **Tip...**
>
> **Smart Tip**
> To get the best pricing, stick to floor stock— the paper the printer already has on hand, advises Maria Smith of Thomson-Shore Inc. If you specify a special paper that must be ordered, your costs will be much higher.

Paper Stock

Now you'll need to decide what stock, or type of paper, you want for your text pages. Like choosing which color of white you want from the house paint swatches at the home improvement center, this can be tough. There are lots of choices.

First you need to decide on the weight of the paper. Your choices range from 40- to 70-pound papers, with a higher number indicating a heavier paper. As a general rule, you should go with 60-pound paper. Anything less is on the flimsy side, and anything more will probably be more expensive than what you need. Colors run from cream to white.

More Color

Next, you'll need to decide on the ink color for your text. This is generally pretty simple: black. But if you are planning something different, or you've got a kid's book, you might want to use another color or two. Don't get too carried away with ink colors. The more you choose, the more expensive the print job will be. And ink colors other than black—unless used cleverly—can make your book look unprofessional.

If you have color or black-and-white photos that you'll want reproduced in black-and-white, the printer will have to re-shoot them as halftones. This means, in a nutshell, that they get re-photographed through a fine screen to make them sharp and clear on the printed page. If you don't use halftones, you end up with the muddy mess you can achieve yourself by running a photo through a copier. If you want color photos in your pages, you'll need to ask for color separations, which simply means that the printer separates each photo into four separate negatives, one for each of the four print process colors.

While we're on the subject of artwork, if you've got photos or graphics that are centerfolds (covering a two-page spread), or that have no white space around them on the page, you'll need to tell the printer you've got bleeds. This means you have to account for the portion of your material that's tucked within the binding or trimmed off the book page during the binding process.

Fantastic Fonts

From the mod and trendy Allumi PTF to the staid and stalwart Garamond, there are hundreds of fonts, or typestyles, to choose from. You can have a lot of fun playing with different fonts for chapter heads or title pages, but when you're

---

Shaving Points

Book design is as much art as technique. There's a lot to learn, but it's also a lot of fun. While the material we're exploring here may sound daunting, it's really not. Remember that with your publishing program, you'll be able to view your final product more or less as it will come from the printer in book form. You can always re-size margins, change fonts, and move graphics—whatever it takes to give your book a professional sparkle.

If you end up with 205 pages, for instance, which is an awkward 13 pages more than an even 12 signatures (16 pages per signature), you might tinker with your fonts, your margins, or your points to shave off those extra pages. You could eliminate your running heads or bump your folios (page numbers) onto the same line as your running heads, instead of placing them at the bottom of the page.

---

producing running text, stick with something simple. Don't force your readers to strain their eyes trying to decipher a weird typeface—they won't. Different fonts take up surprisingly different amounts of space on a page, so this can be a factor in your final product, too.

Point Taken

Typed characters are measured in points—72 points to one inch. The smaller the point, the smaller the type, and the more print you can fit on a page. Most books are printed in 10 pt (or point) to 12 pt fonts (unless it's a children's book or large-print edition for the visually impaired). If you go smaller or larger, your print gets more difficult to read.

Take the Lead Out

Leading (pronounced "ledding") refers to the amount of space between lines of text. Word processing and publishing programs usually figure the leading for you. This is a nice feature since a page with cramped leading or with oversized leading looks amateurish and is hard to read. Leading is measured from baseline to baseline (from the bottom of the first line to the bottom of the second line). Standard leading consists of your font's point size plus 2. For instance, if you have 10 pt type, you'll go with 12 pt leading, which is written as 10/12 and expressed as "ten on twelve."

Checklist of Book Design Elements

Design Element	Font	Point size	Graphics (if any)	Dimensions (1-inch margin, etc.)	Placement (top of page, centered, right-hand page, etc.)
Main text					
Top margin					
Bottom					
Left margin					
Right margin					
Leading					
Chapter heads					
Major heads					
Subheads					
Tip boxes					
Sidebars					
Running heads					
Folios					
Quotations					
Pull quotes					

Going Marginal

You've got four margins to consider: top, bottom, left, and right. How you proportion them makes a big difference to the final size of your book. The more margin, or white space, the less text you can fit on a page. As a very rough rule of thumb, you'll want to allow at least a half-inch of margin on all four sides—any less and your book will look skimpy and cheap. Also, you need to allow a certain amount of "extra" margin for the printer to trim in production. If your margins are too small, you can lose essential white space, or even worse, text on the page.

Running Ahead

A running head is the book title or chapter title that runs across the top of each page. Some books place the book title at the top of each verso, or left-hand page, and the chapter title at the top of each recto, or right-hand page. Others use only the book title as a running head; still others don't bother with a running head at all.

Some publishers place the folio, or page number, on the same line as the running head, while others put it at the bottom of each page. Where you place yours is entirely up to you. Again, peruse other books whose style you admire and emulate them.

Head of the Chapter

Chapters commonly start on a right-hand page, which sometimes means the left-hand page across from the chapter opener is blank. Chapter titles are usually in a larger point size than the text and can be in a different font, which gives them a nice design touch.

Besides your chapter titles, you'll want to break up your text with major heads and subheads, particularly in nonfiction books. Major heads are headlines that define the topic of a particular section in a chapter. Subheads are miniheadlines that define a subtopic within the major head area. Place major heads in a larger point size and, if you like, in a different font than your regular text—but not as large as your chapter titles. Subheads are generally the same size as your text, but in a different font or in boldface.

Got It Covered

Your cover is not only protection for your book's pages but also your sales pitch—the only real way you have of attracting that potential reader's attention at the bookstore and guiding him to the checkout counter. As your most important sales tool, its makeup should not be a hit-or-miss affair. Start thinking "cover" early on in your book's planning stages, and don't stop thinking and planning it until the final moments of preproduction.

> **Bright Idea**
>
> Try to get a celebrity— not necessarily Oprah or Tom Cruise, but an expert in your niche market—to write a foreword. Then you can splash, "Foreword by so-and-so" on your front cover.

Front Cover Story

The front cover is your first-line sales pitch. As the element of your book that prospective readers look at first, it has to sell your story in a critical eight seconds. Make sure your cover contains these components:

- *Color*. The human eye is attracted to color—that's why so many packages on the supermarket shelves are splashed with reds and yellows. Your book does not have to have a four-color cover, but, if you go for just one or two colors, make sure they fit your theme and have a strong design to pull the eye in. For example, take a look at the black-and-white photo with orange print that graces the cover of John Berendt's celebrated *Midnight in the Garden of Good and Evil* (Random House Inc.).

- *Design*. Simply stating your book's title and your name doesn't draw readers in. A strong design does. This is why a book cover designer is so important. If you're not a graphic artist, and you don't have a graphic arts-savvy friend or relative who'll design a cover for you, spend the money to hire one.

- *Title*. Print the title in letters large enough to make a statement. Remember, you're selling the book here.

- *Subtitle*. In nonfiction, a subtitle is important; it tells browsers what your book will do for them and what they can expect inside. *Raising Radishes*, for instance, tells the reader only that it's a gardening book. When we add, "How to Earn Big Money from Your Own Backyard Garden," we have a book that people interested in making money will want to read. A book called *Are We There Yet?* doesn't really explain what it's about. If we add, "How to Vacation with Your Kids without Losing Your Mind, Your Money, or Your Temper," we've got a book most parents would be interested in.

- *Sales pitch*. Your cover is the ideal place to add anything that makes you an expert on your book's topic, or that makes the book itself stand out from the competition. If you've written a book on how to help kids excel in school, and you're an award-winning teacher, for instance, you could put something like, "California's

Teacher of the Year Shares Secrets for Parents." The author of a book on dog obedience might trumpet (tastefully) below his name, "Founder and President of the Dog Can-Do Obedience Academy and American Kennel Association Judge." Your credentials can make a big difference. Testimonials from opinion molders who've read a pre-publication copy can add a nice punch as well. A book

Smart Tip

If you plan to sell your book primarily by mail order (which includes online sales), make sure your front cover photographs well. A small or "thumbnail" photograph won't reveal a lot of detail and may even make a detail-heavy cover come across as too busy.

on helping kids excel in school might add a line like, "A must-read for every parent—Dr. Benjamin Spock."

- *Author's name.* Don't forget this on your cover—seeing your name in print is one of the most satisfying aspects of authorship. Once you've got one successful title under your publishing belt, readers will look for more books written by you.

Back Cover Sensation

The back cover is as important as the front—your last, best chance to sell your book to that browser. While the front cover acts as a teaser, the back closes the sale by explaining how your book will solve the reader's problems and/or enhance the reader's life. Use the following elements to press home your point:

- *Bookstore section.* By this stage of your preproduction, you should know what section of the bookstore or library your book fits into (reference, crafts, business, religion, etc.). Print this section in small but legible text at the top left of your back cover. That way the bookstore knows where to put it so readers and store personnel can find it easily.

- *Headline.* Here's your opportunity to reinforce what your book will do for your reader. Instead of, "How to travel with your kids so you all have a good time," nab that bookstore browser with something like, "Make your next family trip a memory instead of a nightmare." Don't use the same text you used for your subtitle—get creative and keep it snappy. Your headline must make your browser want to read on.

- *Features and benefits.* Now write a short, concise description of just what your book will help the reader accomplish and with what tools. Tell people how they will lead better lives after reading your book. Will they learn the secrets to financial success? The secrets of successful gardening? How to live longer or healthier, or enjoy more romantic relationships? This section of your back cover is a sort of mini-outline of each chapter, written as a tempting list of tidbits. If your book has pullout charts, worksheets, illustrations, or other helps, mention them here. Remember that your goal is to whet the reader's appetite so she will thumb through the book and then take it straight to the checkout register.

- *Recommendations.* After your features and benefits, add a few endorsements and/ or testimonials from opinion molders in your niche market. Endorsements are glowing words about your book like, "Every paparazzi-hounded Royal should have a copy of *Simply Snubbing* on her nightstand. —Queen Elizabeth." Testimonials are explanations of how your book changed or enhanced a life like, "I couldn't have developed the Theory of Relativity without first having read *Hair-Raising Genius.*—Albert Einstein." Again, these words of praise do not need to come from tabloid-type celebrities, but they should be people recognizable and impressive to your target readers.

- *Author, author.* At the bottom of your back cover, write a short paragraph explaining why you're an expert on this subject. Let browsers know they're in the best possible hands when they buy your book and take your advice.

- *The big finale.* Finish off the copy on your back cover with a bang—a final hook that turns a looky-loo into a buyer. Tell your reader one more time what your book will do for him: "Buy this book, and you'll never suffer credit woes again."

- *Price tag.* List your book's retail price in tactfully small print at the bottom right, along with the Bookland bar code and ISBN. If you have a hardcover book with a dust jacket, the price goes on the inside front flap at the top right.

Growing a Spine

Yes, even your book's spine deserves design attention. This is usually the only part of your volume bookstore browsers will see on the shelf. There isn't a whole lot you can do with a book's spine, so make sure your title is clearly visible and legible, and that it stands out as much as possible.

This is yet another place where color can make a major difference. Go to the bookstore; stand in the reference, religion, or romance section and look at which book spines leap out at you. You'll find that there aren't many. You don't want to color your background and print chartreuse and magenta simply to make your spine stand out from the crowd, but if you can use color wisely, do it. It also helps to make your print as large and striking as possible. You want your book to boldly proclaim itself, not timidly whisper.

Besides the title, your book's spine should also include your last name and your publishing company's name and logo. People don't generally buy books based on the publisher, as in, "Oh, wow, another book from Arithmetic Press!" But it doesn't hurt either, and if you plan to enter various publishing industry book design competitions, you can get points knocked off your score if you don't have your logo on your book's spine.

Smart Tip

Tip...

Don't think books sell based on their covers? Most book sales reps and distributors carry only book covers and dust jackets to show booksellers and other buyers. Buying decisions are based on covers, not on content.

Cover Stock

OK, with all this advice tucked under your hat, it's time to start making publisher/printer decisions. While you're designing your cover, you'll need to decide between hard and soft formats. Softcover is less expensive, which is an obvious advantage for both you as the publisher and for your buyer—but less isn't always more. Readers want some books printed as case-bound, or hardcover volumes.

Professional and business books are often case-bound—doctors, salespeople, CEOs, and other white-collar types will more readily buy an expensive hardcover in their field than an inexpensive softcover, believing that a hardcover edition has more merit. Hardcover books also get more serious review attention.

Coffee table and gift books are also generally bound in hardcover—it makes for a more impressive and longer-lasting presentation.

Taking Stock

If you're going with softcover, you'll need to choose a cover stock, or paper. The two standard choices are 10 point C1S and 12 point C1S. Translation: C1S is cover coated on one side with untreated stock on the other side. The 12 point stock is slightly heavier than 10 point and, therefore, more expensive.

You'll also need to decide on a cover finish. The standard choices are gloss lamination or matte lamination. Lamination means the paper cover is treated with a plastic coating that protects against moisture, scuffing, and fingerprints. Gloss lamination provides a shiny finish; matte lamination does not.

Make sure you specify a lay-flat, or curl-resistant laminate, or your covers will roll like surf after a storm when any humidity is present. Cost differences in laminates are minimal—about a nickel more per book for matte than for gloss. And although you may pay marginally more for lay-flat, you really only want lay-flat. You'll be sorry, and so will your readers, if you elect not to use it.

In a Bind

Once you make a decision on the hardcover vs. softcover issue and how you want the spine to look, you will need to choose a binding. If you go with hardcover, you will probably want a Smythe-sewn (pronounced "Smythe-sewn," with the "y" pronounced as a long "i") binding, in which the signatures are sewn together and then glued into the cover. This is the most durable case-bound binding, and the one most publishers choose.

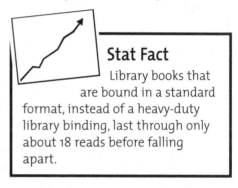

Stat Fact
Library books that are bound in a standard format, instead of a heavy-duty library binding, last through only about 18 reads before falling apart.

Your hardcover itself won't look very interesting, so you'll need an eye-catching dust cover or jacket. If your jacket will consist of just a few artistic hues, you'll need to tell the printer what ink colors you want to use by referring to the Pantone Matching System (PMS) of ink colors. PMS numbers designate specific ink colors. It is sort of the same thing as the house paint samples you find at the home improvement store. PMS numbers ensure that the "burnt orange sienna" you have your heart set on is the same one the printer is looking at. PMS colors come in swatch books that you can flip through. If your printer is in Michigan and you're in Nebraska, go to a local printer or graphic designer and ask to look at their PMS colors. Note the numbers you've chosen and let your long-distance printer know.

You'll also need to specify how you will provide your jacket art. If you go with a professional book designer, you may send it to the printer camera ready, which basically means that you send the original artwork ready to be photographed and then printed. Or you might send your cover as disc to film, which means the artwork has been done using a software program and transferred to a CD or zip disc for the printer to use.

Perfectly Bound

For softcover books, you will probably want to stick with the publisher's premier choice, perfect binding. This is the type of binding used for virtually every softcover at the bookstore or library. The cover is glued onto a tidy, squared-off spine on which

▲

Ideal Specs

Use this sheet to fill in your ideal specs before you go on to that RFQ (request for quote) you'll send to printers:

Trim size: _____

Hardcover or softcover: _____

Cover stock: _____

Gloss or matte lay-flat laminate: _____

Disc-to-film or camera ready:_____

Four-color/PMS number(s): _____

Binding type:_____

Paper stock (weight and color): _____

Bleeds: _____

Halftones: _____

Color separations: _____

Text ink—black plus any PMS color(s): _____

you can print your title and author/publisher information. Perfect bindings can also be Smythe-sewn.

Perfect binding is more expensive than other softcover bindings but has the double advantage of being more durable as well as being the only one most bookstores and libraries will buy.

If you are not concerned with these markets, though, and you're planning to sell via mail order, at seminars and workshops, or to specialty stores only, you've got several other choices:

- *Spiral binding*. Wire is used to bind the pages of a book together in spiral binding. The blank notebooks you find at Walmart or the supermarket are spiral bound.
- *Comb binding*. This type of binding involves a long piece of thin plastic covering "teeth" you often see holding Junior League cookbook pages together.
- *Saddle-stitch binding*. This isn't stitched at all but stapled through the center, like the programs handed out at high school graduations or community theater productions. If your book is 72 pages or less, and you're marketing it as an inexpensive pamphlet or report, this could be the binding to use.
- *Velo binding*. A plastic strip holds the pages (perforated at the left margins) together. Gary S., the military memoirs publisher in Panama City Beach, Florida, uses velo binding for his books.

You might go with spiral or comb binding if you are producing a workbook for a seminar or workshop that will only be used by one reader during a brief period, or for a Junior League or chamber of commerce cookbook where buyers do not expect a "fancy" binding job. For everything else, stick to perfect binding. It's the best!

Pricing and Selling

We've explored the costs to set up shop as a self-publisher and the costs to have a book printed or e-published. But just having your book in hand doesn't mean your fling with financing is over. There are other factors that contribute to the cost of that book, from distributors to storage to shipping. You need a way to get your books from your storage facility to your readers.

You can use wholesalers, distributors, direct mail, specialty stores, and a host of other venues. But nobody is going to beg you to sign on—it's up to you to make the first move. In this chapter, we'll investigate the elements involved in pricing and selling your book.

The Sticker Price

You'll need to decide on a sticker price for your book. You can't forecast profits if you don't know how much you'll charge. An industry rule of thumb is to base your price on your production costs multiplied by 5 or by 8. Note that this rule applies to traditional printing methods only—not print on demand (POD), which we explored in Chapter 6.

In addition to or perhaps in explanation of this rule of thumb, you'll want to consider that book prices are based on two defining elements:

1. *Your production costs.* Obviously, you must charge enough to cover your expenses including not only printing but also editing and artwork.
2. *Comparable retail prices.* If all the other softcover inspirational books on the shelf are priced in the $12.95 to $16.95 range and yours is priced at $30, it's not going to sell. Even if it's a million times better than the competition, people will perceive it as overpriced and give it a thumbs down. This is yet another reason to get out there and do your market research!

Let's take another look at *The Night Garden*, the title Glowworm Press printed at a per-book cost of $1.37, and let's decide that, based on comparable books in the marketplace, we're going to price it at $12.95. That leaves us with a per-book profit of $11.58, right? Well, not exactly. Now we have to take into account the other costs that you will encounter in addition to printing.

Divvying Up Discounts

The traditional method for getting books from your office or garage to your readers is to engage a distributor to sell them to bookstores on your behalf. You can also sell directly to booksellers yourself, but since there are more chains and fewer independents, this is becoming more difficult. Chains generally buy from distributors and wholesalers, and not from publishers. Whichever route you choose (and you should try both), you will need to give a percentage or discount off the book's retail price.

Distributor/Wholesaler Dance

Wholesalers and distributors play a big part in the publisher's world. New publishers are often confused about the difference between wholesalers and distributors—and no, they're not the same. A wholesaler is basically a mega-warehouse stacked to the rafters with millions of books. Wholesalers sit back and wait for booksellers to order books; they don't actively sell.

Distributors, on the other hand, act as sales representatives, designing catalogs that showcase their publishers' books, making marketing suggestions to help sales, and visiting booksellers with the sole purpose of convincing them to stock your title (as well as those of their other publishers). They also handle fulfillment, or orders from booksellers, including shipping, invoicing, and collecting payments—saving you lots of time.

Distributor Dating Game

Steve C., the independent publisher in Hinesburg, Vermont, says the terms "wholesaler" and "distributor" are often misused. "A distributor handles all your trade [bookstore and library] sales, on an exclusive basis. It will generally take about a 67 percent discount and may even levy added costs that you will have to pay. Distributors obviously give a large part of that big discount to the stores and wholesalers they sell to, and they have to pay a percentage to their sales reps. Some distribution companies are National Book Network, Publishers Group West, and IPG," explains Steve.

There are many distributors to choose from, and they may require different discounts. Keep in mind that besides a hefty discount, distributors can and often will charge you for a slew of other services, including setup (to set you up in their system), catalog advertising, book fair advertising, and warehousing. After you add all this up, you're looking at as much as another $1,000 or more.

Some distributors are generalists, while others specialize in niches like education, Christian themes, the outdoor-enthusiast market, the health and fitness market, or books for the business-oriented, etc. If your title fits neatly into one specialty, this might be the place to start. If not, investigate the generalists.

> **Tip...**
>
> **Smart Tip**
> Quality Books, a distributor based in Illinois, deals solely with the weighty library trade and doesn't require an exclusive contract. Quality Books has an excellent reputation for working with small publishers, so try to develop a relationship with them. (See Appendix for contact information.)

Turning Heads

So what will turn a distributor's head and make them want to represent you?

1. *Your book's saleability.* A business book distributor is likely to be far more interested in Bill Gates' sales secrets, as told by his secretary, than in Bill Gates' home décor, related by his housekeeper.

2. *Your book cover and design.* A book with a savvy cover or dust jacket looks like the product of a professional publisher. If everything—including the binding, layout, margins, leading, and the blurb on the back cover—is sharp and skillful, you've passed one of the biggest tests.

3. *Your marketing plan and promotional budget.* Distributors will do their part to sell your book with catalogs, booths at industry shows, and more, but they want to know that you've got a major campaign underway as well.

4. *Your product line.* Distributors prefer seasoned publishers with several titles under their belts. If this is your first title, you can't do too much here except push the sales value of your book. You can also discuss other titles you're working on, if that's the case. If not, don't invent; it won't ring true.

Just because you decide on a distributor doesn't mean they'll choose you. It's a distributor dating game. You will have to convince them that your book is worth representing—and more than that, worth making a significant effort for. The trick here is that distributors like exclusive contracts—they do not want to deal with you if you are also working with another distributor. And since you will be tied solely to that distributor, you'll rely on them for the majority of your bookstore sales. If you find you don't like their style, you're stuck for the life of the contract. So carefully choose the one that's best for you.

You'll find a list of distributors in the Appendix at the back of this book, but instead of choosing one sight unseen, get out there and do some additional research. Visit booksellers in your area and ask the manager or buyer about the distributors who service the books similar to yours. Then visit the distributors online and see how the titles they carry stack up as compared to yours. Get a feel for their services and general attitude. For the ones that look promising, place a call or send an email to the

Interviewing Potential Distributors

These are questions you should ask any potential distributor in order to evaluate whether there is a good fit between your needs and their services.

1. What book genres do you handle? _____

2. How many publishers do you have on board? _____

3. How many trade accounts do you service? _____

4. What other types of accounts do you service, if any (i.e., libraries, specialty stores, airport shops, or convenience stores)? _____

5. What sales volume do you expect for my book this year? _____

6. What percentage do you pay for each sale? _____

7. When do you pay sales? _____

8. How do you handle returns? _____

9. What do you charge for warehousing? _____

10. Will you insure my books? _____

11. Do you pay shipping? _____

12. What extra fees can I expect to incur? _____

13. What is the standard length of your contract? _____

new-accounts reps. These are the folks you want to woo. We've provided a list of the questions you should ask when interviewing potential distributors above.

Wholesaler Heaven

"The fact that a distributor has sales reps may get you greater distribution, but if you can create demand for your book (through good reviews, radio shows, etc.) you can get very good distribution without these people," Steve C. advises. "You do need wholesalers—the people who take a 55 percent discount. The big ones are Ingram and Baker & Taylor. There are a number of smaller ones that can help reach certain markets, including a few remaining consignment wholesalers that are very open to small-press books (New Leaf and Quality Books are examples). Hardly any librarian or

> **Fun Fact**
>
> *Charleston Receipts,* a fundraising cookbook published by the Charleston, South Carolina, Junior League, first went to print in 1950—and is still a hot seller today.

bookstore owner wants to order books one at a time from small presses. Their job is easier if they order hundreds of books at a time from the same place—in other words, a wholesaler."

Even though you may have a distributor that sells your book to wholesalers for you, you'll still need a relationship with a wholesaler yourself. Booksellers and librarians who haven't been approached by your distributor may hear about your book and want to order it, and they generally prefer to order it from a wholesaler, for two reasons:

1. Publishers have a reputation for filling orders in a matter of weeks instead of overnight as wholesalers do.

2. In terms of paperwork, it's far easier to order the works of hundreds of publishers from the wholesaler and receive a single invoice than to pay a different publisher for each title.

Wholesalers are not quite as picky as distributors, but you will still have to do some courting. The two giants of the wholesaling world are Ingram, which holds the lead position, and Baker & Taylor, which focuses on servicing libraries as well as booksellers. There are also a number of smaller wholesalers who have a far better reputation for dealing with small presses—Bookpeople and New Leaf are two shining examples (see the Appendix for contact information). Like distributors, wholesalers demand a discount, generally 55 percent off the list price.

Decide which wholesaler you want to work with in the same way you would seek out a potential distributor, and then go about courting their business in essentially the same manner. You can use the "Interviewing Potential Wholesalers" form on page 135 to help you with this process.

The Bottom Line Revisited

Now you know that distributor and wholesaler discounts can range from 55 percent up to 67 percent. Gulp! This means that if our hypothetical publisher has *The*

Interviewing Potential Wholesalers

To evaluate potential wholesalers, be sure to ask these questions:

1. What book genres do you handle? _____

2. What percentage do you pay for each sale? _____

3. When do you pay sales? _____

4. How do you handle returns? _____

5. Do you charge for warehousing? _____

6. Will you insure my books? _____

7. Do you pay shipping? _____

8. What extra fees can I expect to incur? _____

9. What is the standard length of your contract? _____

Night Garden priced at $12.95, and the distributor or wholesaler demands a 60-percent discount, Glowworm Press is really selling its title at $5.18. They still have to deduct production costs of $1.37 per book, so the per-book profit comes in at $3.81—less than before the discount but still a tidy profit margin.

Ship Shape

Yet another expense to consider is shipping—to and from the distributor's warehouse, to the independent bookseller, from the printer to you. Shipping is another of those costs that can vary dramatically depending on departure sites, destinations, and the number of books being shipped. It is not cheap. All you have to do is think back to the days when you schlepped a bag or backpack filled with books home from high school every day, and you'll remember that books are heavy. What this means for the self-publisher is that, rather than going through FedEx, UPS, or the U.S. Postal Service, you'll need to get bids from freight services.

Return to Sender

There's yet another variable here, and that's returns and damages. Some self-publishers have a terrific relationship with their distributors and wholesalers; others consider them a necessary evil, with the emphasis on "evil." One reason for this

sentiment is that some companies go extremely heavy on the returns. They will order 100 books from you on Tuesday, return them to you on Wednesday morning, and then reorder them on Wednesday afternoon.

This can play havoc with your profits—you not only have to take back the books you thought you'd sold and erase the payments you thought were coming your way, but, to add insult to injury, you have to pay shipping both going and coming (and going again). And if the books are damaged in the return process, you can't resell them.

"Unfortunately, I have not had a good experience," says Anna J. in Temple, Texas. She had trouble with a wholesaler for over a year. "I finally got the problem settled; now I don't get orders from them (which is better than receiving damaged returned books and inaccurate bills for books returned). I'm currently in the Ingram Express

Cinderella Story

As a neophyte in the book trade, you may discover that, even though your book looks professional and has good sales potential, you can't land a distributor. Like those reviews you may not get, this is a fact of life and not a direct insult. Distributors can be snooty, but you can win them in time. Re-contact them every few months and woo them with your solid sales figures, great reviews, news coverage, and endorsements. Sooner or later, they'll say, "Yes."

IBPA (Independent Book Publishers Association) has devised a special Trade Distribution Acceptance Program to deal with this difficulty for newcomers to the publishing industry. Each summer and winter, a committee made up of reps from Ingram and Baker & Taylor (the "Big Two" of wholesaling); Borders; Barnes & Noble; independent booksellers; and Independent Publishers Group (IPG), which is a distributor, reviews submissions from IBPA members. In a sort of Cinderella story, titles they feel are saleable are picked up for distribution by IPG.

program, which is specifically for small publishers, and it is a headache. They order books that I send them; I have to give them a 55-percent discount. Then they send the books back to me even while they're ordering more of the same books! It has been most frustrating."

Steve C. warns that "every publisher hates the Ingram returns, which are a big percentage of its purchases—and usually in damaged condition—and you are expected to pay for their return postage!" But Steve concedes that, "if you want to sell to bookstores, you deal with Ingram."

Not every self-publisher we interviewed has had a bad experience with a wholesaler or distributor. "Wholesalers and distributors are a necessary evil as the chain stores will deal only with them," says June H. in Michigan. "I have a contract with Partners Distributors in Holt, Michigan, and Ingram Books in LaVergne, Tennessee. I've had no problems with either."

Your best bet is to check references with other self-publishers and go with the one that has the best reputation. To some extent, you will have to accept that the process may not always be smooth. In some instances, it may be better to make certain tradeoffs, like budgeting for the expense of return postage, in order to achieve the sales goals that you set for yourself. How much should you allow for returns? Industry experts recommend that you pencil in a figure as high as 20 percent.

You do have some small measure of control here. Although your printer, distributor, and wholesaler will insist that you pay shipping to and from them, you in turn can insist that independent booksellers pay shipping on any returns they send back to you. You'll still have to absorb the cost of the books, but you can let them pick up the transport tab. Just make sure you state your return policy in your book sales contract.

Storage Story

If you print 5,000 books and have them shipped to your home office, you're going to have to decide where to stash them. You could cover them with tablecloths, slipcovers, and bed linens, and use them in place of furniture. But barring this scenario, you'll have a problem.

If you live in an area where dampness and/or humidity are not significant factors, you could warehouse your books in your garage. Otherwise, you'll need to rent a climate-controlled storage facility. You don't want creeping mildew to spot all your pages, or your covers to stick together or curl.

Storage prices will vary with your location and the size space you rent, but as a ballpark figure you can pencil in $70 to $100 per month.

Trade Sales and Alternative Venues

OK, you've got those bound galleys out, bundled up your review packages, along with your finished book, sent them off to everybody who's anybody, and dealt with distributors and wholesalers. Good! But you've still got lots more to tackle. You can't sit back and wait for the sales reps to sell for you, especially if you haven't yet been successful in lining up a distributor.

Besides the traditional trade outlets of bookstores and libraries, there are many alternative venues in which to sell your books. We'll take a look at bookstores and libraries, and then everything from direct mail to premiums to museum shops.

Bookstore Bonanza

When you sell directly to bookstores, you'll need to give them a 40 percent discount. This is the industry norm, and they expect it. If you've lined up a distributor, it's easier to let them make sales to the trade while you concentrate on other venues. But you can sell directly to bookstores whether you've got representation or not. The catch here is that the major chains, from Borders to Books-a-Million, usually can't order directly from you unless you've got a wholesaler—corporate policy won't allow it. But you can ask. Sometimes they'll go around their own rules to carry the titles of local authors and publishers. Some bookstores even have a special section set aside to showcase the works of local talent.

Local talent aside, if you don't have a distributor you'll do better to focus on independent booksellers. These are the mom-and-pop places you can still find in quaint or funky downtown areas and outlying suburban strip malls, if you look. Some bill themselves as "used book" sellers, but they often carry new titles as well.

Because these stores generally do not have the budget for major orders, you won't want to spend months canvassing them door-to-door in the manner of an itinerant salesperson. But you should definitely approach every independent bookseller in your area. Remember, you're a local author and publisher, which means you're a local celebrity. Independents will be charmed to carry your title, and they'll do their utmost to sell it for you. Expect to give independent booksellers 40 percent off your list price.

Appearance Is Everything

Even when chain superstores stock your book, you won't find it on view in the window or on display at the front of the store. Instead it will be tucked discreetly out of sight on the shelf with all the other business books or romance novels or whatever.

Those snazzy cardboard displays, called dumps or point-of-purchase displays (POPs), are generally reserved for the products of the major New York publishing houses and the books that have been on *The New York Times* bestseller list for the tenth week running.

Bright Idea

Talk to sales reps and distributors who specialize in the markets you want to reach. The best way to find them is to ask local merchandisers who their reps are. You can also check with national organizations in those specialties. For instance, if you're selling a cookbook, you could check with the National Specialty Foods Association, which can give you leads to reps and distributors for shops that buy gourmet goodies.

Publicity Freebies

You may think that since you've ordered 3,000 copies of your book from the printer, you've got 3,000 copies to sell. But if you do all the publicity that you should, you'll give away as many as 500 copies—absolutely free—to various book review sources, industry experts in your niche market, TV and radio program producers, and other opinion molders. The numbers add up fast.

And you'll have to add in shipping by postal carrier for each one of those books. As an estimate, you can figure that a 1-pound book shipped Special Standard Mail, or book rate, via the U.S. mail costs $1.59. If you send out a total of 500 books during the course of your publicity campaign, that's $795!

There's not a whole lot you can do about this situation since booksellers only have so much display space. Naturally, they're going to give it to the books they expect to sell the best or those that come with dumps for the display areas.

Your best solution is to either stop worrying about it and trust that your books will sell themselves based on your other marketing and PR efforts, or design and build your own dumps. This will add considerably to your advertising budget, but if market research shows it can really be effective—and your wallet can take it—give it a shot. Interview local booksellers to find out if they can use a dump and where they would prefer to have it placed. There's no point in springing for a five-foot-high floor model when a small counter display would be more effective.

Libraries and Educational Markets

Colleges and other educational buyers will often accept 20 percent discounts. However, educational markets will only purchase certain types of books. If your niche is romance novels, for instance, you can count them out. However, if your book is a nonfiction title like *My Hero: How Romantic Fiction Affects the Female Mind*, you might just find a buyer among psychology, sociology, or women's studies professors.

Libraries, which can be sizable buyers, will pay full retail price for books with special (and more expensive) library binding. For most other books, they expect a 40 percent discount but will take what they can get. Public librarians can be a terrific buying market and may buy just about anything they think will be good for their patrons—that they can fit into their budgets.

Besides traditional public libraries, you can also sell to the thousands of private libraries all over the country. Many churches; synagogues; genealogy societies; film, art, and sports institutes; professional and social organizations; and hospitals and corporations house their own collections. If your book subject would be of interest to any of these groups, try to make sales! Don't forget to offer a fair discount of up to 40 percent.

Smart Tip

The best time to pitch your book to public librarians is during June or December—right around budget appropriation and spending seasons.

The Amazon of Bookstores

A nifty alternative to brick-and-mortar bookstores is the ace of the virtual booksellers' world—Amazon.com. Amazon caters to independent publishers. They'll provide you with a publisher's website; scan in your book's photo; set you up with an author interview, a book blurb, your comments about your book, a sample passage of your choice, and space for readers' reviews. Your title appears prominently on the site's search results, and, as another bonus, your book is offered with 24-hour shipping—and Amazon.com handles order fulfillment.

What's the catch for all these goodies? Not much—there's no contract to sign and no exclusive. All they ask is that you keep your titles in stock and give them a 45-percent discount on the list price of your book. What have you got to lose?

Premium Grade

There are lots of creative venues for making sales other than bookstores and libraries. One of these is custom publishing or premiums, two different names that mean the same thing. You are familiar with premiums—those freebie cookbooks given out as advertising incentives by the local natural gas board, the amortization books handed out by the local bank, and even the oven mitts emblazoned with the name of a nearby supermarket.

Your book just might be the stuff of a terrific premium. Take a look at your subject matter and evaluate it in terms of what companies or organizations might benefit from it. You could pitch a sinful dessert cookbook to a dairy products company to showcase their butters and creams or to a chocolate manufacturer to feature recipes for their product. This is where the term custom publishing comes in. You may need to customize your text so that instead of "2 pounds of chocolate," your recipes read "2 pounds of Chocoholic-brand chocolate," or whatever it may be.

Your customization might be as simple as adding the store's name to the title. A home improvement chain might be interested in selling copies of your do-it-yourself remodeling manual to its customers. You would simply add the store name to your existing title: *Handy Hal Superstore's Home Remodeling for the Hammer-Impaired.* Or you might not change anything—a lingerie manufacturer might like to give each customer who

Smart Tip

Tip...

When you sell customized publishing or premiums, give your customer discounts based on volume—perhaps 40 percent for 500 to 1,000 copies, and 50 percent for amounts over that. Have the customer pay for shipping.

orders over a certain amount from its spring catalog a "free" copy of your romance novel. And hospitals might like to tuck copies of your new-baby inspirational book into their take-home kits for parents.

Obviously, the more changes you make, the more advance notice you will need. You can't change your cover or your text after your books are already printed. You'll need to approach potential customers very early in the game—before your initial printing or before any reprints.

Your other option is to purchase stickers or rubber stamps to add to your cover or title page, ones that say something like "With Best Wishes from Grace Avenue Maternity Hospital," for example.

> **Bright Idea**
>
> Why not sell your book to nonprofit organizations, either as a customized printing or as is? You can offer a deep discount, feel good about helping a worthy cause, and generate a little money and publicity all at the same time.

The Catalog Game

Another nontraditional venue for selling your book is through mail order catalogs. Don't confuse this arena with your own mail order sales—here we're talking about selling quantities of your books to a third-party mail order retailer. There are thousands of mail order catalogs out there, and each one works hard to find one-of-a-kind merchandise for its pages. Your book could be ideal.

As with premium sales, match your subject matter to the catalog. A book on golf techniques might be the perfect match for a catalog of goods for the novice golfer. An aromatherapy title might be just the thing for a health-products catalog. And an inspirational gift book on fathers and sons could sell well in a general interest catalog, especially around Father's Day.

Sell to catalog merchandisers the way you do to anyone else—sell early, sell assertively, push your book's sales potential, and offer a fair discount for volume sales. You can find catalog merchandisers by doing a search on the internet.

Specialty of the House

Bookstores aren't the only retail shops capable of stocking your book. There are also all sorts of specialty stores and boutiques that can be terrific sales outlets. Use the same criteria we explored above for catalog merchandisers. Think about what kind of match your book can make with what sort of shop. There are hundreds of specialties to choose from including:

- Outdoor activities—camping and hiking gear, or canoe outfitters
- Boating
- Health food and vitamins
- Arts, crafts, and hobby shops
- Toys
- Children's and infants' supplies
- Automotive
- Luggage and travel
- Beauty shops
- Gardening
- Computer and software
- Educational
- Fine furniture and home décor
- Cards, stationery, and gifts

> **Tip...**
>
> ### Smart Tip
>
> Take a ghostly sheet from June H.'s sales book. "I sell anywhere I can," says the horror writer from Rochester Hills, Michigan. "For the last two years, I have sold books at a Halloween event in Stone Mountain, Georgia, called *A Tour of Southern Ghosts* and [have] done quite well. Look around at the small stores or local events that tie into the types of stories you produce," offers June.

Museum-Quality

When you think alternative retail, don't forget about museum shops. There are thousands of museums and historic homes all over the country, from the mammoth Metropolitan in New York City to the diminutive Franklin D. Roosevelt vacation-home site in Warm Springs, Georgia. Each one has its own shop crammed with merchandise. Your book could be on display as well.

Once again, think about how your title might match the subjects on display or the general ambiance of the museum or historic home. A book about World War II or the Depression might do well at the Roosevelt home, since he was a fixture during both traumas, but a regional title on travel in Georgia might also be a big seller.

Stepping into the Spotlight
Publicity

As a general rule, books don't sell themselves. Unlike hot dogs at a ball game or iced confections peddled from a cart on a steamy city afternoon, people don't notice books without prompting. One of your biggest tasks as a self-publisher is to publicize your book as effectively, creatively, and energetically as possible. Start thinking about your book, your personality, your budget,

▲

and your niche market and how you can tie them all into a glittering promotional package. In this chapter, we'll explore the very best ways to get your book noticed by the people who count, from pre-publication reviewers to post-publication venues.

Pre-Publication Pow

After you've written and designed your book and sent it off to the printer, it's time to focus on selling it. Note that we didn't say you have received your completed volumes back from the printer—the prime time to start your sales campaign is before your book is ever released. In fact, most major reviewers won't accept a finished product. They only want to see a work in progress.

Setting the Date

Once you are active in the publishing industry, you will see the terms "publication date" or "pub date" bandied about. Most people assume this refers to the date the book comes back from the printer and (hopefully) floods those bookstore shelves. Well, it's not. A book's publication date is entirely fictional.

Its purpose is to give you time to get your product from the printer to the distributor and into stores, well before entering the welcome glare of the limelight you'll generate with your marketing blitz. Set your pub date at six weeks to two months before your book is ready for shipment from the printer. Then swing into pre-publication action! Time pre-publication reviews, media appearances, press releases, and news articles so that prospective readers are primed to snap it up by the time your book actually arrives on bookstore shelves.

Bound for the Galleys

Pre-publication reviews can do as much or more to ensure the success of a book than just about any other marketing technique you can employ. A favorable review in a trade publication can net significant sales and generate terrific additional publicity. But trade reviewers are picky. They won't review every book that comes down the pike, and they won't review anything that looks like a finished product. Their reasoning is that if the book is already printed, it's not new enough to warrant their attention.

Instead of a tidy book with a dust jacket or shiny four-color cover, you put together a bound galley to send to reviewers. This is your book on standard 8.5-by-11 copier-quality paper, regardless of what the actual trim size will be. The pages are perfect bound, but with a plain-Jane cover: nothing but a title page printed in black ink on a white background. This is one place where it's fine to have a general printer copy and bind your book—short-run printers such as Odyssey Press (acquired in November 2011 by Yurchak Press in Landsville, Pennsylvania) focus a lot of their business in bound galley printing. Or you can check prices with a POD printer. The book printer you use will send you F&Gs, which are the folded-and-gathered signature pages of your book. These are what you can have quick-copied by a general printer and bound to make your bound galleys.

Since this is an advance promotional copy of your book, it's perfectly acceptable to send it without the table of contents, dedication, acknowledgments, index, or other final round of layout material. It's also OK to send a bound galley without illustrations—unless of course it's a children's picture book or other title that depends on illustrations to tell the story.

If you leave out the table of contents, index, illustrations, or other matter, make sure you note that they'll be included in the finished book. And of course, make sure you've done all your copyediting and proofreading. You want the galley as clean and sharp as possible. That said, always state on the cover that it is an "unproofed" galley since things do change between galleys and final printed book.

Announcements and Accompaniments

You can't send a bound galley out into the cold review world all alone—it will immediately get lost in the crowd. Fashion a one-page cover letter to accompany it. This should briefly describe the book and explain why you, the expert, are the perfect author for this subject.

If at all possible, give your letter a hook to attract special attention to your topic. For instance, if the headlines are filled with news of a scientific breakthrough on aging and your book is about living longer and healthier, you could tie into the media frenzy. If your sci-fi adventure is about life on Mars, you could tie into current news stories on Mars exploration, for example.

You'll also need to make up an announcement form to glue onto the galley itself. Because of the avalanche of books reviewers often get buried under, your galley can easily get lost from your vital information if you don't use glue. And this information is critical: Reviewers can't tell the public your book's ISBN, publication date, or price if your galley has gotten separated from your letter. Take a look at the sample "Book Announcement" on page 148.

▲

Book Announcement

The Night Garden: How to Enjoy Your Garden After Dark

Author: Peter Moss
Publication date: October 15, 20xx
Price: $12.95
ISBN: 0946555-23-X
Vital statistics: Trade paperback, 6 inches by 9 inches, illustrations, and index
Number of Pages: 192

Publisher: Glowworm Press, 1 Firefly Lane, Luminescent, FL 10000
Distributed by: Friendly & Reliable Distributors Inc.
Contact: Sally Luna (850) 555-0000, www.glowwormpress.com

The Pre-Pub Revue

Once you have your bound galleys, you'll want to send them out for review—three to four months before your pub date. You should target both book trade and general interest publications.

Trade Reviewers

The major publications for trade buyers—the ones that have the greatest impact—are *Publishers Weekly* and *Library Journal*. Don't neglect the rest, though. The more pre-publication reviews you can garner, the better your book's chance of success.

The following is a list of publications you'll want to include on your mailing list. While most are interested in a wide range of materials, they all have their own guidelines. Some will accept only children's books; some won't review textbooks; and others shy away from mass-market paperbacks and poetry.

Although we've provided you with some tips on who reads what, it's up to you to check with each publication to make sure they review your book's genre (and to make sure they still exist—this business changes fast!). While you're at it, get the name of the editor for your genre (with the correct spelling . . .). Address your package specifically to him and add his title as well—that way if he's moved onto another publication or gone to Tahiti for two months, his substitute can receive the materials.

The two top dogs in the general book publishing world are:

1. *Publishers Weekly*. This is the penultimate pre-publication review machine. If you get a rave response here, you've just about got it made. The entire trade goes by what *Publishers Weekly* says is good—bookstores, libraries, and wholesalers alike. The main area of interest for *Publishers Weekly* is just about anything that will appeal to the general public. On top of which, the magazine began to acknowledge that the world of self-published books had changed. "In recognition of the boom in self-publishing and as an acknowledgment that valuable works are being published outside traditional publishing, PW is giving self-published authors an opportunity to present their titles to the publishing trade." This "opportunity" came in the form of a quarterly supplement called *PW Select*. You can pay to be listed in the supplement ($149 at this writing) and you can submit your book for potential review; the editors pick 25 titles to review each quarter. Your book, however, must be deemed of interest to the general reading public.

> **Smart Tip**
>
> Be sure to send a bound galley to Quality Books, based in Illinois, a company that distributes independent publishers' products to libraries. Unlike most wholesalers and distributors, Quality Books wants to see your pre-pub product rather than wait for the finished book.

2. *Library Journal*. Almost as powerful as *Publishers Weekly*, *Library Journal* is the reviewer of choice for public librarians all over the country, as well as for wholesalers who sell to libraries. An A-plus here can mean sales of 1,000 to 5,000 copies—an entire print run. Not surprisingly, *Library Journal* looks for books that will appeal to the broad readership of a public library.

Both of these important trade publications have a heavy online presence and can be subscribed to as digital editions.

Other magazines that are very important to the book world include:

- *Kirkus Reviews*. Another major trade reviewer, *Kirkus Reviews* is read by booksellers and librarians. *Kirkus Reviews* takes on fiction and nonfiction of just about any genre but poetry, mass-market paperbacks, and picture books for the toddler set.

- *School Library Journal*. The junior version of the venerable *Library Journal*, *School Library Journal* reviews fiction and nonfiction for children and teens, including picture books. Despite the name, *School Library Journal* is read by public librarians, as well as those in school settings.

- *ALA Booklist*. The ALA stands for American Library Association, which tells you that this is another journal targeted toward librarians. *ALA Booklist* reviews

▲

Molding Opinions

While you're in your bound galley review phase, don't forget to send copies to opinion molders in your niche market. If your book is targeted toward physicians, for instance, send copies to doctors who can give you a favorable review, an endorsement or testimonial, or perhaps even write the foreword. If your book's niche is crafters, send galleys to noted crafters and to crafting publications.

Sending galleys to opinion makers is a good way to generate early interest in your book and get readers looking forward to its appearance on bookstore shelves. You may even make advance sales.

Send as many bound galleys as your budget will allow and get creative about who's an opinion maker. Anna J., the self-publisher in Temple, Texas, sent her book targeted toward siblings of critically ill children to nurses and social workers—people who have the power to suggest it to families in need.

fiction, nonfiction, and reference (but not textbooks) for children, teens, and adults.

- *Choice*. This journal also targets librarians, with a focus on those in academic and research settings. *Choice* is the place to go if your book has a technical or scholarly bent. Recent reviews include an encyclopedia of dinosaurs, a documentary history of sports in North America, a volume examining Lewis Carroll's use of earlier childhood literature, as well as the layperson-oriented *Marketing for Dummies* (John Wiley and Sons).

- *ForeWord*. A trade journal targeted toward booksellers, librarians, and publishers, *ForeWord* specializes in the products of independent and university presses. Although they don't want to see textbooks or technical tomes, *ForeWord* is open to just about everything else, including e-books and audiobooks.

General Interest Reviewers

The following is a list of publications that review books for the general public. As with trade journals, it's up to you to double-check all the contact information before sending out your galleys. Life is not static. Reviewers move on or retire; newspapers change their guidelines. Part of effective PR is staying on top of details.

- *The New York Times* Book Review Section. This is the *Publishers Weekly* of the general interest world—the supreme review mechanism. If you're a smash in the pages of *The Times*, you can expect the orders to roll in. A bonus to a review here is that it may be syndicated, which means it will appear in other newspapers nationwide. *The Times* is interested in just about everything but technical tomes.

- *Los Angeles Times* Book Review Section. The West Coast *Times* is not as big a draw as the Big Apple version but can do well by you. This *Times* takes on most general interest books.

- Book reviewers at other major metropolitan newspapers. Send galleys to other major newspapers such as *The Boston Globe*, *Chicago Tribune*, *The Philadelphia Inquirer*, and *San Francisco Chronicle*. If your budget will stretch to it, also send galleys to book review editors at newspapers in Atlanta, Louisville, St. Louis, San Diego, Seattle, and other points around the country. But use common sense. If your book has a strong regional appeal, as in *Smoky Mountains Gardening*, don't send it to out-of-the-area reviewers.

Significant Others

Steve C., the independent publisher who has produced more than 20 books, believes in the power of advance reviews. "There are some important publications that need to receive bound galleys three or four months in advance of the official date of publication—otherwise, they won't review the book," the Vermont resident says. "The most important of these are *Library Journal* and *ALA Booklist.* Without review there, you sell no books to libraries and miss out on the best chance to make back your initial investment quickly.

"Other significant publications that need advance galleys include *Publishers Weekly* and *The New York Times*," Steve says. A favorable *Publishers Weekly* review will help with bookstore sales and is useful to quote in your publicity to show that you've been reviewed by a prestigious publication. That can open doors for you that might otherwise be closed to a new self-publisher. *The Times* probably won't review your book—certainly not if the editors notice that you are a self-publisher. But it's worth trying anyway

Smart Tip

Sending a bound galley for review doesn't guarantee that your book will be written up in a trade or general interest publication. Most major publications receive thousands upon thousands of galleys each year, more than they could ever read and make room to review in their pages. Don't be deterred by this, and don't feel you've failed or been slighted if you don't get reviewed.

because if they do, a review from *The Times* all by itself may sell 10,000 books and propel the book to continuing publicity elsewhere.

"A great many other publications do not want advance galleys and prefer to receive finished books when they are available," says Steve. When submitting your galleys to publications other than the biggies, it is important to check into their policies—particularly if the publication is subject- or genre-specific. "Making the wrong type of submission can cost a review and can cost many book sales."

The Post-Pub Revue

Once your book has been printed, you can send out more review copies. But instead of bound galleys, you'll send the finished product, along with a tidy review package (which we'll discuss in the next section). Send your finished book to:

- All the sources to whom you previously sent bound galleys (Often, the receipt of the actual book will prompt a review.)
- Magazines, journals, and other publications in your niche market
- Any opinion makers you didn't catch the first time around, or whom you would like to thank or woo with the finished product
- Local media, including newspapers, regional magazines, TV, and radio
- National media (Your chances for success here are far slimmer than with local media, but if you follow up—over and over again—you can get noticed.)
- The major wholesalers: Baker & Taylor and Ingram
- Book review magazines

Reviewing the Package

When you send review copies of your finished book, you'll put together an entire package full of goodies that reviewers, editors, TV and radio producers, and other media types can use to fill in their own blank spaces and promote your book at the same time.

Here are the elements you'll want to include in your review package:

- *Cover letter.* This can be basically the same letter as the one that accompanied

> **Bright Idea**
> The best way to get testimonials and endorsements is to ask. It's a two-way street. Opinion makers are helping you, but in return you're giving them an absolutely free opportunity to get their names in the press before their market niche and yours.

your bound galleys. Update it to reflect your finished book and any newsworthy hooks you can devise.

- *Sample review.* Write up your own review of your book—it's not tacky; it's smart. Editors often don't have the time or the person-power to read and review your book, but they'd like to include it in their pages. If you write a review for them, they can use it as is, use snippets with their own comments as a frame, or paraphrase it. And if you have written the review, you know it will be favorable. Read reviews of other books similar to yours to get ideas of how to write your review.

- *News release.* This is your review written like a news story. Make it as topical and newsworthy as possible. Publications that don't use reviews will use a news release—it helps them fill space on a page or on the air. As with your sample review, they do not have to write it up unless they choose to because you've done it for them.

- *Copies of other reviews.* Add good-quality copies of other reviews of your book. Remember that the purpose here is to blow your horn, and the more A-plus publicity the better.

- *Testimonials and endorsements.* Print up a page of testimonials and endorsements, and add it to your package. Word-of-mouth—even on a printed page—sells.

- *Interview questions.* Make up a list of ten questions for interviewers to ask you. Radio and TV interviewers especially like this feature, but print media writers also find it a plus. They don't have to take the time to read your book to ask you intelligent questions about it. Design your questions to highlight the important points of your book and to divulge a few tips. Once you whet people's appetites for what they will get if they buy the book, they'll be eager to do so.

- *Demo tape announcement.* If you've allowed for a demo interview videotape in your budget, add a sheet to the packages you send to national TV shows, letting them know that you have a demo available for review. Producers like demos so they can see for themselves that you're personable, presentable, and interesting.

- *Photo.* Add a professional-quality, black-and-white photo of your book or of yourself. Most of the time this won't be used, but it doesn't hurt either.

- *Your shiny new book.* Don't send a copy that has been damaged in transit or

> **Tip...**
>
> **Smart Tip**
>
> Some budget-conscious publishers send a press release instead of a cover letter to all but the most important and most likely reviewers. This way, they can ask that the recipient request a book only if interested.

splashed with coffee while gracing your coffee table. This is your calling card, so it must look sharp. Order a rubber stamp that says "Review Copy" and stamp the surface formed by the outside edges of the pages when the book is closed. This way nobody can return your review copy to the bookstore—which could result in having it sent back to you for credit.

Traveling Man

You'll want to take into account some sort of dollar figure for promotional travel. How much depends on how you plan to promote your book and how much you can afford to spend. Promotion is one of the very most important aspects of self-publishing. If you don't get the word out, you don't sell books.

Are you thinking all-out media blitz, flying out to guest on as many TV stations around the country as will have you? Or will you stay more focused on your local market, with a plan to drive to every niche market event (like games, meets, conventions, or shows) within a 400-mile radius? Or do you plan to do the majority of your promotions through the internet and through radio interviews that you can conduct from your home phone? In this case you will not need much of a travel allowance at all.

Sending yourself on an author tour where you stay at the Ritz and get around by limousine is not a must. It's perfectly acceptable to go the Motel 6-and-minivan route. Perhaps you won't even need to budget money for lodging. Do you have friends and relatives with whom you can stay, or an RV to use as a temporary base? If you have a limited budget, there are many ways to keep your travel expenses reasonable.

Guest Spot

Once you've sent out all those review copies, you may start getting requests from the media. There's nothing quite like the thrill of that first phone call from a producer asking if you'd care to guest on a radio or TV show. Of course, you'll say, "Yes!"

But after the initial glow of accomplishment wears off—and as airtime nears—you may

Bright Idea
Always follow up an interview with thank-you notes to the show's host and producer. This is a nice personal touch that shows your appreciation and leaves the door open for further interviews down the line. Be sure to enclose your business card!

find yourself starting to get nervous. What will you wear? What will you say? How will you say it? And what if—the ultimate horror—you absolutely freeze up?

To perform well in the media arena, it's essential that you do your homework and prepare for the task. Here's how:

- *Realize that everybody gets butterflies.* OK, maybe not Jim Carrey, but every other star of stage and screen. This is healthy. It keeps you sharp. And once you get past the first couple of interviews, you'll learn to relax and have fun while you're at it.
- *Realize that you're the expert here.* You have written an entire book about your subject. By this time, you know your material inside and out. You have also

---

Good Morning World

It's fairly easy to get an interview on local radio and TV—depending, of course, on where you live. The producers of *Good Morning Apalachicola* are hungry for stories and will be delighted to have you on. But the producers of *Good Morning Manhattan* may have more than they can handle already. And national shows—the ones that give you the greatest exposure and the greatest endorsements—are extremely difficult to get on.

But this doesn't mean you should give up. It can be done. Be persistent. Send publicity material every month or so and be creative. Producers of these shows are flooded with mail, faxes, and phone calls from interview hopefuls on a daily basis. They can't and won't follow up on anything that doesn't reach out and grab their attention. Think about how you can tie into another media or news event, or how you can hook them with a clever ploy that will make your package stand out from the crowd. If your book is about travel, for instance, you could send your PR kit wrapped up in a road map, tucked into an oversized "passport," or stashed in a cardboard "suitcase."

Although most self-publishers go it alone, hiring a publicist is an option here. It can be an expensive one. The advantage is that the publicist may know more than you do about PR and have more contacts. The disadvantage, aside from the costs, is that you may very well know your market better than anyone else. If you choose to explore this avenue, start by checking in with self-publishing organizations like IBPA (Independent Book Publishers Association).

▲

written up all sorts of publicity materials from your sample review to your galley cover letter to your news release. You have already got down on paper just about everything any interviewer is likely to ask. You know your stuff.

- *Ask the producer if she'd like to send you a list of ten interview questions before the airdate.* She will probably accept in a second. And by doing this, you appear professional, make her job easier, and give yourself a heads-up on what the questions will be. You also will not have to worry about being hit with something for which you haven't thought out an answer.

- *For radio interviews, keep your phone line free.* You do not want that distracting call-waiting beep in the background with your mom calling from Nebraska to ask what the garage man meant when he said her distributor cap is clogged, or your daughter phoning from the mall to ask if she can get her navel pierced. Tell friends and family who are likely to drop by that you'll be unavailable during airtime. If possible, have the phone company temporarily disable your call waiting, give the radio station a number that doesn't have call waiting (like your fax or internet line), or tell everyone you know not to call at airtime.

- *For TV interviews, dress like you would for a business meeting—professional but not formal.* You want to look polished but not stuffy. Of course, you should dress to match the show's ambiance and your own subject matter. If your book is for golfers and you're being interviewed on the links, you'll look pretty silly standing around in a business suit. In this case, you'd wear your golf duds. If you'll be demonstrating painting techniques from your crafts book, wear something that looks artistic but workable.

- *Practice—but not too much.* Have a friend or family member "interview" you so you can practice what to say and how to say it. But don't overdo it. If you memorize your lines, you will end up sounding wooden during the actual interview. And if the interviewer asks a question that's not on your list, she may throw you for a loop. It's best to feel comfortable with your material but stay loose. It's OK to improvise a little.

- *If your budget allows, hire a professional videographer to make a demo disc.* This serves two purposes: It allows you to "practice" with the real thing—a live interview—and get all those first-time

Bright Idea

You may want to spring for a demo disc—a "pretend" videorecorded interview about ten minutes in length, which national-caliber TV shows like to see before asking you on as a guest. If you decide to go this route, hire a professional videographer. Expect to pay $200 to $400, depending on prices in your area.

nerves out of the way in a situation where they can be edited out. It also gives you a professional edge with producers.

- *Most producers will give you an idea of how long the interview will be.* For radio, an interview is usually about ten minutes—unless you're the only guest on an hour-long phone-in show. But some media interviews—especially for TV—are astonishingly short. You've barely been introduced, and it's over. If you know the interview will be brief, state your most important points first so you get them out there before you're gone.
- *Don't be shy.* For TV interviews, look at the camera—which is the viewing audience—as well as at your host.

Adventures in Autographing

One of the most terrifying things in the author's world is the book signing. Unlike interviews, where you have a mission—to answer questions asked by an experienced host—the book signing sets you out on the floor of the bookstore with nothing to do but sit there and try to look interesting.

It's only in the movies, or when you reach Stephen King caliber, that you'll find a line of book buyers snaking across the room to have their copy autographed. The truth is that very few people show up for book signings. If you sell a half dozen volumes in an afternoon, you can consider that you did exceptionally well.

So why bother? Because of the accompanying publicity. Even if few people show up at the bookstore for an autograph, you can use a signing event to garner a write-up in the local newspaper, get a mention on local TV and radio, and convince bookstore management to prominently display your title (at least temporarily).

Since you will need do these autograph sessions, try these tips for book signing success:

- *Make sure you've got all your publicity lined up in a timely fashion.* Supply the bookstore or specialty retailer with a poster and fliers about two weeks before the event. Have local media get the word out no more than a week ahead of time (although earlier is fine if they'll repeat the news within a few days of the event).
- *Set your signing for a time and day when the store will be busy, say on a Saturday afternoon.* One ideal date—especially if your book would make a nice gift—is Black Friday, which is what retailers call the Friday after Thanksgiving, the kick-off of the holiday shopping season.

- *Try tying into the store's own events.* Some bookstores, for instance, host a weekly kids' story hour. Offer to read your tale aloud and then have your book signing directly afterward.

- *Make an effort to greet shoppers, who are often as shy in this setting as you may be.* Smile and say hello as they pass by. Offer a few words of chat about your book if they slow down to look. Be friendly and accessible.

Bright Idea

More fun with desktop publishing: Make up bookmarks featuring your title and a quote or a few tips from your pages, and hand them out at signings. Give a large supply to booksellers to display and hand out at their checkout counters.

Advertising and Marketing

You may have wondered why we have not talked about advertising yet. The reason is that it doesn't really work for books. As a new publisher with a limited budget, you can spend your money in far more effective ways by concentrating on publicity and promotions rather than by running ads in magazines, newspapers, or other media.

We covered how to publicize your new book in Chapter 9. In this chapter, we'll discuss some additional avenues for promoting and marketing your book, including word-of-mouth, book fairs, direct mail, and seminars. Developing your own website is discussed in the next chapter.

The Golden Word

Even though books are a print medium, you can still sell more through word of mouth than just about any other source. Its power is astonishing. One of these terrifically effective techniques is writing articles for magazines, journals, and newspapers—which works much better than any advertising possibly could. People glaze over when it comes to ads, but they do read articles, and not only read but heed. Your credibility as an expert soars if you're in a magazine. People reason that you must be a pro, and as your credibility takes wing, so will your book's desirability. And the benefits don't stop with the reader. People won't tear out an ad, but they'll tear out an article and pass it along to friends and relatives, so you get the word-of-mouth effect even in print.

"Word of mouth is a powerful thing," agrees June H., the horror maven in Rochester Hills, Michigan. "Donate a copy of your book to the local library. Get in touch with the chamber of commerce and get some leads on speaking engagements for writers' groups and anyone else who needs a speaker. One can sell an ample amount of books at these events.

"And do not forget the book trade shows—my personal favorite is the Horror Writers Association, which I attend each year and set up a table to house my books for sale. Volunteer for panels at the events and bring along more books to sell."

"Talk to anyone and everyone who will listen," advises June. "Call your local radio and TV stations, and request an interview. Call bookstores and ask for the event coordinator and set up an autographing—that's one good way to get stores to stock your books. Send a copy to Amazon.com and Barnes & Noble online, and ask your friends to write blurbs about how they enjoyed—or didn't enjoy [in the case of a horror title]—the book."

Gary S., the military memoirs publisher, agrees. "We are in the startup phase of our

Bright Idea

If you think the topic of your book lends itself to some limited advertising, barter an article or two, or a monthly column, in exchange for a quarter-page or larger ad. This method can work wonders with smaller publications, if they target a specific market suited to your book.

company, so we haven't done much advertising," says the resident of Panama City Beach, Florida. "We attend veterans' functions. This is how we make our contacts and sell our books—largely personal contact and word of mouth. Also, my company has appeared on the web page directory of the Association of Personal Historians [www.personalhistorians.org], and our books are prominently displayed on local booksellers' racks."

Headline Fever

What publications should you submit to? Take a look at your niche market, then go for the trade or professional journals they read, whether it's *Dog World* or *Direct Marketing*. If you're going for a general audience, you can also target general interest publications—the ones you find in the supermarket checkout lines (not tabloids like *The National Enquirer*, but titles like *Woman's Day* or *Self*.) General interest magazines are much more difficult to get into than trade and professional publications, but if your topic and your writing skills are terrific—and if the editor is in the right frame of mind—you can do it.

The best way to approach the issue is to head down to your local public library and sit down with the latest copy of *Writer's Market* (Writer's Digest Books), which is also available online if that is the format you prefer. Thumb through this hefty volume—you'll be amazed at the number of publications in every imaginable specialty. Pick out the ones that might be good targets for your articles.

Back at home, call the magazine or journal to find out which editor to send your piece to. Then send a one-page query letter describing the article and asking the editor to contact you if he's interested.

The most important thing about writing articles, of course, is that you tie them into your book. You want people to recognize not only you as an expert but also your book as an expert source. Try these tips for getting the most from print exposure:

- *Your article does not have to be long*. Magazines usually have plenty of material for their main copy but are always hurting for those fillers—the one-page to one-sidebar length piece to fill in the gaps. Make your story in the form of "Ten Tips for Cooking Lean" or "Ten Ways to Help Your Child Excel," etc. These are the perfect length and are also great for people to snip out and mail to a friend or stick on the fridge.

- *Mention your book in the text so readers understand where to turn for more information*. Have the publication add an endnote that says something like: For more information or for a free tip sheet, call or write to Glowworm Press at Box 17, Luminescent, FL 10000, (850) 555-0000, www.glowwormpress.com.

- *Expand your horizons.* Tweak your material so that it fits the subject matter of as many magazines or journals as you can match. If your book is about gardening, for instance, you could devise articles like these:

  - For culinary magazines—"Cooking with Your Garden's Bounty"
  - For parenting magazines—"Helping Children Learn Science in a Garden"
  - For ecology journals—"Gardens as Environmental Lifesavers"
  - For business magazines—"Using Gardening to Combat Office Stress"
  - For regional magazines—"Gardening in the Wine Country"

> ## Smart Tip
> Despite *The New York Times* and other bestseller lists, a bestseller is just a name. If your book on raising radishes sells better than any radish-raising tome on the market, or better than any of the other titles your company publishes, you can honestly call it a bestseller.

My Fair Book Fair

As June H. says, book trade shows (commonly called book fairs) are events not to be missed. The major-league highlights of the season are the annual BEA, or Book Expo America, which is held each spring in a metropolis like New York or Chicago, and the Frankfurt Book Fair, held each October in Frankfurt, Germany, and conveniently timed to coincide (more or less) with Oktoberfest. There are also dozens of smaller, regional book fairs held all over this country each year. See the Appendix for a listing of contact information for several prominent book fairs.

These events are terrific places to see and be seen. You can schmooze with other independent publishers, pick up tips and industry gossip, look over the competition, make friends and contacts—and also make sales. A major book fair is the place to sell your title to a big publisher and land that legendary five-figure contract, to sell the foreign rights for another hefty sum (more on this in Chapter 13), or to catch the eye of a distributor. The smaller fair is a terrific place to meet your readers and local booksellers, and sell directly to them.

Exhibit space at smaller book fairs will cost you in the range of $200 to $2,000. Booth space at the big fairs can go for thousands of dollars a pop, but you can often band together with other small presses and share a booth. Independent Book Publishers Association and other independent publisher organizations often sponsor booth spaces. Even BEA usually has a small press section with lower-priced booths. These booths often have lesser visibility as well, but for those attendees who know how to work the show and find things that others are overlooking, these small press booths can offer some great finds.

Take-Along Kit

Book fair organizers will provide you with a cloth-draped table for exhibiting your wares. You'll want to bring:

- *A box of your books* (enough to display and sell—but check with the event to be sure you can sell books on the floor). Don't overpack but don't run short, either. Even regional events can attract as many as 18,000 patrons.
- *Brochures.* Make up a brochure that encapsulates your review package. Start with a thumbnail photo of your book cover; then add an enticing overview of your books, some stellar testimonials or endorsements, snippets of outstanding reviews, and whatever else you think will sell your title. As with your other materials, observe good design sense. Don't clutter your brochure with so much information that it turns readers off.
- *Bookmarks or other give-away goodies.* The book fair is a great place to hand out bookmarks, tip sheets from your text, or other sales freebies that will make readers remember your book and decide to buy it.

Mail Order Magic

Mail order, or direct mail, can be magic in terms of sales for the self-publisher. In fact, some self-publishers sell almost exclusively by mail order without worrying their heads with the book trade. Mail order is an art in and of itself and can be very expensive. If you plan to take it on in a big way, read everything you can about it before you take the plunge. You'll find a list of sources in the Appendix at the back of this book.

Winged Success

Direct mail can take the form of sales letters, fliers, brochures, postcards, or any other printed material you send winging into the mailboxes of potential readers. You can use any direct-mail format that works for you, from a letter describing your book to a one-page flier or multipage brochure.

▲

The Participation Effect

One of the quirky things about direct mail (and human nature) is that people are far more likely to respond to an offer they have to actively do something for than one they do nothing for. In other words, people like direct-mail offers in which they're asked, for example, to paste a "yes" or "no" sticker on the reply card. That's why all those Publishers Clearing House packets are full of stickers, reply cards, and tear-offs. They work. Call it the participation effect.

Of course, these gimmicks cost money, but if you can afford them and they fit your style, by all means use them. If not, think how else you might incorporate the same idea into your order form. If you're offering a discount for early ordering, for instance, you might let your customer "flag" the discount by checking a box on your form. Make sure your form is clear, easy to understand, and easy to fill out. See page 171 for a sample.

Experimentation, testing, and—always, always—market research will give you the best idea of which format is the best for your company. We're going to talk here about sales letters, but you can and should apply these same success secrets and tips to any other direct-mail pieces you design.

Since most people today are flooded with direct-mail pieces, yours needs to leap off the desk or table and instantly capture your potential client's attention so that she'll pick it up instead of tossing it aside. Then, when she does pick it up, it must keep her attention so she'll read it through. Besides interest and attention, the main thing to aim for in your letter is the sense that you're writing to her personally with the answer to her gardening or personal finance dreams or problems, for example.

The Hook

If this sounds daunting, try reading all those direct-mail pieces that come to your mailbox. The best ones to study are those that pitch books, but carefully examine all of them, even those selling winter underwear or summer flea sprays.

What do they have in common? For one thing, they start off with something that immediately hooks your attention. Maybe it's a description of the book, enticing you to read on with tidbits of the information you'll harness when you buy the book. Maybe it's a description of the benefits of having read the book, like a healthier financial picture, a healthier mind and body, or a garden that's the showplace of the neighborhood. Try the same approaches with your sales letter. Experiment until you hit on something that sounds good to you and matches your particular niche.

Then go to work on the body of the letter. Again, analyze the ones you've received. What makes them work? Notice that they spend a lot of time describing the benefits of the book. You'll want to do the same thing. Emphasize the benefits of your book throughout your body copy, repeating them as often as you can, using different descriptions so they stick in your customer's mind. If you've got testimonials, use them too. They lend credibility to your book and your company, and they add another dimension to your copy by showing that it's not just you who thinks your products are great—it's real people just like your prospect.

> **Bright Idea**
>
> Join any organizations that match your target market. Volunteer for things that will get your book and your publishing company recognized and thought well of. Most people respect volunteers within an organization and consider them experts in the organization's area of interest.

After the main body of your letter, tell your customer what she needs to do to buy your book. Put in a convenient order form that she can send back, or make your phone number easy to spot so she can call and order if she'd prefer. If you've designed a discount with a time element or a freebie, this is the place to mention it.

Prospecting for Attention

Be sure to check out the sample sales letter we have provided on page 167 and look over the following sales tips:

- *Grab that reader's attention.* Remember to relate it directly to your book and how it will benefit your customer.

- *Use time-proven winning words like "secret" and "free."* Everybody wants to know a secret, and everybody wants something for free! Like what? How about something like: "Learn the secrets of financial security for life!" Or you might say: "Receive a free gardening calendar when you buy The Night Garden!"

- *Where you have space, try for headlines of ten or more words.* Generally speaking, longer sells better than shorter when it comes to headlines.

- *Don't write for thousands of prospective readers.* Write to just one reader, as though you're speaking to him or her personally.

- *Save the flowery prose for a poetry contest.* Instead, use everyday language that the average person can relate to.

- *Don't focus only on the features of your books.* Spend time highlighting the benefits, too.

- *Try indented paragraphs, underlined words, and two colors.* These pack more of a punch and out-pull plain text. But use elements like boldface type, underlining, and italics sparingly. If you use them for no particular reason, or too often, they become annoying instead of intriguing.

- *Keep your materials clean and free of grammar and style errors.* Have someone you trust as a spelling, punctuation, and grammar star check your work before you commit to a print run.

- *Relax and enjoy yourself.* Have fun! It will come across in the marketing materials you produce.

Winning Ways

OK, we've seen what direct mail looks like and how to design your own for optimum effect. Now let's review some sure-fire techniques for winning customers:

- *Give away freebies with prompt purchase.* Remember that everybody likes to have something for free. Everybody likes a gift. Depending on your style, budget, and target market, you can give away something substantial (but still relatively inexpensive) or a mere trinket. If your books focus on home décor, for instance, you could include a color chart, a measuring guide, or designer's notebook.

- *Time-date your offer.* Say something like: "If you respond within the next 30 days, you'll receive a free _____." You might also try: "This offer is good only through _____." This encourages readers to buy now instead of at some nebulous time in the future.

- *Write a riveting headline.* Your letter must compete with scads of others crammed in your customers' mailboxes. Penning your headline before your copy will help you focus on the basic need or desire your product satisfies and the appeal your copy should make.

- *Offer testimonials from satisfied customers.* Use real first and last names, and real hometowns. Remember that you must notify testimonial-givers that their names and hometowns will be used and get their permission.

- *Remember the participation effect.* Give your customers plenty to look at, lots to read, and, if possible, something to stick, paste, or tear off.

> **Tip...**
>
> **Smart Tip**
> Accept credit cards and toll-free calls. It's much easier for your customer to fill in a credit card number on a form, or call and give it to you over the phone, than to sit down and write out a check.

Glowworm Press

Hello Charlie Gardener!

I'd like to offer you a very special invitation—*and a free gift.*

I've chosen you to receive this offer because I know you love gardening, just as I do. You treasure the fragrance of roses after a rain and the fresh scent of moist, rich earth under your fingers. Now you can enjoy a brand-new book just for gardeners. **The Night Garden** is the only book you'll find that reveals the secrets of tending to your garden after dark. You'll learn:

- *How to plant and grow organic vegetables after dark. Even if you work all day, you can have a bounty of fresh vegetables on the table for supper.*
- *How to grow night-blooming flowers that fill your home and garden with thera-peutic scent. You'll sleep better than you have in years.*
- *How you and your family can use your garden as a source of rejuvenation and renewal. Instead of watching TV on warm summer evenings, you'll be out enjoy-ing your own private sanctuary.*
- *How to attract nocturnal wildlife into your garden, while you and your family gaze on in wonder.*

The Night Garden is the perfect book to read alone or to share with family and friends. With all the tips and tricks you'll learn, you'll find yourself referring to it again and again. I'm so sure you'll be delighted with **The Night Garden** that I'm offering you a special publisher's edition printed on luxurious cream stock, with illustrations by noted garden artist Lel Lorin, for only $14.95—that's 10 percent off the retail price!

Free Gift!

As an added bonus, I'm also offering you a free gift: a special gardener's calendar that helps you plan your hours in your private backyard getaway. Packed with full-color photos and handy gardening tips, you'll treasure the garden calendar almost as much as **The Night Garden.**

I hope you'll take advantage of this offer. *I can't offer it for long.* Just fill out the enclosed reply form and pop it in the mail to me. If you're not pleased for any reason, just send it back in its original condition, and I'll cheerfully refund your money. Don't take too long! Because of demand, my offer must end June 1st.

Best regards,

Peter Moss

Author and Independent Publisher

P.S. I'm so positive you and your family will love **The Night Garden** that I'm also going to send you a hand-crafted cricket house for your own garden! It's absolutely free, along with the garden calendar. All you have to do is circle the cricket on the reply form when you send it back.

1 Firefly Lane • Luminescent, Florida 10000 • (850) 555-0000 • www.glowwormpress.com

The List

A mailing list can make or break a direct-mail campaign, and a good list can be worth more than double your ad budget. You can target your audience more effectively with a mailing list than with any other medium.

Say you decide to go with an alternative and advertise on TV. We don't recommend it, but for the sake of making a point, let's look at the following example. You might choose *I Love Lucy* reruns or *The X-Files* or the *Tonight Show*. Although each will have its demographic profile, you'll get a fairly indiscriminate selection of viewers. You have no way of knowing if they're junior teens whose main reading passion is *Goosebumps* (Scholastic Inc.), homemakers who like to do arts and crafts, sailing enthusiasts, or maximum security prison inmates whose mail is carefully monitored.

When you rent a mailing list, however, you can target your audience to a tee. For a health and fitness book, you can choose Midwestern women who have bought health and fitness magazines; or you might target Northeastern men who buy marine equipment and earn more than $50,000 per year for your book on sailing adventures in Maine.

The Response, Please

In the mailing list world, there are two types of lists: the compiled list and the buyer or response list. A compiled list is made up of people with the common thread of a group or organization—for example, members of alumnae organizations or car clubs; members of professional organizations from doctors to contractors; or even people who have attended different types of vacations, tours, seminars, or workshops. A compiled list can also be made up of people with certain demographic characteristics in common such as: people who live in Manhattan and make more than $30,000 a year, and who are between 45 and 70 years old.

The main point to remember with compiled lists is that unless you rent a list comprised of people who have previously bought books similar to yours, you can't know that those doctors or contractors or car aficionados have ever bought a book by mail in their lives.

Now, the other type of list—the buyer list—is the one you want to shoot for. Why? The people on it are already known to order books through the mail. They might be buyers of gourmet cookbooks, or books on vegetable gardening, or Disney collectibles editions, but the main idea here is that since they've already bought books similar to yours, they're likely to buy yours as well. This may not be the case with people on compiled lists. This doesn't mean you should never use compiled lists. It does mean, though, that you should use them carefully. List brokers are experienced at this sort of thing, so let them advise you on what's best for your particular situation.

Going for Broke

Where exactly do you get mailing lists?

- Rent them from any number of list brokers, which you'll find in your local Yellow Pages under "Advertising—Direct Mail," or within the pages of direct-marketing magazines like *Catalog Age* and *Target Marketing*. We've provided the names of a few list brokers in the Appendix to get you started.

- Rent or swap lists directly from your competition—other publishers engaged in selling books to similar target markets. Yes, they'll often share!

- Rent directly from associations whose members fit your target market.

- Buy lists from a competitor who has gone out of business. This doesn't happen too often but is worth keeping an eye out for.

- Build up your own list and use it often.

The Rules

As a direct-mail merchandiser, you must follow the rules—specifically, the Federal Trade Commission's Mail or Telephone Order Rule, which regulates direct-marketing businesses (and that includes you). These rules also apply to orders placed via fax, email, and the internet. You can find yourself flailing in rough seas if you ignore the guidelines set forth in the Mail or Telephone Order Rule, so we have laid them out for you below. Unlike a lot of government legalese, the guidelines actually make sense and are easy to follow:

- You must send ordered merchandise within the time period specified in your ad or, if you don't specify a shipping time, within 30 days. The clock starts ticking on this time requirement when you receive the completed order. An order is complete when you have a) received your customer's cash, check, or money order, or b) charged the person's credit card account, and c) have all the information you need to process and ship the order. If the customer doesn't specify essential information, such as quantity or shipping preferences, the order is considered incomplete.

- If you do not specify a shipping time and your customer is applying for credit to pay for the purchase, you have 50 days to ship after receiving the order. This is the one exception to the 30-day shipping rule.

- If you can't meet the shipping deadline, you must notify your customer and offer an alternative option. The customer can either receive a prompt refund or agree to a delay. Your notice must include a new shipping date, instructions on how to cancel the order, and a postage-paid way to reply.

- If your customer agrees to a new shipping date and you can't meet it again, you must send a second notice as soon as possible. Unless the customer signs and returns this second postage-paid notice, you must automatically cancel the order and refund the person's money.

> **Smart Tip**
>
> Get your own complete copy of the Mail or Telephone Order Rule from the Federal Trade Commission at www.ftc.gov. The complete text is available online and can be downloaded as a PDF.

- What happens if you don't ship the merchandise on time and don't notify your customer as required by law? You must count the order as canceled and send a refund.

- If your customer cancels an order, you must refund his or her money. If the customer paid for the order by cash, check, or money order, you must return the money within seven business days. If the order was paid for by credit card, you must credit the customer's credit card account within one billing cycle.

The Mail or Telephone Order Rule applies to almost everything ordered through direct-marketing sources. The exceptions are photofinishing services, magazine subscriptions (after the first issue), COD orders, seeds, and plants.

Seminar Time

As we explained at the beginning of this book, self-publishing and seminars go hand in hand. Many, many self-published authors use their books as a springboard for paid seminar success. This can be a lucrative enterprise that can tidily augment your book's income. It can also be extremely helpful in spreading the word about your subject matter. If you're a crusader for saving the planet or teaching kids self-esteem, for example, your books and your seminars can be the best platform for your work.

Like the world of mail order and the world of self-publishing, however, there's much to learn about seminar production. Before you dive into this arm of your career, read everything you can on the subject. You'll find a few useful books listed in the Appendix to get you started.

Order Form/Reply Card

Yes! Send my copy of *The Night Garden* today!

Just fill in the following information to send your copy winging its way to you:

Quantity	Item	Cost
_____	*The Night Garden* ($14.95 per book)	$
_____	Garden calendar ($10.00 value, free with this offer)	FREE
	Cricket house ($20.00 value, free if you circle the cricket on this card)	FREE
	Florida residents add 6% sales tax	$
	Shipping and handling ($3.95 per book/gift set)	$
	Total Cost	$

Name _____

Address _____

City _____ State _____ Zip _____

Phone _____

☐ Check   ☐ Visa   ☐ MasterCard

Card number _____ Expiration _____ / ____

Signature _____

Glowworm Press • 1 Firefly Lane • Luminescent, Florida 10000
(850) 555-0000 • www.glowwormpress.com

Selling in Cyberspace

Having a website is a must for any serious business these days. People from all over the world can see and buy your books at any time, day or night, on your website. It's just part of doing business in the 21st century.

This is even truer for writers. People love to connect with writers. And if you are a self-publishing writer who has an expertise and do speaking engagements, a website can help you in the credibility department.

If you aren't going to be web-based, for which having a website is clearly a must, then here are some things to consider in deciding that a website is important for your business:

- Websites give you the ability to change content quickly and cheaply, making it easy to keep the information you have out there up to date. Printing a brochure does not afford you that ease of change.
- Customers can readily get information, or more information, on your business just by looking at your website.
- The entire world is your market.
- You can track the results of your marketing efforts more easily with website "hits" and questions/orders you get from your site.
- Your business is open 24/7/365.

Setting Up a Website

If you are one of those people who claim to be computer illiterate and are proud of it, get over it now if you are going into business. If you are adept at using a computer and want to design your own website, that's great, especially if it's going to be an information-only site. But be sure it is professional looking. Just like a physical retail shop, you need your website to express the kind of businessperson you are. Look at the differences in any retail world. When a potential buyer walks into a Cadillac showroom, they expect to have a high-quality experience compared to what they would encounter if they were to be shopping at their everyday Ford dealership. Harley Davidson motorcycle dealerships are spotless works of art; they know that their middle-aged customer base is almost completely different from, say, the young dirt bike buyer. Check out all the websites of different products you are familiar with and get a sense of how their site caters to their buyer base.

If you don't feel like you can create the right website, consider hiring a professional web design company. The cost is typically not out of reach; you can expect to spend around $1,000 for a well-designed site. You will also incur monthly charges to have it "hosted"—someone with a large server that keeps everything coming and going. Hosting fees (from as little as $30 a month to several hundred, depending on the complexity of your web business) usually include a certain amount of monthly changes.

Before you hire a designer, look at lots of other websites and make sure you can give the designer ideas on what you like and don't like in the websites you see.

Find web designers by searching online or noticing who designed the sites you like. The designer doesn't have to be local to design your site—everything can be done, well, online!

You can also buy "template" web designs—you fill the details into a basic design. There are many template companies to choose from, such as www.baskweb.com, www.dreamtemplate.com, www.weebly.com, and www.web.com. You don't have to be a computer programming wiz to use them; they are designed to be put together by anyone with basic computer skills.

Website Design

The design of your site should be simple yet comprehensive. By the time your customers have spent a few minutes on your website, they should have a pretty good sense of your business—not just what you sell but that you care about quality and customer service.

Your Homepage

Your customer will first come to your "homepage" where you will introduce them to your business and tempt them to spend some time on your site browsing other pages—and ultimately be enticed enough to order something.

Your homepage should introduce your business—go ahead and give a little history about how you got started but don't tell every detail about every thought you've ever had about the business. This is a chance for customers to feel like they know you, but don't lose them right at the homepage!

Include a photo of your book and a photo of you on the homepage—the web customer should open to your site and know they got the site they are looking for. Go ahead and include a shot of you and your dog—readers like to know authors!

Smart Tip

Publishers Weekly once a quarter does something called "PW Select," a listing of books that have been self-published. They then review about 25 to 40 a quarter. There are too many to review all self-published books. Read the full interview with PW co-editor Jim Milliott in Chapter 14.

Beware!

You can consider linking to the web pages of other companies for whatever reason—maybe you wrote a book on pizzas and want to encourage people to consider making pizzas who will therefore want your book, by linking to companies that sell pizza-related baking products. But beware of leading customers away from your site—they may not come back!

Keep the homepage simple but informative.

By all means, do some advertising on this page. If you do speaking engagements, you don't have to clutter the page with every date of every seminar you have scheduled. But have an "upcoming" box that tells the next one, or a box that encourages viewers to jump to the page about your schedule of talks. How often you can change this page depends on what setup you have with your website provider.

Include a menu of items along one edge of your homepage with headings that the customer can click on to get to that section of your online store. Think of it like the signs you see overhead in the grocery store or the pharmacy—direct customers to the sections they are interested in.

Drilling Down

Each time the viewer clicks on a button on your website, they get further into your site. This can be accomplished in two ways—one is with a "pop-up window" where, when they click on a category, the new section pops up over the main page, and when they are done browsing that page and close it out, they get brought back to the page they started from. The other "drills" them further and further into your site. Drilling down like this is the most common way websites are set up, but it can get frustrating to your customer if they can't easily get back to a point where they saw something they wanted to look at further. One way to help this is to always have a "home" button on every page—all they have to do is click "home" to get them back to the beginning and find their way forward again from there. It's like having Dorothy's ruby red slippers on your site at all times—only unlike Dorothy, make sure readers know how easy it is to get back home.

The Rest of the Site

Your homepage is one of the most important parts of your website. You may

Bright Idea

Always include your business's name, address, and phone number on every page of your website. Once customers have drilled a few pages down into your site, they don't want to have to backtrack all the way to your homepage just to get your contact information.

want a separate page for each title you have self-published. You need a page for ordering, of course, which is covered in more detail below.

Selling from a Website

There was a time when small businesses used websites mainly as marketing pieces—people came to the site to view your products, then either called an order in or printed out an order form from the site and faxed their order to you. Those days are almost gone. Again, customers expect to be able to sit at their computer and not only see what you have to offer but be able to order it right then and there. While it may be OK that they click over to a site like Amazon and order your book, ideally, once you have them at your site, they might as well order the book there where you get all the profits. The two key things that your site will need—and that your designer will set you up with—is a shopping cart for customers to collect their items in and a secure way to pay for them.

Shopping Cart

If you have just one book, a shopping cart setup can be quite simple. The shopping cart is a simple function that your web designer will build into your site if you say you want it (which you do). If you offer several books, or paraphernalia associated with your book's topic, as your online customers shop, they can click the little button that says "add this item to my shopping cart" and it will join the list of any other items they have already put in the cart. Some carts accumulate items that stay there even after the customer left the site. This feature can translate into more sales—if a customer gets interrupted before completing the transaction, they don't have to go through the entire shopping process when they return to your site. "Abandoned" shopping carts is a big issue with online shopping—customers leave before the sale is done—and this feature can retrieve some of those abandoned carts.

The shopping cart page is where the customer can make changes. Here they can change the quantity of each item (sometimes bad for you, when they decide to change it to 0, other times good when they decide not only will they order a copy of your book for their sister, but make it three, to send one to Mom and Aunt Jean as well).

Also on the shopping cart page will be where they decide what kind of shipping they want. Always offer inexpensive shipping options along with overnight options—shipping charges is one of those things that still bogs down catalog and online sales, so give customers the option of making it very cheap. But you also want them to feel like they can shop online last minute as well, so the ability to have something shipped overnight is a must.

▲

Payment Options

Most anyone reading this has shopped online and knows that credit cards are always an option for paying for your cyberpurchase. While using credit cards online has become very secure, there are still people who have no interest in giving out their credit card number over the internet. Some companies still give those people the option of faxing in their order, and there is always the option of calling—both good reasons to make sure your contact information is available on all web pages.

PayPal is another option for paying online. People with a PayPal account load it up with funds or attach their PayPal account to a credit card, and then funds are withdrawn when you use it to pay for a purchase online. PayPal allows you to send money to anyone with an email address. PayPal became the payment method of choice for eBay traders, so much so that in 2002 eBay bought PayPal. If you allow PayPal for purchase, your site needs to include a PayPal button.

Other Ways to Sell Online

There are other ways to sell online besides having your own website. You can try these in conjunction with your own site or before you get your site up and running.

eBay

The popular auction site, eBay, offers a couple ways to sell your books online. You can list your book in a "fixed price" listing where there is no actual bidding. Or you can sell it with "reserved pricing" where the item does not sell if it doesn't meet a minimum bid. Reserved pricing probably doesn't make a lot of sense for your book sales.

The other way you can sell on eBay is to open an eBay store. This is basically a personalized selling platform similar to your own website, where eBay customers can come find your products. You must be an eBay seller already (which is a very easy process, with simple registration) and there is a nominal fee for the store. However, your products are potentially in front of the eyes of the millions of visitors to this very successful online selling space.

Amazon

This giant in the online bookselling world is now offering online "storefronts" for a monthly fee. Amazon is constantly changing its offerings and has proven very friendly to self-publishing. Check them out frequently to see what's new and how it might fit into your self-publishing venture.

Other Sites

You might be able to work a deal with a website that sells complementary products that might carry your book. Say your topic is horses. One or more of the thousands of

Get People Clicking

There's no point to having a website if you don't do what you can to get people to click on it. Here are some tips for attracting visitors, and possibly buyers, to your website:

- ○ Simply tell all your friends and family and ask them to tell all their friends and family.

- ○ Do the appropriate search engine registration.

- ○ Make sure every printed and online piece you send to anyone has your website URL listed prominently.

- ○ Suggest visitors bookmark your site.

- ○ Trade web advertising with other websites.

- ○ Create contests with giveaways.

- ○ Change your content/product regularly to keep people coming back to see what's new.

- ○ Join online discussion groups.

- ○ If you do public speaking, always mention your site.

- ○ Provide an "expert" column to newspapers and make sure to mention your website.

These are just a few of a long list of ideas for getting people to come to your website in the first place and keep coming back, and to encourage them to tell everyone they know. Click around to other author websites or in any category that interests you, see what catches your eye, and get other creative ideas to drive people to your site.

equine-related websites will likely be happy to carry your book on their website for a share of the profit.

Trades

If you already have your own website, you can consider finding appropriate sites with whom you can trade ads or products. For instance, "banner ads" (those mini-business-card-size color ads you find around the edges of a website) are often traded among companies whose products and services complement each other. You can put hyperlinks on your website to other companies that you recommend and ask that they put your link on their site.

Marketing Your Website

Once you have created your website, don't keep it a secret! While your website may be in cyberspace, be sure your web address is on every printed piece you create for your business—letterhead, business cards, print advertisements, newsletters, radio

Netiquette

The dramatic increase in the use of email has meant that there is a need to understand good etiquette when it comes to emailing. The last thing you want to do is offend a customer. So follow these guidelines for proper emailing:

○ Never use all uppercase letters; it is considered the equivalent of shouting.

○ Spellcheck your emails. Just because email is quick, it doesn't have to be sloppy.

○ Be enticing but also give an accurate sense of what your email is about in the subject line.

○ Create a signature for your email so that every email you compose automatically includes your business name, address, phone number, and email address so the recipient can quickly see how to contact you.

○ Keep your messages short and to the point.

ads—everything that has to do with your business should announce your web address. Put the address in your answering machine message.

E-Newsletters

Creating a newsletter that is sent via email has become a popular way for businesses to keep in touch with their customers. Solicit e-newsletter subscribers on your own website, and on the websites of others. Sending e-newsletters out unsolicited is considered "spam" and can land you in a bit of hot water. But once you create a useful, readable newsletter that might contain a coupon or special or even a giveaway, people will readily subscribe.

Keep 'Em Interested

Once you get visitors checking out your site, there are some ways to keep them there as long as possible. The longer they are there, the more likely they are to order something.

Be sure they know immediately whose website they have arrived at. Make it easy for them to contact you by having a "contact us" button that makes it simple for them to send you a message.

Keep your website fun and changing. Find ways to engage readers with information from your book, links to news stories related to your book's topic, and miniwebinars in the form of videos.

Then, make it easy for customers to use your website to order and pay. Nothing will make them click the exit button faster than to find it is difficult to spend their money!

Don't Avoid Cyberspace

You can see that it is to your business's advantage to sell online. Most authors are already comfortable with computers and the

Bright Idea

For anyone thinking of self-publishing a book, Stephanie Chandler of Authority Publishing recommends blogging as the very first thing an author should do, even before you write the book. It helps you start building the audience and then becomes the foundation for your social media. See her full interview in Chapter 14.

internet and all the trappings that go with it, so it comes naturally to creatively use this marketing and selling option.

It does seem like a no-brainer to be selling online, but you must be prepared to deal with the additional sales. And although the costs for selling online can be very minor, they are still costs—such as website design and maintenance—that need to be figured into your overall projections and budget.

Social Media

The rise of social media presents a fantastic opportunity for all small-business owners to meet and engage with targeted audiences full of thousands of potential customers. The cost of entry into this marketing channel is often only your time. If done correctly, participating in social media will help your business grow beyond your local area through powerful word-of-mouth campaigns.

To get started, there are a few things you should set up right away: a Facebook page, a Twitter account, and a YouTube channel. These social media accounts will become useful tools for you to interact with your audience.

Here are eight great tips on using social media to your advantage from Jesse McDougall, co-owner of Catalyst Webworks.

1. *Before you start any social media outreach, define your target audiences.* How old are they? Do the people in your audience tend to be more female than male? What groups, organizations, or associations are they likely to join? Think about the kind of people you market to and want to use your business—then hang out with them.

2. *Once your target audiences are defined, locate them online.* Search Facebook, YouTube, Twitter, and MySpace for groups, organizations, channels, or discussions that would contain the people you are looking to meet.

3. *Use social media search and organizational tools to help you find your audiences.* Some sites, like Facebook and YouTube, have great built-in search functions that will help you find your audience. To find your audience on Twitter, try using external sites like Twibes and TwittGroups.com.

4. *Once you've found your audience on these sites, join their groups and lists so that you can follow the ongoing conversation.* Do not jump right in with a sales pitch! Listen, instead. Learn the etiquette and major players. Spend a week or more just following along.

5. *Once you're familiar with the etiquette and people involved, jump into the conversation when and where appropriate.* Do not hide who you are or the company you represent. Become a regular voice in the conversation and offer your friendly expertise to others. Invite people back to your website and social media accounts to see what it is you do and offer.

6. *Once you're a regular voice in the conversation, don't be shy about doing a little promotion.* Contests, giveaways, and raffles can be great tools for audience interaction and promotion of your products. Why not give away a book to someone every month? People will love the chance to play in your contest and will invite friends to join in the fun.

7. *As your audience grows, stay creative.* Invent new ways to engage your audience and encourage them to invite their friends. Continue to avoid hard sales pitches. People do not forward commercials to their friends. They forward value.

8. *Finally, do not try to do everything everywhere.* Sometimes it seems there will soon be as many social media platforms as there are websites. To try to maintain a presence on all of them is unsustainable. Focus on the top two or three that have proven to contain the largest number of people in your target audience.

> **Fun Fact**
>
> Deana Gunn is an engineer and co-author Wona Miniati has a business degree. They started their Trader Joe's-related cookbooks on a whim and now have somewhere around 40,000 Facebook fans, are on Twitter, and blog regularly. And now they do self-publishing full time! See their full interview in Chapter 14.

Remember, social media provides you with the opportunity to meet your audience—not sell to your audience. People do not join these social media network to find marketers. They join and participate for friendly interaction and the value that that interaction adds to their day. Provide that friendly interaction, and you will watch your audience grow.

Controlling Your Finances

Whether you're a chronic number cruncher or one of the finance-phobic, you'll want to give your company periodic financial checkups. You may feel that you have already done all the math stuff several chapters back—which is true. But that was for the purpose of figuring out how much it would cost to get started and whether your book would earn enough potential profit to make it worthwhile. Once your publishing company and your first book(s) are a reality, you'll want to do periodic checks to make sure you're still on the right page. If there's a problem, you'll want to find out before it becomes critical.

In this chapter, we will discuss the monthly operating expenses that you will encounter in running your business, and we'll walk you through determining your projected annual net income. You will also learn about financial statements and tips for being prepared when tax time rolls around.

Operating Expenses

Besides your company setup, book production, and promotion costs, your new company will also have the various and sundry monthly expenses that make up the backbone of every business. We will assume that you'll be homebased when you first start out in this business, so we won't worry about the expenses for office rent, utilities, or employees. As a homebased self-publisher, you will need to consider the following monthly operating expenses:

- Phone
- Postage
- ISP (internet service provider)
- Web hosting (so your website, if you choose to have one, has a server to keep it up and running)
- Electronic card processing
- Stationery and office supplies
- Ongoing legal or accounting services
- Loan repayment
- Promotions/marketing (covered in Chapter 10)

Phone Facts

You will definitely rely on phone service for many aspects of running your business. Start with a base rate of $25 per line per month—one for your business, which is separate from your home phone, and one for your fax machine and email. Then add in estimated long-distance charges based on the locations of your customers, your printer, your distributor and wholesaler, and anyone else you will do business with on an ongoing basis. Also figure in what sort of rate you've negotiated with your long-distance carrier.

If you plan to sell books by direct mail or do seminars in various regions around the country, you may want to invest in a toll-free number so customers can call at your cost instead of theirs. There are many good deals to be had on toll-free plans, so shop around. In many instances, you pay a small monthly fee and the incoming calls are charged at your normal long-distance rate. This can be pricey as you receive more calls, but if the number of customers you'll nab increases exponentially as a result, it's probably worth it.

It's likely you will also want a business cell phone. If you have great cell service in your home, you may want your cell phone to be your only phone line. But cell phone coverage is still spotty in some areas of the country; you will want to seem as professional as possible, so having good phone service is crucial.

Also, if you get a "smartphone" and the accompanying cell phone plans, be careful of charges that keep creeping up. Work out the best plan for how you use your phone and be sure you know the details of the plan so you don't get taken by surprise with unexpected charges.

Access to the Net

ISPs, or internet service providers, generally charge a flat rate of up to $50 a month for unlimited monthly service, which gives you access to the World Wide Web and to email. Check with your cable TV provider. Most local cable services also offer internet service.

Web Host

If you've decided to have a website, your potential costs don't end with the fee you pay for having one designed by a professional. You'll also need a web host, which is not a dapper chap in a tuxedo standing at the door with a tray of champagne cocktails. It's the computer or computers that handle all your customer traffic. A web host can be likened to an internet service provider. While you can manipulate your website all you want from your home/office computer, it takes a much larger server to handle the complexities and size of web traffic. That's why you need a host. How much can you expect to pay? Expect to pay in the range of $5 to $75 per

> **Beware!**
> Though the lure of free web hosting is attractive, do your homework first. Someone's got to pay for your hosting, and it's often advertisers whose banners pop up all over your site—and whose content you have no control over. Know what you're getting into before you commit to a free host.

month depending on the services they offer. Investigate the service menu and be sure to sign up for only those things that you really need.

Getting Carded

If you decide to have an electronic credit card terminal so that you can accept orders by internet or direct mail, you'll have operating expenses associated with this. To keep your merchant card service humming along, you will pay a monthly statement fee of $5 to $15. And if you've decided to lease your terminal instead of purchasing it, you'll have that fee of $19 to $72 per month to account for as well. Credit cards are a fact of life—often the ability to accept credit card payments pays for itself several times over in increased purchases, especially online where people are reluctant to use a debit card and often dedicate one credit card to online purchases.

Your Best Pal

Go ahead and set up a PayPal account. Your potential customers will want to be able to pay for your goods using every possible method. PayPal does not cost anything to have a basic account. Head to their website and in minutes you will have an account ready to accept payments. And be sure to load their PayPal button onto your site.

Paper Tiger

Once you've made your initial outlay for office supplies and stationery, your fixed expenses in this category should be fairly low. Staples last a long time, you can reuse paper clips, and you shouldn't have to replace office items like a letter opener and scissors for quite some time after your initial purchase. Your main expense will be paper: lots of paper for your printer and fax machine, fine-quality paper for stationery, and envelopes. Oh yeah, and printer ink. Laser printer toner and inkjet printer ink is pretty expensive! Even ink cartridges for the most basic printer can run $65 to $75 for both the black-and-white and color cartridges. Be sure to

Dollar Stretcher

Be environmentally and economically smart. Reuse that printer paper. Instead of practicing hoop shots into the trash with all those versions of letters, evaluation sheets, and other printed materials that you decided you didn't like, put an x through the bad text and set the pages aside. When you've compiled a tidy stack, load them back into your printer and print drafts on the blank side. Save your "good" paper for the final draft that goes out in the mail.

collect (and use) any loyalty points and discounts you can get from the big-box office supply stores!

Paying the Piper

We've set aside a fixed expense called loan repayment. If you do not borrow money to start your business, you won't need to bother with this one. If, however, you finance your startup costs through any means, you'll need to repay the piper. Here's where you pencil in whatever your monthly fee is.

You may have many more expenses than the ones discussed here, such as employees and the workers' compensation and payroll costs that go with them, auto expenses, and subscription fees for professional publications. We have not included the costs associated with rent, utilities, and employees on our worksheet, but they are common features of financial projections. If they will not apply to your homebased company, of course, you won't need to worry about them. But when you start publishing more books, you may find your business is successful enough to start considering them! Use the worksheet called "Your Projected Annual Income/Expenses Statement" on page 192 and pencil in your estimated operating expenses over the course of your first year.

Making a Statement

Financial checkups don't have to be negative. They can give you a rosy glow by demonstrating how well you're doing—possibly even better than you expected. If you've been saving for a new printer or software upgrade, or if you're hoping to take on an employee, you can judge how close you are to achieving that goal. And if there are problems, you can catch them early by doing regular financial checkups—and then you can make any changes you need to. For instance, if you discover that your income barely covers your promotional or operating expenses, you can change gears along with the number of direct-mail pieces you send out.

An important tool for keeping your finances on track is the income and expenses statement, also called a profit-and-loss statement. This type of financial statement

> **Tip...**
>
> **Smart Tip**
>
> As your company grows, your postage expenses will bloom, too, but for your first year of operation you should be able to keep it to a minimum. If you figure on an average of two pieces of mail per day at the first-class rate, you can pencil in about $20 per month.

charts the revenues and operating costs of your business over a specific period of time, usually monthly or annually. Check out the annual income statements on page 191 for our two hypothetical publishers, Glowworm Press and Bell & Candle Publishing. Glowworm projects an annual income of $6,313, while Bell & Candle projects it yearly earnings at $25,110.

Adding It All Up

And now, the moment we've all been waiting for: the grand total for how much it will cost to get to the end of publishing your first book and what profits you can expect. As we have said repeatedly, these figures will be different for every publisher. You need to do your own careful homework to determine what your expenses and your bottom line will be.

Let's go back to "Your Projected Annual Income/Expenses Statement" worksheet on page 192. You should already have filled in the operating expenses you project, but you're not finished yet. Next, you need to determine your projected income, taking into account both retail and wholesale revenue (use the worksheet on page 194 to arrive at a projection for profits from your first book). After you have an idea of what your projected gross income will be, then you need to subtract your expenses from this figure to arrive at a net income figure. Your expenses will include not only the operating expenses that you have already listed, but also the "cost of sales," which includes:

- The total for your projected company startup costs, from the worksheet on page 74.
- Your projected production costs for your first book, from the worksheet on page 97.
- The additional costs of distributor fees, returns, a travel budget, shipping and postage, which were discussed in Chapter 8. Use the worksheet on page 194 to help you calculate these additional costs.

Add all these elements to arrive at a figure for the cost of sales. Once you subtract both your operating expenses and the cost of sales from your projected gross income, you will arrive at the projected net income for your company's first year.

To give you a few typical scenarios, we have once again used our two hypothetical publishers, Glowworm Press and Bell & Candle Publishing, to show you how to arrive at a projected annual net income. Look at the calculation of gross income and cost of sales for these companies in the "Annual Book Profits" chart on page 193. Yes, they do make a profit! Also take a look at the "Annual Income/Expenses Statement" for the companies on page 191.

Annual Income/Expenses Statement

INCOME/EXPENSES STATEMENT

For the Year Ended December 31, 20xx

	Glowworm	Bell & Candle
Projected Income		
Retail sales	$16,835	$49,900
Wholesale sales	$7,770	$24,950
Gross Income	**$24,605**	**$74,850**
Projected Cost of Sales		
Company startup expenses *(total from worksheet on page 72)*	$3,561	$10,764
Production costs *(total from worksheet on page 92)*	$7,542	$19,226
Other costs of doing business *(distributor fees, returns, travel budget, shipping, and postage)*	$3,519	$12,080
Gross Cost of Sales	**(–$14,622)**	**(–$42,070)**
Operating Expenses		
Phone	$900	$900
Toll-free line	$0	$1,200
Electronic credit card processing	$300	$300
Postage	$240	$300
Legal services (beyond startup)	$360	$400
Insurance (remaining six months)	$850	$1,150
Accounting services (beyond startup)	$300	$350
Office supplies	$120	$150
Internet service provider (remaining six months)	$120	$120
Web hosting (remaining six months)	$180	$300
Loan repayment	$0	$2,000
Miscellaneous	$300	$500
Total Operating Expenses	**(–$3,670)**	**(–$7,670)**
Projected Net Annual Income	**$6,313**	**$25,110**

Your Projected Annual Income/Expenses Statement

For the Year Ending _____

Projected Income	
Retail sales	$
Wholesale sales	
Gross Income	$
Projected Cost of Sales	
Company startup expenses *(total from worksheet on page 74)*	$
Production costs *(total from worksheet on page 97)*	
Other costs of doing business *(distributor fees, returns, travel budget, shipping, and postage)*	
Gross Cost of Sales	(–$)
Operating Expenses	
Phone	$
Toll-free line	
Electronic credit card processing	
Postage	
Legal services (beyond startup)	
Insurance (remaining six months)	
Accounting services (beyond startup)	
Office supplies	
Internet service provider (remaining six months)	
Web hosting (remaining six months)	
Loan repayment	
Miscellaneous	
Commercial office only: *Rent*	
Utilities	
Employee payroll & benefits	
Total Operating Expenses	(–$)
Projected Net Annual Income	$

Annual Book Profits

		Glowworm Press	Bell & Candle Publishing
Projected Income			
	Retail price	$14.95 per book x 1,300 copies sold = $16,835	$24.95 per book x 2,000 copies sold = $49,900
	Distributor wholesaler price (at 60% discount)	$5.18 x 1,500 copies sold = $7,770	$9.98 x 2,500 copies sold = 24,950
	Gross Income	**$24,605**	**$74,850**
Cost of Sales			
	Company setup expenses	(−$3,561)	(−$10,764)
	Production costs	(−$7,542)	(−$19,226)
	Distributor fees (setup, warehousing, etc.)	(−$500)	(−$1,000)
	Returns	20% of $7,965 = (−$1,593)	20% of $24,950 = (−$4,990)
	Free copies for publicity	200 copies (included in production costs) (−$0)	500 copies (included in production costs) (−$0)
	Travel budget	(−$1,000)	(−$5,000)
	Shipping to distributor	(−$200)	(−$300)
	Postage (to send publicity copies to reviewers)	$1.13 x 200 copies = (−$226)	$1.58 x 500 copies = (−$790)
	Gross Cost of Sales	**(−$14,622)**	**(−$42,070)**
Operating Expenses			
	Total Operating Expenses	**(−$3,670)**	**(−$7,670)**
Net Income			
	Net Income after all Expenses	**$6,313**	**$25,110**

▲

Your Bottom Line

Use this worksheet to calculate your annual projected income and expenses. Make copies and work up several different scenarios, then go with the one that works best.

Annual Book Profits for _____

(Your company name)

Projected Income		
	Retail price	$ _____ per book x _____ copies sold = $ _____
	Distributor/wholesaler price (at 60% discount)	$ _____ per book x _____ copies sold = $ _____
	Gross Income	**$ _____**
Cost of Sales		
	Company startup expenses (total from worksheet on page 74)	(–$ _____)
	Production costs (total from worksheet on page 97)	(–$ _____)
	Distributor fees (setup, warehousing, etc.)	(–$ _____)
	Returns	20% of $ _____ profit from sales to distributor/wholesaler = (–$ _____)
	Free copies for publicity	_____ copies (included in production costs) (–$0)
	Travel budget	(–$ _____)
	Shipping to distributor	(–$ _____)
	Postage (to send publicity copies to reviewers)	$ _____ x _____ copies = (–$ _____)
	Gross Cost of Sales	**(–$ _____)**
Operating Expenses		
	Total Operating Expenses	**(–$ _____)**
Net Income		
	Net Income after all Expenses	**$ _____**

Getting a Grip

The whole point of doing financial checkups is to get an overview of your profits—or losses—and then get a grip on them. If you discover, after inking in your expenses, that you're not going to be able to afford that trip to the book fair in London (much less the price of a London broil at the supermarket), don't panic. Get a grip!

First, realize that the first year in the life of your company is generally the most expensive. You've had all those setup costs,

Smart Tip Tip...

To draw up a monthly income statement, you'll need to prorate items that are paid annually, such as business licenses and tax-time accounting fees, and pop those figures into your monthly statement. For example, if you pay annual insurance premiums of $600, divide this figure by 12 and add the resulting $50 to your insurance expense.

from buying equipment to software to registering your business name. Those are one-time fees that you won't incur again unless, or until, you splurge for a hardware or software upgrade, for example.

Second, your book won't cost as much the next time around. When you go back to the printer for another run, those reprints will have far fewer production costs. You won't need to pay for copyediting or proofreading because those are already done. You won't have cover design or illustration costs—those are already done. And you won't have to pay for the printer to put the book on film because that's already done.

Raising Cain

You've got other options for raising your income as well. One way is to bump up your book's list price. You may think this is akin to raising Cain, but it's not. If you increase your retail price from, say, $12.95 to $14.95, readers are not likely to see an appreciable difference. It is not the same as jumping from $12.95 to $20.95. Before you do raise your price, however, engage in some last-minute market research. In most cases a raise of a dollar or two doesn't make a huge difference, but there are ceilings for most products beyond which most consumers won't budge, and your book may already be there.

Another way is to shoot for those alternative sales outlets, the ones where your discount is not as high. Try for more library sales, more specialty store sales, and more direct sales garnered through your website and by writing articles for publication. Use more of the same creative energy that goes into getting your book written and designed to boost your profit potential. That's a big part of being a self-publisher.

▲

Tip...

Smart Tip

Use your book's second printing as a promotional tool. A reprint is proof that readers are buying it and it's in demand. Spread the word!

Uncle Sam Speaks

When you earn money from your book, someone will be queuing up for a piece of the action: Uncle Sam. If your budget allows, you should engage an accountant. You probably won't need her for your daily or monthly concerns, but it's well worth the expense to have someone in the know at the reins when it comes to April 15, or for those questions that come up now and again.

Your tax deductions should be about the same as those for any other small or homebased business. You can deduct a percentage of your home office, so long as you're using it solely as an office. These deductions include all normal office expenses plus interest, taxes, insurance, and depreciation (this is where the accountant comes in handy). The IRS has added in all sorts of permutations such as: The total amount of the deduction is limited by the gross income you derive from the business activity minus all your other business expenses, apart from those related to the home office. And you thought that interactive software game was complicated! Basically, the IRS does not want you to come up with so many home office deductions that you end up paying no tax at all.

Driving Yourself Crazy

What else can you deduct? Acceptable deductions include business-related phone calls; the cost of business equipment and supplies (again, so long as you're truly using them solely for your business); subscriptions to professional and trade journals; and auto expenses. Your auto expenses accrue when you drive your vehicle in the course of doing business or seeking business. In other words, you're chalking up deductible mileage every time you motor out to conduct research, do a book fair, give a seminar or a guest spot on TV or radio, visit your printer, or take a cross-country spin on an author tour.

To keep from driving yourself crazy, keep a log of your business miles. You can buy one of several varieties at your local office supply or stationers, or you can make one yourself. Keep track as you go. It's no fun having to recreate a year's worth of driving adventures

Tip...

Smart Tip

Tax questions? Beard the lion in its den and call the IRS. First go online at www.irs.gov to find the toll-free number for your region. You may have to go through voice mail or the on-hold-forever period, but once you get a live being on the line, they're surprisingly friendly.

at tax time to guesstimate how many miles you drove to how many places and for what purpose during the year.

Let Me Entertain You

You can deduct entertainment expenses like a book launch party or a dinner to wine and dine a distributor. Keep a diary of all these expenses as well, especially if they come to under $75 a pop (you do not technically need to keep receipts for these). And if you're entertaining at home, have your customers sign a guest book.

Remember that you must have a business-related purpose for entertaining, like a sales presentation. General goodwill toward potential customers or sales reps doesn't make it, so be sure your diary contains the reason for the festivities.

Planes, Trains, and Automobiles

When you travel for business purposes, you can deduct airfares, train tickets, rental car mileage, and the like. You can also deduct hotels and meals. And you can even—under certain circumstances—deduct recreational side trips you take with your family while you're traveling on business. Since the IRS allows deductions for any such trip you take to expand your awareness and expertise in your field of business, it makes sense to also take advantage of any conferences or seminars that you can attend. You can stay abreast of events in your target market or see how the competition's doing.

Smart Tip

The IRS loves documentation. The more receipts and logs you accumulate and carefully organize, the happier you will be if that horrid "A" word (audit) rears its ugly head.

Looking Ahead
Small Press to Publishing Giant

OK, you've successfully written your book, have it stocked in bookstores and other outlets, and launched an ongoing promotional campaign. Is that all there is? Well, no, not by a long shot.

For the savvy self-publisher, there are many avenues left to explore—other outlets for your talents and your message, and other ways to augment your income. In this chapter, we will investigate these other avenues, from making a deal with a mega-publisher to selling subsidiary and foreign rights, and more.

Let's Make a Deal

The publishing industry is rife with stories of writers who became self-publishers because no traditional house would buy their work. They later sold that same "unsaleable" property for hundreds of thousands of dollars. This doesn't happen to every independent publisher, of course, and not every self-publisher wants it to happen—some would rather keep all the control and profits for themselves—but it's definitely worth considering.

Selling Out

In Cinderella scenarios, a big publishing house sees your book at a book expo, or picks up on all your terrific publicity, and approaches you with an offer. In other cases, it's up to you to make the first move, going after a traditional publisher the same way you go after reviews from trade magazines and opinion makers.

Why would you want to sell out after you've done all the work of grooming your book for success all by yourself? The simple answer is money. In the Cinderella scenario, it's hard to say no to a mega-publisher that courts you with a staggering sum for your book. And in the you-court-them scenario, you can land significant earnings upfront by selling out and then using those earnings to bankroll your next successful book.

The Acquisition

The Cinderella scenario is not as uncommon as you might imagine. It's unlikely that you will be wooed with a million-dollar contract, but it's perfectly likely that you'll be courted with a reasonable offer. Traditional publishers send talent scouts called acquisition editors to book fairs, like the yearly colossal Book Expo America, to seek out likely titles and snap them up.

And why not? You've done the hard part. Besides writing your book, you've designed it and laid it out in a format that sells. You've conducted all the market research—you've found a niche market, written for that market, and promoted to it. You've done the testing that proved the market is viable and lucrative. So what publisher wouldn't like to have a piece of the pie?

The Sadie Hawkins Approach

If major publishers do not single you out for attention, you can take the Sadie Hawkins approach and tackle them. Use the same campaign techniques you will use to garner media attention during your pre-publication and early release phases.

Put together a package that includes a cover letter detailing:

○ Why your book would be the perfect purchase

○ Every great review you've ever received

○ A compilation of sterling testimonials and endorsements

○ Magazine reprints and news articles about your book—not written by you

○ A blurb about any subsidiary rights you've sold and any particularly large orders you've filled

You'll have to do your homework here, too. You won't send a children's picture book to a publisher of technical tomes, or a cookbook to an aviation publisher. Do your research. You'll find hundreds of publishers listed in the pages of *Literary Marketplace* (R.R. Bowker, www.bowker.com) and *Writer's Market* (Writer's Digest Books, www.writersmarket.com). Once you've identified potential candidates, ship your query package off to all of them. Note in your cover letter that you're sending multiple queries (i.e., you're sending your query to other publishers)—it's considered courteous if you do and irreparably rude if you don't.

It's flattering to have a New York publisher take interest in your book. It's validation from the most cliquish sector of the industry—sort of like being the wallflower at the senior prom and suddenly having the homecoming queen or football star ask you to dance.

It can also be dangerous. Self-publishers often are so thrilled by this coveted attention that they give away their books. And the big houses—no dummies—take full advantage. They'll usually offer a 10 percent royalty, or even less.

Demanding More

As the publisher, you deserve a lot more. Remember, you have done all the work up to this point: You've burned the midnight oil to create the product; taken all the financial risk to make it a reality; and put in countless hours to make it a promotional success. Don't take the first offer—instead do some heavy negotiating and be sure to include the following:

- *Cost plus.* Your contract should give you a fee of two to three times your book's production costs, plus 10 percent of the projected sales.

- *Royalty inclusive.* Make sure the contract reads royalty inclusive. This means you get the projected royalties immediately—a major perk compared to the traditional method where you wait for months at a time until the publisher tallies up its quarterly earnings and then divvies up your share.

- *Easy on the rights.* Don't give away all rights to your book—you don't have to. Give the buyer North American rights only, which is permission to sell the book in the United States and Canada. You still retain the foreign rights, which can be considerable.

- *To the trade only.* Specify that the buyer gets the rights to sell only to the book trade—libraries and bookstores. This gives you the option to continue selling to non-traditional outlets and also lets you continue to sell by direct mail.

Dollar Stretcher

One week after Stephen King offered the first installment of his e-serial, *The Plant*, in July 2000, he had already sold more than 152,000 downloads.

- *Electronic egress.* Do not give away e-book and e-publishing or electronic rights. Either retain them for yourself or give the buyer a short-term option to purchase those rights separately.

- *Audio outlet.* Don't give the buyer audiobook rights unless they normally release audiobooks along with the print version.

- *Out of print.* Make sure all rights revert to you once the book is out of print. If and when the buyer decides not to publish it anymore, you can pick up right where you left off if you so choose.

- *Release date.* Insist on a specific release date so that the buyer is forced to actually print and sell your books. Occasionally publishers buy books for the sole purpose of removing the competition; they have no intention of actually entering into distribution. When you insist on a specific release date, you nip this strategy in the bud.

Smart Tip

When you sell conden-
sations, it is up to the
magazine to condense your material—they pay for it, not you.

Selling Subsidiary

Subsidiary rights are the rights to morph your book into different forms, including movies and TV (imagine your own miniseries!), magazine condensations or reprints, book club editions, and foreign language editions.

Handled wisely, subsidiary sales can be extremely lucrative. In fact, this—rather than book sales—is where the major New York publishers make the most money. As a self-publisher, you may not find vast fortune with subsidiary sales, but you'll certainly augment your income. You may negotiate a deal that nets you millions of dollars, but it's far more likely that you'll get in the neighborhood of a few thousand dollars.

Even if you only land $300 to $600 for that first magazine reprint right, you stand to make thousands more over the long haul from the additional exposure. Each time readers see your book in any form, it's free advertising and promotion. And the more subsidiary rights you can claim, the hotter property your book becomes.

Hot Serial

You can sell to magazines or periodicals in several ways—as excerpts, serializations, and condensations. A serial is a book divided into installments that run in successive issues of newspapers, magazines, or other periodicals. A condensation is a book that's condensed or abridged, primarily as a space-saving measure, and then printed in a periodical or anthology.

When you sell the rights to excerpts, serializations, or condensations before your publication date, you sell the first serial rights. When you sell the rights after the publication date, you sell the second serial rights. First serial rights are generally considered more of a scoop than second, for the obvious reason that before your publication date nobody (more or less) has yet laid eyes on your story; it's so hot it hasn't even rolled off the press.

When you sell excerpts, choose sections that relate to the subject matter of the publication. If your gardening book has a

Smart Tip

With foreign translations, it is up to the buyer to have his version of your book translated, printed, and bound. All you have to do is deliver a few copies of your original title and the rights to go with it.

chapter on cooking with your bounty, use that chapter (or a piece from it) to sell to a vegetarian cooking magazine. Sell the section on garden furniture to a home décor magazine. Send bound galleys to the magazines you think are the most important and review copies to the rest.

Whichever route you take, make sure the periodical prints something like this at the end of the article:

> Reprinted with permission from *The Night Garden*, by Peter Moss © 2007. Available for $14.95 + $3 shipping/handling from Glowworm Press, Box 17, Luminescent, FL 10000, (850) 555-0000, www.glowwormpress.com.

Join the Club

You know book clubs—those mail order houses that send blurbs urging you to buy the first five books for $1 and receive a free tote bag if you join. As a casual browser you may have tossed the catalogs, or added them to an ever-growing stack of mail on the kitchen counter.

But as a publisher, these book clubs should have a whole new dimension to you. If they buy your book, you'll have great advance sales and you can use the fact that your title is a Book of the Month Club pick, for example, as a terrific promotional blurb. Send bound galleys to the major clubs like Quality Paperback Books, along with any that specialize in your market niche. Then follow up with review copies if you didn't get a response the first time around. You'll find lists of book clubs and their contact information within the pages of *Literary Marketplace* (R.R. Bowker).

Foreign Affairs

You can sell your book to foreign markets in two different ways, as foreign rights and as translation rights. As you can probably guess, foreign rights give publishers in English-language countries a license to reprint your book, while translation rights give foreign publishers the license to reproduce the book in their own language.

Not all books lend themselves to foreign sales. If your title is *The Truth about Social Security*, a foreign audience will not be interested—it's a country-specific topic. But if your title is *Reversing the Aging Process*, you've got something of interest to almost any human on the planet.

For foreign rights, you can sell the British, Australian, or other publisher F&Gs (folded and gathered signatures) from your print run so that all they have to do is bind the books with their own covers. Or you can offer them the camera-ready copy or print-ready film that they can print as is.

Foreign publishers usually get hooked on books at book expos. The mega-event of the year internationally is the annual Frankfurt Book Fair, which takes place in Germany every October (see the Appendix for contact information).

The Reel Story

You can also go after movie and TV companies and sell the film rights to your book. These are far more difficult to land than other types of subsidiaries. Hollywood types are notoriously fickle and are unlikely to look at anything unless it's already a hot property in print. Nevertheless, it does happen. Even nonfiction occasionally hits the silver screen.

The trick with film companies is that they frequently purchase the rights to your book and then—because of their own funding woes—fail to actually produce the movie. This can be extremely disappointing. In an effort to save themselves the full expense of buying film rights, movie and TV companies often purchase options to the film rights, which gives them a period of time (typically from six months to two years) to find the funding and buy the full rights.

Movie-making is astonishingly expensive, and many movies never make a substantial profit. So if and when you do sell your film rights, make sure you negotiate a percentage of the gross profits and not the net.

Because the movie field market is so complex, it might be in your best interest to have an agent—or even better, an attorney—who specializes in publishing and entertainment to walk you through negotiations. Choose your mentor with care. Agents especially can sometimes put their percentage of your profits ahead of your best interests. Start your search for an agent or attorney by asking for referrals from publishing industry associations. Then make sure you check references thoroughly and interview any potential candidates to make sure their vision (and their values) match yours.

> **Fun Fact**
> Clark Gable initially turned down the role of Rhett Butler in MGM's movie version of *Gone with the Wind* (1939), fearing he wouldn't measure up to the Rhett millions of American women had envisioned while reading the book.

▲

The Adventure Continues

Once you are a publishing pro, you will want to take advantage of all your hard-earned expertise with another exciting project. With the greater part of your learning curve behind you, as well as a growing professional reputation, you can launch another book of your own or publish the works of another author.

> ### Smart Tip
> **Tip...**
>
> If your publishing niche is very narrow, you'll want to publish similar titles. Take advantage of the niche market and promotional contacts you've already established. If you go with a different genre title entirely, you may want to establish an imprint, which is a different company with its own name under the umbrella of your main firm. Consult your attorney on just how to proceed.

Launch Pad

A new book is a natural. Hopefully you have located a niche market, established yourself as an expert, found readers eager to hear what you have to say, and found promotional opportunities and outlets to sell your books through. Take advantage of those eager readers by giving them another product to purchase. Your book doesn't have to be on exactly the same topic, so long as it caters to the same market. If your last cookbook was on desserts, make this one on main dishes, cooking for campers or boaters, or culinary skills for kids.

Your new project can take the form of a full-length trade paperback or hardcover, a series of reports on short topics related to your previous book, an audiobook, a video primer to complement your existing title, an e-book or POD adventure, or any combination of the above. Do your research, keep promoting and selling your existing book, and have fun!

Be aware that there is always the possibility that your market, production costs, promotional opportunities, and sales outlets may change. So it's up to you to stay in touch with your niche and with new developments in the publishing industry.

Somebody Else's Baby

Once the word gets out in the industry that you're a publisher, you'll find there's no shortage of authors eager to have you publish their baby. It's a kick to be on the other side of the fence as the final word on accepting or rejecting manuscripts, instead of being the one on the receiving end of all those rejection letters.

The first rule, of course, is to be nice. Don't trample on someone else's feelings, but don't accept a project that you don't feel you can put your own heart and soul into, either.

Keep in mind that even though somebody else writes the text, you will still be responsible for the book layout and design. You'll have to make sure it's properly edited, which can mean requesting that sensitive authors make sometimes heart-wrenching changes. You'll be in charge of all the promotional work including writing sales copy, back cover blurbs, and sample reviews.

You'll have to consider advances, royalties, subsidiary rights, what happens if you decide to let the book go out of print, and other financial issues. It can be a lot of work. So if you don't believe in a project, chances are you won't be very happy putting so much effort into it—and it may show in the final product.

When you do find a project and an author you believe in, the experience can be almost as magical as seeing your own book to fruition. Helping someone else to success is more satisfying than you might imagine.

Bestseller or Bomb?

Success in the self-publishing industry is achieved by following the tried-and-true business methods of persistence and plain, old-fashioned hard work—along with a healthy dose of optimism. If we've illustrated anything in this book, we hope it's that becoming a successful self-publisher

▲

involves a lot of work. It is rewarding and sometimes exhilarating work, but hard work nonetheless.

We also hope we have managed to convey that becoming a self-publisher is not the same as becoming an overnight success. It takes diligent market research, loads of planning, and abundant creativity to achieve bestseller status.

Words of Wisdom

When we interviewed the self-publishing entrepreneurs included in this book, we asked them to give us some words of wisdom for neophytes—and we got them! Following are stories of success and failure from these entrepreneurs. We hope their hard-won lessons and advice will help you as you start up your own self-publishing business.

A Revolution

Jim Milliot is co-editorial director at *Publishers Weekly*, where he has worked for ten years. He's seen a few things and here's what he has to say:

> "Self-publishing has been totally revolutionized over the last three or four years, with the advent of digital printing and digital book creation. It's all moved from the old vantage press days of [authors] paying $20,000 for bound books to paying hundreds of dollars for an e-book and a little more than that for a print book that can now sell online. The whole thing has no resemblance to what it was five years ago.

> "On the PW website (publishersweekly.com) there is 'PW Select.' For a $129 fee you get a guaranteed listing. Traditional publishing would send us the book before it's published, but with self-publishing it's often simultaneous. We just ask that it's been published in the past year.

> "Today you have a better chance to make money back pretty much [simply] with Amazon and B&N [Barnes and Noble] putting you on their websites. Online distributors, like Smashwords, distribute your e-book on their website and get it out to other retail stores or online stores that sell e-books. You don't have to be beholden to someone to distribute your book physically to bookstores anymore. Of course, the downside is that there are hundreds of thousands of people doing that now and millions of books competing.

> "The best people to do this are those who have a platform—people who have a radio show or a popular blog or something like that. On the

other hand, if you're a famous columnist you can get a big advance from a traditional publisher.

"I don't know if it's 50-50 but there's a divide in self-publishing between people who just want to publish a book because they want to get down their own memoirs for their children but aren't expecting to make money, and people who have dreams of hitting it big.

"Certainly a large portion of people publishing books want to use [self-publishing] to get more public speaking or increase their speaking fees. It gives them a little more credibility if the first book sells and also gives them something to sell too.

"Author House and Author Solutions are the biggest of the self-publishers, Create Space from Amazon is right up there, and there's also Lulu and Barnes & Noble's PubIt!. There are others, and they're all pretty straightforward about the costs involved. If you do your homework, you're not going to get ripped off, but you are going to have to pay for things . . . you have to expect that. It's not like in the old days when you would turn your manuscript over to a vanity publisher, give them your money, and you had no idea what they were doing. I've been following this for a long time, and there were certainly stories 10, 20 years ago where someone gave their money to a publisher and got 10 copies. Now you're doing it yourself and they help you, so it's not like your money will disappear into some black hole.

"People know more about self-publishing today; it's much more transparent than it used to be. The number of titles is growing fast. The numbers of sales is a little bit murkier, but the number of books coming out from self-publishers is more than doubling every year the last few years. I have a hard time believing that it's going to keep growing like it's been growing, but who knows?"

Custom Publishing

Stephanie Chandler is the founder and CEO of Authority Publishing (authoritypublishing.com), which specializes in custom publishing for nonfiction books, and BusinessInfoGuide.com, a directory of resources for entrepreneurs. A frequent speaker at business events and on the radio, she has been featured in *Entrepreneur* magazine, *BusinessWeek*, Inc.com, *Wired*, and many other media outlets. Stephanie is also a blogger for *Forbes*. She tells about her entry into the self-publishing world.

"I started in 2008, self-publishing my first book. I also got a few traditional contracts. Then I decided that I wanted to help other people do what I had done.

"I studied the pricing from service providers and their offerings. We came up with our prices and landed somewhere in the middle. It was important to me to hire editors and designers with a lot of experience; I didn't want to outsource overseas to get things done.

"Most of the people I work with come from referrals from other people who have worked with them. I'm a huge fan of elance.com and find providers there. They have a review section that tells you what other people have to say. I'm kind of slow to hire and fast to fire. I've been known to move on very quickly. I run my entire business off of contracts; I have no actual employees.

"To do this kind of business, you need a cover designer, interior designer (which is a totally different skill set), professional editors, virtual assistants, a marketing assistant, and research assistant. You also need a good printer. After researching for the right printer, I chose to do most of my work with Lightning Source.

"Certainly doing lots of media interviews, publicity campaigns on a huge span of internet, radio, and professional speaking are great ways to captivate an audience and sell a lot of books. I read a great book called *Speak and Grow Rich* by Dottie Walters, and now I do about 20 speaking engagements a year. I tell people to start speaking locally at local associations and build to larger speaking engagements.

"I do some marketing, since I had a marketing business before, but we don't offer a ton of marketing services primarily because it's so hard to meet author expectations and I don't want to sell something that doesn't dazzle people. I do online classes for author marketing and a lot of education for authors. I think it's more important to empower them to know what to do on their own than to try to do it for them."

Stephanie Chandler's books are:

- *The Conference Catcher: An Organized Journal for Capturing Ideas, Resources, and Action Items at Educational Conferences, Trade Shows, and Events* (Authority Publishing, February 2011)

- *Booked Up! How to Write, Publish, and Promote a Book to Grow Your Business* (Authority Publishing, October 2010)

- *LEAP! 101 Ways to Grow Your Business* (Career Press, September 2009)

- *The Author's Guide to Building an Online Platform: Leveraging the Internet to Sell More Books* (Quill Driver Press, May 2008)

Dinner and a Book

Deana Gunn is a self-published author who, along with co-author Wona Miniati, has published:

- *The Cooking with Trader Joe's Cookbook: Dinner's Done!*
- *Cooking with All Things Trader Joe's*
- *Cooking with Trader Joe's Cookbook Companion*

"Moms are looking for great dinner solutions that are healthy, homemade, easy, and convenient, so around five years ago we came up with the idea of doing a cookbook based on Trader Joe's food selection. We thought it was a winning idea and wanted to get it out quickly so we decided to self-publish it. We also wanted a lot of creative control. We wanted a binding that would lay flat, a certain format, and full-color photos for every single recipe. This is expensive for most traditional publishers to do so we decided to do it ourselves. The book came out just nine months after the inception.

"We're not affiliated with Trader Joe's; we're completely independent. We approached them after we had the books written and asked them if they were interested in partnering with us or distributing the book in their stores. They said they liked the book but it wasn't part of their corporate policy to carry books, so we forged ahead on our own. We were careful to be respectful of their rights. We were familiar with 'fair use,' and knew we could use the name as long as we didn't try to represent ourselves as part of the business or use the company logo. There are similar books, like how to play with Lego or the unofficial guide to traveling to Disney World. Ultimately, we published before the holidays in 2007.

"That first book was very popular and had multiple printings. We just did a second edition. Initially our marketing was very grassroots, very much word-of-mouth and such. A lot of editors wrote about it in late 2007, running little articles based on the food from the store. People started talking about it. In the spring of 2008, Borders called to tell us they were going to carry it nationwide and we set ourselves up with top wholesalers. Barnes & Noble followed. Next, we came out with a sequel, *The Trader Joe's Companion*. Other people started coming out with imitations but we had a jump on them. So now we've put out the fourth and fifth books! The newest one is *The Skinny Dish, Trader Joe's Diet*.

"We both create the recipes and collaborate closely on everything. We've actually expanded, and the last two books were written by different authors. We still served as publishers and worked closely as a team. We do all the different stages: marketing, managing the blog and the website, as well as our social network.

"Neither of us have formal culinary training. I see that as a plus since our recipes are very appealing to the average person who shops at Trader Joe's. It's family friendly, great for a party. We met in engineering school in college at MIT. I went off to grad school and became a rocket scientist and Wona went off to Stanford and got her business degree. We both worked in our fields for a long time, but cooking was always a great passion. Then we discovered Trader Joe's and loved it. Once we started having kids and being busy with young kids and careers, Trader Joe's offered great time-saving options. It let us cook conveniently at home, eat very healthy, and make our own baked foods.

"We both started doing this as our full-time jobs in 2007. It takes a full-time effort to do the writing, photography, collaborating with our designer, getting the book out—printing, fulfillment, and so on. We use a broker in San Francisco that manages the printing which is done overseas, then we do the fulfillment.

"We've been approached by many, many publishers over the years. When *The Wall Street Journal* featured the cookbook, there was a lot of interest from agents and publishers. But it made the most sense for us to do self-publishing because we already had our distribution and other pieces in place, and we wanted to maintain control over everything.

"We also now work as publishers for other book projects. We formed Brown Bag Publishing right away and now when other people come to us with manuscript ideas, we're looking at them. We offer royalties and now we are more of a traditional publisher than a self-publisher. We will work with authors as a team.

"The Trader Joe's books are selling about 150,000 copies each. The caution I have is that self-publishing is very tricky; make sure you have an idea that is compelling. If we had put out *The Deana and Wona's Cookbook*, we probably would have sold 50 copies; you need to find a niche that isn't too general or too common."

A Self-Publishing Lulu

Patrick Schwerdtfeger (80shortcuts.com) has published:

- *Make Yourself Useful: Marketing in the 21st Century*
- *Webify Your Business: Internet Marketing Secrets for the Self-Employed*
- *Marketing Shortcuts for the Self-Employed: Leverage Resources, Establish Online Credibility and Crush Your Competition*

"I did *Make Yourself Useful: Marketing in the 21st Century* with Lulu. Then I also did *Webify Your Business: Internet Marketing Secrets for the Self-Employed* with Lulu. The second book did quite well and Wiley asked to publish it. They expanded it and changed the title to *Marketing Shortcuts for the Self-Employed*; it was released in June of 2011.

"I did a little research and it seemed . . . Lulu was a good bet. They weren't the cheapest but were a big player and provided a pretty good service. So I went with them and they did a great job. My experience with self-publishing was that it was tremendously easy and the service is tremendously good.

"Marketing was a big part of it. The second book was initially an email course. You could sign up on my website and receive an email every day for a year, which ended up being quite popular. In fact, a lot of my readers suggested that I compile it into a book. It ended up as 60 chapters, all of which were emails, so they were about one or two pages each. Most people on that list ended up buying the book.

"In the new version of the book, we took 6 chapters away and then added 26 so it has 80 short, punchy chapters. This allowed me to blog the content and create a video for every single chapter. Marketing is all about getting content out there. If the content is out there in piecemeal format, no one's going to go through the trouble of trying to put it all together again—it's not worth their time—so they buy the book. Getting the content out there does not cannibalize your sales; it actually promotes your sales. Use blogs, articles, podcasts, videos; I even summarized it into 300 marketing tips on Twitter. I keep repurposing the content.

"I took a sort of crooked path immediately before getting into self-publishing and speaking. I was in the real estate business and I did a podcast to try and get clients. I put it on iTunes and it became one of the most popular mortgage-related podcasts on iTunes—I kind of ended up with a couple of unlikely successes early in the game and people started asking me how I had done it, so that was kind of my entry into speaking.

"In 2009 I spoke at 127 events and got payment for 6, [the following] year I spoke at 57 places and got paid for 31 and travelled to 30. I finally made a decent income this year after making nothing at it for years.

"It's easier to self-publish now, but there are more books out there and more competition. I can't brag about being a bestseller, so you take the good with the bad.

"The thing that I've done in my life that was truly successful was becoming a keynote speaker—that's a process I've gone through myself. The only reason I wrote the first book was to get speaking gigs, and that worked out very well for me."

Publishing with Authority

Donna Hartley's books are self-published through Authority Publishing. They are:

- *Fire Up Your Life!*
- *Fire Up Your Intuition!*
- *Fire Up Your Health!*
- *Fire Up Your Healing!*

"I was in a major plane crash in Los Angeles in the late 1970s and walked away from it—I had injuries but nothing compared to other people on the plane. I was lucky to be the last one to make it out of my section before the plane exploded. I am now a motivational speaker.

"I tried for over 15 years to get published by a traditional publisher. I went to New York and nothing clicked. I stayed in New York City and met with publishers, but nothing really finalized. I was frustrated because I am a speaker, and I do speak a lot, so I wanted to publish.

"I finally went with a small publishing company in 2000 and had a bad experience with them on all levels, including financial. So when people were asking me for the book, I decided to go out on my own and have complete control over the books . . . . Now when I speak, I have books in the back of the room.

"I did a lot of research for about a year and eliminated different self-publishers. Then I went with Authority Publishing in Sacramento, which is only two hours from my home. I wanted to meet who was going to be in charge with my books and knew that I could have communication with them if things went wrong. I didn't want to be in a big house where I would be just a number. Stephanie Chandler was delightful. I found when I talked with the editors, designers for the cover, and the whole team, everybody I was going to work with were kindly. And they communicated—I wasn't waiting two weeks for a response to an email.

"That's what I was looking for from a self-publisher. I wanted somebody with a track record that had done it. I was looking for four books. Could I have gotten the books done cheaper someplace else? Absolutely. I wanted quality and a long-term relationship.

"My first two books came out in June of 2011. I have another one coming out in May or June 2012, and the fourth a year after. I'll have all four books out in a three-year period. I've been working on my books for years. I wanted to have continuity with the same editors and the same designers, have that formula down so the books would look like they go together when they were on book racks. I wanted paperback and [the cover price at] $15 or under—I was anxious, in these times, to keep it economical for people to buy them.

"I market the books through speaking, social media, and lots of radio. Radio is inexpensive so I do radio shows all over at weird hours. I send a pitch and a media package out every week to radio stations, and land a few every month. Then I can send people to Amazon to buy the book. I also do interviews, get in the local newspapers, and sometimes on the local TV shows. When the third book comes out, I will hire a publicist to do a national campaign.

"You have to position yourself and have enough to offer your readers. I have three books out there, and while not all of them will appeal to every reader, one book probably will. You kind of have to strategize when you self-publish. I really do believe it's all in your own marketing.

"When the economy was going great, I did 60 [speaking engagements]; now I'm happy with 30. That is important—anyone self-publishing has to get a platform and get out there and speak. There are tons of social groups and associations and community groups. In every agreement I write that I want to have a book signing. Also with self-publishing you can package your books however you want, so instead of $15 each, you can make them two for $25. I'm very happy with my small, self-publishing house!"

▲

All in One Page

Jim Horan runs the One Page Business Plan company. He does speaking engagements and he self-published several One Page titles:

- *The One Page Business Plan for the Creative Entrepreneur*
- *The One Page Business Plan for the Busy Executive*
- *The One Page Business Plan for Non-Profit Organizations*
- *The One Page Business Plan for the Professional Consultant*
- *The One Page Business Plan for Financial Services Professionals*
- *The One Page Business Plan for the Creative Entrepreneur* (Spanish Edition)
- *The One Page Business Plan for Women in Business*

"The short story is that on April Fools Day in 1990 I got kicked out of corporate America. I was a Fortune 500 CFO. It was the best damn thing that ever happened to me! Perhaps the most painful, as well. It was the recession of 1990. I wandered around for two years and did not get a job. It took me a few years to figure out that it wasn't because of the recession; it was that I didn't really want to find a job. I reinvented myself as a consultant and called my company Rent a CFO. I worked with 20 million-dollar companies. I saw this complete absence of and terror about the thing called a 'business plan.' The worst thing that could happen to somebody in business, any entrepreneur, is being asked: 'Do you have a business plan and can I see it?' And not having one.

"I would ask people about their business and found that I could get a business plan together in about 90 minutes. The concept of the one-page business plan came to me in 1994. I took it to an entrepreneurial support group and they suggested I go out and do some public speaking. I told them I was scared to do that but they told me to just get over it and go out and do it. Then people began asking me if I had a book. I went back to my support group and asked them what should I do, and they told me to just do it. I explained that I got C's and D's in English. Again, they just told me to get over it.

"I joined a self-publishing organization in Berkeley, California, called the Bay Area Independent Publishers Association. They help everyday people get their books written and are an affiliate of Independent Book Publishers Association. The short of it is, working with a book coach and editor in the fall of 1997 I published the first book. The book coach guided me through the process. I experimented with three editors and then I met Rebecca Soloman-Show. Her company was called Entrepreneurial Authors. I thought, that's me, I'm an entrepreneurial author. So she edited some of my pages and she was the magic that I needed—she made light edits and we were 'off to the horse races.'

"I did the second book, the nonprofit book, probably three years later. After that we did a book a year. We did the publishing ourselves, contracting with a graphic designer for the book layout. I read Dan Poynter's book and did a lot of the things he said. We then sent out 20 to 25 RFQs for printers and finally met someone who had done the Olympics printing from Salt Lake City. He introduced me to his printer; they were 30 percent lower than the lowest bid we received. We've used them now for 14 years. We've created seven titles and sold tons of books, made 3.5 million dollars. Then we made $10 million in software!

"I remember meeting someone who had sold 30,000 copies of his dog book. He told me that when you finish your book—and it's hard to do that—that's only 5 percent of your overall effort. It is what you will do with the book that actually counts. I've built a global cottage industry around 'one-page business plan' and I was only able to do that because of self-publishing.

"I did my public speaking and did a speaking engagement at a bookstore where I picked up one of Tom Peters' books. I sent him an email and told him, 'I've done something incredibly brilliant or outrageously stupid: I've simplified the business plan to a single page.' Most business plans are very long and aren't worth the paper they are written on.

"Tom responded back in 48 hours and wanted to see the book. He then responded that he thought it was a brilliant book and wanted to write the foreword—the highest-profile person in any industry was asking to write the foreword to my book!

"The point is that I took a chance. I was at the bottom of the ant pile and wrote to someone who earns $100,000 a speech. Not only did he respond but he wrote the foreword for each book. It helps to take a chance and get someone who is high up and respected in your industry to get involved with your book project in some manner—a testimonial, a foreword, anything can help. It sure didn't hurt me to ask!"

Helping Thousands

"Read, read, read, and research, research, research before you get started," advises Anna J. in Temple, Texas, who we have heard from throughout this book. "I just decided to do this because I knew my book was needed. I jumped in without really looking. Of course, then I think that if I had researched too much, I might have been too intimidated to start, and that would have been a pity. I have now helped thousands of people who heretofore had nothing to help them through one of the most difficult passages of their lives. I have a binder full of thank-you letters and cards from people who have been touched by my books. I know I've made a difference in this world.

"So maybe, instead, the best advice I can give is to decide why you want to publish. Is it to make money? Is it to develop a new line of books never thought of before and thus too risky for the big publishers? Is it to make a difference? Decide now what you will consider 'success' and write it down.

"For my husband and me, we felt we would be successful if we helped even only one family," Anna says. "We have done that. We consider our publishing company a great success. For us, the bottom line is that we know we're providing useful resources that are helping people all over the world, and that is more valuable than money. If you are publishing for altruistic reasons, you have a different perspective on business."

Ever Erratic

"In retrospect, my wife and I made a mistake by quitting our nice day jobs before starting the company," says Steve C. in Hinesburg, Vermont. "Small publishing provides too erratic an income (at least until you have a collection of steady-selling backlist) to count on as your only source of income while raising a family. Therefore we took on some side ventures—the book fulfillment and the software—to provide a steadier income.

"I'm terribly proud of what we accomplished with those aspects of the business, but they diverted a lot of effort away from publishing, the main thing I wanted to do. I now think it makes a lot more sense to keep your day job while you write and publish your first book, or maybe your first several books. Or at least, if you're married, one of the two of you should keep the day job until the books are providing enough steady income to support the family.

"I think I'd have a lot more books in print today if I had done it that way—my regular job was a more reliable way of supporting the family than the new ventures I took on all at once," the veteran publisher says. "Again, I can't regret what was accomplished. The software program in particular is very successful, and I take great pride in it. But we'd be farther along in book publishing if we had phased into it directly from our regular jobs, rather than taking on the side ventures."

Swing Low

Gary S. in Panama City Beach, Florida, who has kept his day job while moonlighting in self-publishing, concurs with Steve. "Keep overhead low at first," the environmental protection agent advises. "Book production and storage is a big expense. Try out the print-on-demand option first until you see how well the books will sell."

"One thing I wish I had done was visit with some other publishers face-to-face," Anna J. says. "I think this might have helped me. I've been reading lately where some publishers form co-ops, and that seems like something worth investigating. Perhaps I could have found a mentor. There were so many things that I learned the hard way. It would have been nice to have someone to hold my hand through the beginning stages of my business.

"The one thing I neglected to do which I really think would have made a difference for my business was creating a real business plan," adds Anna. I have since hired a lawyer who is helping me prepare to become a nonprofit organization, and the time I have spent brainstorming with her and developing a solid business plan has been invaluable. That should be part of everyone's startup expense—and it will cost a couple of thousand dollars, but it will give you a solid foundation. I think that if I had done that, I would have distributed a lot more books by now."

> **Fun Fact**
> Many authors have gone from writing books to screenplays or vice-versa, including F. Scott Fitzgerald, Sidney Sheldon, and Nora Ephron, who penned the ever-popular *Sleepless in Seattle* (1993).

Love What You Do

"Love what you do," Anna also advises. "This is a tough business, but if you love what you do, then you will be successful. Don't let others define success for you. You will know in your heart if you are successful or not. Success is not measured in dollar signs but in the way you feel about your business. Love what you do, and maybe your books will make a difference in someone's life—then you will be successful."

June H. in Rochester Hills, Michigan, agrees. "Any privately owned business overtakes your life from time to time and so, therefore, you must truly love it," June says. "And if you truly love it, don't let anyone say it can't be done—because it can. Be passionate about it and believe in yourself."

▲

The Happiness Factor

If you're the type of person who can handle the ups and downs of entrepreneurship in general, and the yin and yang of creativity and number crunching that makes up the self-publisher's world, you'll probably thrive. If not, you may discover during your company's first year of life, or beyond, that the business isn't for you. You may feel that instead of a bestseller, you're dealing with a bomb.

Whether or not you're earning money, the success of your business is contingent on a happiness factor. Because it involves a good deal of work and responsibility, you may discover that you'd be just as happy—or more so—working for someone else. And that's OK. With everything you will have learned, you'll be a great job candidate.

None of the people interviewed for this book, from a newbie to a veteran with 15 years' experience, seems to have any intention of packing it in. Rather, they seem to have a sense of delight at doing what they enjoy, helping others with the same interests, and being a part of the larger world.

Ten Tips for Self-Publishing Success

1. *Read.* Read everything you can find about the business of self-publishing.

2. *Read even more!* Soak up everything available about running a small business.

3. *Join in.* Join groups, take classes, ask questions, and do market research.

4. *Write from the heart.* Be passionate and let your readers share your sentiments.

5. *Produce the best book you possibly can.* Don't skimp on your cover, copyediting, or proofreading. Cross every "t," dot every "i," and check every fact.

6. *Send pre-publication materials to every industry source and opinion molder.* Then follow up where appropriate to start collecting endorsements and testimonials.

7. *Maintain a steady post-publication publicity campaign.* Track down every possible PR opportunity and then follow it up.

8. *Don't be afraid to blow your own horn.* Your book's future depends on it!

9. *Send thank-you notes after all reviews, interviews, speaking engagements, articles, and other PR opportunities.* It's common courtesy and also leaves the door open for further opportunities.

10. *Have fun.* After all, isn't that at least half the point?

Success and Failure

But is it all sunshine and roses? Surely, we hear you asking, even the most successful self-publishing professionals hit some bumps on the road to achievement. So we asked our interviewees about their worst—and best—experiences in the business.

Stress!

"My worst experience has been with my most recent printer," says Anna J. "The books were not done as well as I thought they should have been done, and I had a terrible time getting any satisfaction from the printer. Then they went bankrupt! It wasn't hard to see why, but it was a very stressful and costly experience."

Steve C. counts a different sort of trauma as his stress memory. "The worst was a book that didn't get any library reviews, and that we'd counted on selling to college professors as texts or recommended reading for their courses; but we weren't successful in that form of marketing," the Vermont resident recalls. "I won't tell you the title of the book, because it's a great book, and it's still actively in print; but we've spent a lot of money on promotion that didn't work and, after several years, we still have half the first printing of 5,000 copies."

June H., the horror writer, also went through a publisher's horror scenario. "My worst experience was when I assigned the same ISBN to two different books," she says. "Ultimately, I retired the first book—which wasn't a big seller anyway—and notified the distributors and bookstores of the error. I still get backlash from that mistake, but it's improving."

Springboard to Success

"My best experience came from last year's anthology," June says. "Two of the contributors were beginners, and since then one has published two e-books, and the other has sold more than a dozen short stories since their work first appeared in my book. I hope that, in some small way, the success of that book was a springboard to their other projects."

Gary S. in Florida feels his books help others, too, garnering long-awaited acknowledgment for men who laid their

> ### Bright Idea
> Joining a writer's group can be a wonderful way to keep you motivated, pick up tips from other writers, and talk shop to your heart's content. Most groups allow members to share their work once a month (or whenever they meet) and receive free friendly and constructive critiques. Plus, you'll be surprised how much you can learn about your own writing by critiquing someone else's!

lives on the line for their homes and families. "It's been a very gratifying experience writing and publishing books for veterans," the Panama City Beach resident explains. "Really, I would say that it was an honor to be involved in it. I can't say that I've had a bad experience thus far. It's all been positive." What more could anyone ask?

Steve C.'s books make a difference in the quality of people's lives as well. "The best experience has been my wife's books on caring for the dead," Steve says. "Her latest is a 640-page book that sells for $30, and we're quickly going through a printing of 10,000 copies. She gets a lot of publicity. Any time a newspaper, magazine, or television program covers abuses by the funeral industry, she gets interviewed, and that helps to create a continuous market for her books."

Goose Bumps!

"My best experience?" Anna J. says. "There have been so many! There was the time I was first introduced as an 'author'—what a thrill! There was that first letter I got from a stranger thanking me for my book. I will never forget the time a woman called me from a Chicago library. She told me she had read the review of my book in Library Journal and wanted to know how to order my book. I didn't know about the review (I got a letter from them later), and I got goose bumps while she talked to me.

"I think that the best experiences come when you least expect them. . . . I was just recently at the 'Meet the Author' session of an international parenting conference. It felt so good to attend the sessions with a little green 'Author' ribbon attached to my nametag—somehow it seemed to validate so much of what I have done, but it was during lunch one day that I felt most honored. I could not find any parents I knew to eat with on the last day of the conference, so I just decided to eat at the first available table. I asked a woman sitting alone at a table if I could eat with her, introduced myself, and put my things down.

"When I came back from the buffet line," Anna recalls, "the lady said, 'I didn't realize who you were!' She then proceeded to tell me that her son had the same heart defect my son did, and that she had bought my book from a social worker in Boston. She told me that my book had helped her. There were over 1,000 people at that conference, and it catered to parents of children with mental retardation, autism, Down syndrome, and a host of other special problems. There were only a handful of us 'heart' parents there, so having this happen was quite extraordinary."

> ### Smart Tip
> Tip...
>
> Don't get so busy that you don't take the time to give back to your community. When you're asked to speak for free at a local writer's group or a school, say, "Yes!" It's an honor—and it's free publicity as well.

Honors

"Recently I was asked to attend some parenting conferences as a vendor," says Anna, the mother of two. "This was an honor to me because the doctors didn't charge me to attend their conferences—they let me set up a table free of charge and were very supportive. Perhaps the greatest honors to come from the medical field for me recently have been: 1) to write a chapter for a medical textbook (a chapter from a parent's perspective), and 2) to be a guest speaker at a major children's hospital for their first parenting conference. Not only was I asked to be a speaker, but I was also asked my opinion on topics to be addressed during the conference. When others value your opinion and want to hear what you have to say, that makes everything else worthwhile."

A Job Well-Done

This seems to be the attitude of all the self-publishers who so generously helped with this book—the joy in a job well-done and the desire to make a difference for others. If you go into this business with the right stuff—a willingness to work hard, to learn everything you can, the confidence to promote yourself and your business, and the drive to succeed—chances are you will.

Appendix A
One Day at a Time: Basics of the Publishing Process

So you've got a great idea for a book. You know in your heart you've got a winner. Now you just need to realize the dream. But where do you start? No matter how much time you spend deciphering the ins and outs of book publishing, you can expect essentially the same basic steps to apply to the process:

▲

- *Market research.* Take the time to make sure you have a saleable product. After all, the book business is a BUSINESS, which means you need to make money to survive. Spend time both online and in the bookstore researching similar, competitive titles. If you choose to shell out the money for it, this is the right time in your process to access Nielsen Bookscan and find out the most detailed sales information on your competitors.

- *Create a P&L.* A profit/loss statement is an essential tool in figuring your production and printing costs in relation to estimated income for the book.

- *Hire an author.* Most of the time, you will already have an author in mind (particularly if the book concept is one being shopped TO you), but this is the point at which you solidify your potential scribes so that you may prepare to extend an offer. Or perhaps the author is you.

- *Extend a verbal offer and negotiate author's contract.* At this point, you will not only be negotiating money, but other essential elements of the author contract like due dates, payment dates, marketing responsibilities, author copies and discount, and subsidiary rights (like audio, script, etc.). Don't ignore the contract phase if you are the author—if you ever decide to sell, you will want some of the contract already in writing.

- *Execute contract.* All parties involved should receive an electronic or paper draft of the contract for final review. Many authors (and rightfully so) will want to have an agent or lawyer look over the legalese before signing their skills away, so be prepared to wait a few days and possibly to make edits to the document. Once everyone is in agreement, have them sign and date the final document, send copies for their records, and file the originals in your office. If an initial payment is due to the author, send it now.

- *Wait, wait, wait.* This is the hardest part for some publishers—to wait for the final manuscript. The writing process usually (hopefully) lasts only a few months, so be patient. It can be a good idea to arrange some interim due dates with your author to keep him on track and to be sure you are getting the manuscript you want, being mindful not to micromanage. If you do find that your author is not performing up to professional standards, you have options like extending the due date or termination of the contract. You DID specify nonperformance options in the contract, right?

- *Request ISBN, LCCN, and CIP.* Log onto www.isbn.org and www.loc.gov to find out more about the process. Note that obtaining CIP information from the Library of Congress can take up to two weeks, so be sure to send in the appropriate information with enough lead time. Keep in mind that the Library of Congress does not typically provide CIP for single, self-published works, so make sure your book is eligible.

- *Premarketing.* What? I have to sell my book before it's actually a book? You bet—and in the book trade, advanced marketing is truly the key to your sales success. For example, if you want your book reviewed by industry publications like *Publishers Weekly*, you must send pages about three months prior to the book's publication. This is the time to create and send advance press releases, send manuscript pages to publications for review, start doing the legwork for setting up author interviews, planning author appearances, and requesting advanced praise for the back cover copy. You will find that the time goes quickly, so don't burn daylight—get marketing!

- *Check availability of freelancers.* While the author (or you, if you're the one with your fingers on the laptop keys) is writing, now is the time to assemble your design team. You will need an editor (again, you, if you've got the skills), a cover designer, an interior designer, copyeditor or proofreader, and indexer. Many book designers offer multiple services, so shop around. If you are planning to hire freelancers you haven't worked with yet, be sure to check references and get plenty of samples of their work. And always use a contract that allows you to get your money back if you are not satisfied with the work or if important deadlines are missed.

- *Acceptance of manuscript.* If someone else is writing the manuscript, your contract should specify that you, as publisher, have a specific amount of time to either accept the manuscript as-is or request changes if the end product is far from your expectations. Thirty days is a typical amount of time for most publishers to accept a manuscript. This is typically the point where a publisher will make final payment to the author.

- *Manuscript edit.* This is your chance, as publisher, to mold the original manuscript into your ideal book. Ideally, there should be three rounds of editing: a substantive edit in which you consider the "big picture" and move chunks of text around and arrange chapters; a line edit in which you fix grammar, spelling, and clarity; and a copyedit in which you dot all the "i"s and cross all the "t"s.

- *Interior design.* Once the text is the way you want it, it's time for the interior designer to get to work. Trust your designer to create a look and feel of design elements that will complement your text. You will want to try out two to three different designs before deciding on one. Most designers will create some examples and allow one to two rounds of changes prior to your final decision.

- *Cover design.* Like interior designers, your cover designer will create examples based on the concept of the book for you to peruse and will allow a certain number of "rounds" in your selection process.

- *Author review.* Once the interior is designed, allow your author to view the pages and make any necessary editorial changes. The key word here is "necessary."

Some authors have a nasty habit of trying to do an editor's or designer's job (or, better yet, thinking they know more than the pros), so be sure your author knows what you expect of him. Your author should be looking for factual errors and any major boo-boos that stand out or were missed by the copyeditor. We are, after all, human.

- *Indexing.* When all editorial and design changes have been made and you are absolutely sure the pages are complete, it's time to send them off to the indexer. This is a job that you should not attempt yourself unless you are trained to do so. Indexing is time-consuming, to say the least, so it pays to pay a professional. Turnaround time is usually about one to two weeks.

- *Send to printer.* The pages are designed and indexed, the cover is gorgeous, and you've backed up all files. Now, send your baby to "bed."

- *Digital prints/proofs.* A few weeks after you send files to the printer, you will receive digital prints, what used to be referred to as "bluelines," or "blues." These are unbound, untrimmed proofs of what your pages and cover will look like. This is your absolute, final chance to make any changes. At this point, you should only change items that MUST be fixed, like typos, incorrect page numbers, etc. Before you mark up your digital prints, though, know what your printer charges for changes. Some printers charge per page changed, and the cost can be as high as $100 per change. Other printers include a set amount of changes in your printing price. Be sure to ask. Most printers request that you turn around digital proofs in one to two days in order to keep your book in the printing queue. If your book is about graphic design, or somehow the cover is key to the book's topic, consider doing a "press check" and approve where you can see the actual colors on press.

- *BBD.* The bound book date, or BBD, is the date you have books in hand, available to sell.

Appendix B
The Grass Is Greener: Tips and Tricks for Great Grassroots Marketing

Most small and self-publishers don't have million-dollar marketing budgets. Most publishers regardless of size, in fact, are on a fairly tight budget when it comes to spreading the word about their books. There are only so many hours a day and inches of copy that media outlets can devote to shameless self-promotion, which makes the competition tighter than Scrooge's wallet. Here are some tips to help you develop a strong grassroots marketing network.

- *Think locally*. For now, at least, put your dreams of *The New York Times* "Bestseller List" aside and work on making your book a hit on the local scene. Think of the process as a ripple effect. Success in your town breeds success in the neighboring town, then the next town, then the state, and so on. Focus on making lasting (i.e., for more than the release of your first book) relationships with the local media. In other words, do more than send out a press release. Get to know reporters, radio and TV personalities, and local bookstore owners on a personal level. Join a local organization like Rotary or Lions Club—you'll be surprised how the power of networking can spread the word about your book.

- *Make your book a component of a bigger news story*. It's all fine and dandy to send out a press release announcing the release of your latest book, but . . . zzzzzzz. Bor-ing! News people want NEWS, so give it to them. Focus your release on a timely event or current issue, then quote the author or yourself (as publisher) as an expert, citing the recently released book. For example, say you have a new book about the history of women's colleges. You do your homework and find a newly released report that proves graduates of women's colleges earn more money and secure higher-ranking jobs. There's your release! Lead with the report and include quotes from the author about the importance of women's colleges. You've practically done the reporter's job for him.

- *Put your holiday greeting card list on steroids*. Beef it up! Create a database of everyone—and we mean EVERYONE—you know, from relatives to passing acquaintances to the people who work at your favorite coffee joint. Then, use the list for good. Send postcard announcements of a book's release, host a book reception, invite them to events. Most people will find they know more people than they think. And those people know people . . . and so it goes.

- *Get yourself some loyal fans, because they get results*. It pays to have friends and relatives beat the drums on your book's behalf by hounding their local booksellers to stock the book. Some discretion is necessary on their part, though. They don't need to explain that they are your third cousin on your mom's side twice-removed and they're just trying to help you out. They simply need to go in and ask about the book and tell the fine folks at the bookstore that they are looking forward to its release, as are their 100 best friends.

- *Think outside the bookstore and consider unconventional sales venues*. Most local businesses will agree to put a few copies of your book near the cash registers, even if books aren't their main source of revenue. Does your town have a local farmers' market or flea market? Look into scoring some booth space. What about any conventions or festivals nearby? Find out how you can get in the door. And bring that trusty friend database back into play by calling in some favors with local businesspeople. Local libraries and places of worship often offer seminars and workshops, so find out how you can help out and do some cross-promotion at the same time.

- *Speaking of seminars, start offering them to your adoring public.* If you are a professional with a new book, you have at minimum ten different seminars in you. Create a brochure or prospectus-style booklet that details all of the workshops you offer. Distribute them to churches, colleges and universities, libraries, local civic clubs, the YMCA and YWCA . . . anyplace you can get a room filled with people. Many colleges and universities offer non-credit classes and are actively looking for people to teach them. All of these events offer ample opportunity to sell your books at the back of the room.

- *Don't ignore social media.* Start a Facebook page for your book or use your existing personal Facebook page to post updates about your book's progress, sales, great publicity. If your book's topic is appropriate for it, start a blog—and post it to your Facebook page. Get a Twitter account and post occasional but regular Tweets. Add your book's publication to your LinkedIn page. You need to toot your own horn and social media is a great place to do it.

These are just a few ideas to kick-start your grassroots marketing efforts. Spend some time having your own personal "blue sky" meeting and brainstorm every crazy marketing idea you can conjure. Even if you walk away with ten feasible ideas out of the 100 you started with, that's ten great ideas you didn't have before!

Appendix C
Self-Publishing Business Resources

The ultimate jackpot for the savvy, successful self-publisher is a wealth of resources—a publisher's clearinghouse of places to go and people to contact for information on everything from book fairs to wholesalers. We've compiled a list of resources to help get you started on your own personal information blitz.

▲

These resources are a starting place. They are by no means the only sources out there, and they should not be taken as the "Ultimate Answer." We've done our research, but businesses—like people—do tend to move, change, fold, and expand. So as we've repeatedly stressed, do your homework. Get out and start investigating. Don't be afraid to ask questions. You'll be amazed at how much you'll learn!

As an additional tidbit to get you going, we strongly suggest the following: If you haven't yet joined the Internet Age, do it! Surfing the net is like waltzing through a vast library, with a breathtaking array of resources literally at your fingertips.

ABI Forms

R.R. Bowker, 630 Central Ave., New Providence, NJ 07974, (888) 269-5372, www. bowkerlink.com (Click on "Bowker Link" under the "Data Services" drop-down menu.)

Associations

Association for Postal Commerce (Post Com),1421 Prince St., Ste. 410, Alexandria, VA 22314-2808, (703) 524-0096, www.postcom.org

American Booksellers Association, 200 White Plains Rd., Tarrytown, NY 10591, (800) 637-0037, (914) 591-2665, email: info@bookweb.org, www.bookweb.org

American Library Association, 50 E. Huron St., Chicago, IL 60611, (800) 545-2433, www.ala.org

Association of Science Fiction and Fantasy Artists, P.O. Box 65011, Phoenix, AZ 85082-5011, www.asfa-art.org

The Direct Marketing Association (DMA), 1120 Avenue of the Americas, New York, NY 10036, (212) 768-7277, www.the-dma.org

Graphic Artists Guild, 32 Broadway, Suite 1114, New York, NY 10004, (212) 791-3400, www.graphicartistsguild.org

Independent Book Publishers Association (formerly PMA), 627 Aviation Wy., Manhattan Beach, CA 90266, (310) 372-2732, ibpa-online.org

National Association of Independent Publishers Representatives (NAIPR), PMB 157, 111 E. 14th St., Zekendorf Towers, NY, NY 10003, www.naipr.org

National Mail Order Association, 2807 Polk St. NE, Minneapolis, MN 55418-2954, (612) 788-1673, www.nmoa.org.

National Speakers Association, 1500 S. Priest Dr., Tempe, AZ 85281, (480) 968-2552, www.nsaspeaker.org (This is the place to go if you're planning on doing paid seminars.)

Small Publishers, Artists and Writers Network (SPAWN), PMB 123, 323 E. Matilija St., Suite 110, Ojai, CA 93023, (818) 886-4281, www.spawn.org

Small Publishers Association of North America (SPAN), 1618 W. Colorado Ave., Colorado Springs, CO 80904, (719) 475-1726, email: span@SPANnet.org, www.spannet.org

Society of Children's Book Writers and Illustrators, 8271 Beverly Blvd., Los Angeles, CA 90048, www.scbwi.org

Book Clubs

Book of the Month Club, c/o Bookspan, 15 East 26th, 4th Floor, New York, NY 10010, www.bomclub.com

The Literary Guild, www.literaryguild.com

Quality Paperback Book Club, www.qpb.com

Note: These are the biggies, but there are hundreds of book clubs to choose from—some are imprints of venerable Bookspan, while others are stand-alones. Check them all out via the *Literary Marketplace* at www.literarymarketplace.com.

Book Designers and Cover Artists

Dunn + Associates Design, Kathi Dunn, P.O. Box 870, Hayward, WI 54843-0870, (715) 634-4857, www.dunn-design.com

Knockout Design, Peri Poloni-Gabriel, 5304 Velvet Bent Ct., Naperville, IL 60564, (630) 718-0861, www.knockoutbooks.com

Opus 1 Design, Pam Terry, Owner/Senior Designer, P.O. Box 3653, Beverly Hills, CA 90035, (800) 590-7778, (323) 935-6666, www.opus1design.com

Book Expos and Fairs

Book Expo America (BEA), 383 Main Ave., Norwalk, CT 06851, (800) 840-5614, www.bookexpoamerica.com

▲

The Center for The Book (book fairs and other literary events), Library of Congress, www.read.gov/cfb/

Frankfurt (Germany) Book Fair, www.frankfurt-book-fair.com

Reed Exhibition Companies (handles four foreign book fairs as well as Book Expo America), www.reedexpo.com

Bookland Bar Codes

Bar Code Graphics Inc., 875 N. Michigan Ave. #2650, Chicago, IL 60611, (800) 662-0701, www.barcode-us.com

General Graphics, P.O. Box 3192, Arnold, PA 15068-0092, (800) 887-5894, www.ggbarcode.com

Book Printers

Bang Printing, 3323 Oak St., Brainerd, MN 56401, (800) 328-0450, (218) 829-2877, www.bangprinting.com

Central Plains Book Manufacturing, P.O. Box 648, Arkansas City, KS 67005, (877) 278-2726, www.centralplainsbook.com

Data Reproductions Corporation, 4545 Glenmeade Ln., Auburn Hills, MI 48326, (800) 242-3114, (248) 371-3700, www.datarepro.com

Hignell Book Printing, 488 Burnell St., Winnipeg, MB R3G 2B4, CAN, (800) 304-5553, (204) 784-1030, www.hignell.mb.ca

McNaughton & Gunn, 960 Woodland Dr., Saline, MI 48176, (734) 429-5411, www.mcnaughton-gunn.com

Thomson-Shore Inc., 7300 W. Joy Rd., Dexter, MI 48130, (734) 426-3939, www.thomsonshore.com

Books

The Complete Guide to Self-Publishing, by Marilyn Ross and Sue Collier, F&W Publications Inc. (Cincinnati, OH)

The Entrepreneur Next Door, by Bill Wagner (Irvine, CA: Entrepreneur Press, 2006)

The Fine Print of Self-Publishing: The Contracts & Services of 48 Self-Publishing Companies—Analyzed, Ranked, and Exposed, by Mark Levine, Bascom Hill Publishing Group (Minneapolis, MN: 2011)

Guerrilla Marketing for Writers: 100 Weapons to Help Sell Your Work, by Jay Conrad Levinson, Writer's Digest Books (Cincinnati, OH: 2000)

Jump-Start Your Book Sales: A Money-Making Guide for Authors, Independent Publishers and Small Presses, by Marilyn and Tom Ross, Writer's Digest Books (Cincinnati, OH: 2000)

Literary Marketplace, R.R. Bowker, www.literarymarketplace.com

Print-on-Demand Book Publishing: A New Approach to Printing and Marketing Books for Publishers and Self-Publishing Authors, by Morris Rosenthal, Foner Books (2008)

The Self-Publishing Manual: How to Write, Print and Sell Your Own Book, by Dan Poynter, Para Publishing (Santa Barbara, CA: 2007)

Ultimate Guide to Direct Marketing, by Al Lautenslager, Entrepreneur Press (Irvine, CA: 2005)

Consultants

About Books Inc., 1618 W. Colorado Ave., Colorado Springs, CO 80904, (719) 632-8226, www.about-books.com

Mary Embree, email: maryembree@gmail.com

Para Publishing, Dan Poynter, Box 8206-240, Santa Barbara, CA 93118-8206, (805) 968-7277, www.parapublishing.com

Copyeditors and Proofreaders

Archer Editorial Services, Laura Poole, Senior Editor, 112 Blue Ridge Ct., Durham, NC 27703, (919) 596-7047, www.archereditorial.com

Bibliotechnica, 119 Middle St., Hadley, MA 01035, (413) 586-4267, www.bibliotechnica.com

Quinn's Word for Word Brainstorm Editorial Services, 10573 W. Pico Blvd., #345, Los Angeles, CA 90064, (310) 838-7098, www.writingandediting.biz

▲

Distributors

Consortium Book Sales & Distribution, 34 13th Ave. N.E., Suite 101, Minneapolis, MN 55413, (612) 746-2600, www.cbsd. com

Independent Publishers Group (IPG), 814 N. Franklin St., Chicago, IL 60610, (312) 337-0747 (trade or publisher inquiries), www.ipgbook.com

Partners Publishers Group, 2325 Jarco Dr., P.O. Box 580, Holt, MI 48842, (517) 694-3205, www.partnerspublishersgroup.com

Publishers Group West, 1700 Fourth St., Berkeley, CA 94710, (510) 809-3700, www.pgw.com

Quality Books, 1003 W. Pines Rd., Oregon, IL 61061, (800) 323-4241, www. quality-books.com

Unique Books, 5010 Kemper Ave, St. Louis, MO 63139, (800) 533-5446, www. unique booksinc.com

e-Publishers

Bookface Technologies, www.bookface.com

Booklocker, www.booklocker.com

eBook Shoppe, www.ebookshoppe.com

Helpful Government Agencies

Bureau of the Census, www.census.gov

Federal Trade Commission, www.ftc.gov

Library of Congress, www.loc.gov (For ISSNs, LCCNs, CIP data blocks and other Library of Congress services, click on "Resources for Publishers.")

Patent and Trademark Office, (800) 786-9199, (571) 272-1000, www.uspto.gov

U.S. Copyright Office, (202) 707-3000, www.copyright.gov

U.S. Postal Service, (800) 843-8777, www.usps.com

ISBN and SAN Provider

R.R. Bowker, www.bowker.com (click on "Bowker Publisher Services") or www. isbn.org

Magazines and Publications

ALA Booklist, 50 E. Huron St., Chicago, IL 60611, (800) 545-2433, www.ala.org

BookWire (an e-zine from R.R. Bowker, the people who bring you *Books in Print*, ISBNs, and other publishers' tools), www.bookwire.com

Choice, 100 Riverview Center, Suite 298, Middletown, CT 06457, (860) 347-6933, www.ala.org/acrl/choice/home.html

ForeWord Reviews,425 Boardman Ave, Suite B, Traverse City, MI 49684, (231) 933-3699, www.forewordreviews.com

Library Journal, 160 Varick St., 11th Fl., New York, NY 10013, (212) 380-0700, www.libraryjournal.com

Publishers Weekly, 71 West 23rd St., #1608, New York, NY 10010, (212) 377-5500, www.publishersweekly.com

Sharing Ideas, 9420 Reseda Dr., Suite 610, Northridge, CA 91324, (818) 788-5460, www.sharingideas.com

Speaker, National Speakers Association, 1500 S. Priest Dr., Tempe, AZ 85281, (480) 968-2552, www.nsaspeaker.org

Target Marketing, North American Publishing Company, 1500 Spring Garden Street, 12th Floor, Philadelphia, PA 19130, (215) 238-5300, www.targetmarketingmag.com

Writer's Digest, 4700 E. Galbraith Rd., Cincinnati, OH 45236, (513) 531-2690, www.writersdigest.com

Note: Most magazines will send a sample issue free of charge if you call and ask. So do it!

Mailing Lists

ALC, 4300 Route 1, CN-5219, Princeton, NJ 08543, (800) ALC-LIST, www.alc.com

Allmedia Inc., 5601 Democracy Dr., Suite 255, Plano, TX 75024, (469) 467-9100, www.allmediainc.com

Info USA, (800) 321-0869, www.infousa.com

Note: Check into any issue of magazines like *Catalog Age* or *Target Marketing*—advertisements for list brokers, managers, and owners abound.

Merchant Card Services

1st American Card Service.com, www.1stamericancardservice.com

Merchant Express, 20 Trafalgar Square, Suite 466, Nashua, NH 03063, (888) 845-9457, www.merchantexpress.com

Print On Demand

CreateSpace, www.createspace.com

iUniverse.com, www.iuniverse.com

Lightning Source, 1246 Heil Quaker Blvd., La Vergne, TN 37086, (615) 213-5815, www.lightningsource.com

Lulu, www.lulu.com

PubIt, www.barnesandnoble.com

Trafford Publishing, 1663 Liberty Dr., Bloomington, IN 47403, (888) 232-4444, www.trafford.com

Xlibris, 1663 Liberty Dr., Bloomington, IN 47403, (888) 795-4274, www.xlibris.com

Shipping Supplies

Anchor Box Co., 5889 S. Gessner Rd., Houston, TX 77036, (713) 977-3100, www.anchorbox.com

Associated Bag Company, 400 W. Boden St., Milwaukee, WI 53207-0120, (800) 926-6100, www.associatedbag.com

Software for Publishers

Adobe InDesign, Adobe Systems Inc., www.adobe.com

Quark Xpress, Quark, www.quark.com

PUB123, Adams-Blake Publishing, 8041 Sierra St., #102, Fair Oaks, CA 95628, (916) 962-9296, www.jaya123.com

Publishers' Assistant, 41 Lawrence Heights, Jericho, VT 05465, (800) 310-8716, www.pubassist.com

Publishing Manager, Trilogy Group, www.trilogypublishing.com

Publishing Solutions, 400 W. Cummings Park, Woburn, MA 01801, (617) 274-9001, www.publishingsolutionsgroup.com

Wholesalers

Baker & Taylor, 2550 West Tyvola Rd., Suite 300, Charlotte, NC 28217, (800) 775-1800, (704) 998-3100, www.btol.com

Ingram Book Company, One Ingram Blvd., La Vergne, TN 37086, (615) 793-5000, www.ingrambook.com

National Book Network, 4501 Forbes Blvd., Suite 200, Lanham, MD 20706, (301) 459-3366, www.nbnbooks.com

New Leaf, 401 Thornton Rd., Lithia Springs, GA 30122, (770) 948-7845, www.newleaf-dist.com

Workshops and Seminars

Independent Book Publishers Association, 1020 Manhattan Beach Blvd., Suite 204, Manhattan Beach, CA 90266, (310) 546-1818, www.pma-online.org

Small Publishers, Artists and Writers Network (SPAWN), 323 E. Matilija St., Suite 110, Ojai, CA 93023, (818) 886-4281, www.spawn.org

Small Publishers Association of North America (SPAN), 1618 West Colorado Ave., Colorado Springs, CO 80904, (719) 475-1726, www.spannet.org

Glossary

ABA: American Booksellers Association.

Acquisition editor: a publishing company editor who scouts out potential new acquisitions.

Back matter: all pages in a book after the main body of text.

Back-of-the-room sales: *see* BOR.

Bleed: the area of a page that will be lost when a book is bound.

Bluelines: page proofs printed on white paper with blue ink.

Bookland EAN: bar code for books.

BOR: back-of-the-room sales; books and/or other merchandise that are sold by seminar professionals at a seminar or workshop.

Bound galley: a perfect-bound set of galleys.

C1S: cover coated on one side; a type of paper stock used for softcover books.

Camera ready: ready to be photographed and printed.

Case bound: hardcover.

Cataloging in Publication record: *see* CIP.

▲

CIP: Cataloging in Publication record; a block of information helpful to librarians that includes a book's shelf category and catalog numbers.

Color separation: printing technique in which color artwork is photographed and separated into four different-colored layers of film.

Comb binding: a type of plastic binding.

Content editor: *see* copyeditor.

Copy: text; written material in a manuscript.

Copyeditor: editor who evaluates manuscripts in terms of content, style, and continuity.

Custom publishing: tailoring a book for a specific customer.

Dead tree book: slang term meaning conventionally printed book as opposed to an e-published book.

Direct mail: mail order.

Dump: a cardboard display stand.

e-Book reader: hardware device for reading downloadable books.

F&Gs: folded and gathered signature pages of a book.

Fiction: a tale invented for the purpose of entertainment.

First serial rights: serial rights sold before the publication date.

Folio: page number.

Font: type style.

Foreign rights: the rights to publish a book in a foreign English-speaking country.

Four-color: printing process that utilizes blue, yellow, red, and black to produce all the colors in the spectrum.

Front matter: all pages before the main body of text.

Fulfillment: filling orders for books or merchandise and shipping them to customers.

Galleys: page proofs from the printer—the final copy before a print run.

Ghostwriter: writer who pens a book for someone else to put his name to as author.

Gloss lamination: a glossy film applied to printed cover stock for protection from fingerprints, smudges, and moisture.

Half title page: the first standard page in a book; contains the title and subtitle only.

Halftone: artwork that has been photographed through a fine screen to break the image tones into dots to increase sharpness and clarity when printed.

HTML: hypertext markup language; a language used to put up and edit website content.

Imprint: the identifying name of a publishing company under a parent company.

Independent publisher: a small publisher who may produce his own work and/or those of other authors.

International Standard Book Number: *see* ISBN.

International Standard Serial Number: *see* ISSN.

ISBN: International Standard Book Number; assigned by publishers and used to identify a book by edition, binding, and publisher.

ISSN: International Standard Serial Number; assigned by the Library of Congress to identify serials.

Lay-flat laminate: a type of cover stock protective film that won't curl up when exposed to humidity.

LCCN: Library of Congress Catalog Card Number; used by librarians to identify and order books.

Leading: the space between lines of text, measured from the bottom of one line to the bottom of the next.

Library binding: a heavy-duty binding designed for repeated readings.

Library of Congress Catalog Card Number: see LCCN.

Listserv: email message-sharing group.

Major head: headline that defines the topic of a section in a book.

Mass market paperback: a paperback book with a trim size of 4.5 inches by 6.75 inches; the size of paperbacks commonly found in supermarket and drugstore racks.

Match print: color proof used by the press operator in calibrating final output.

Matte lamination: a non-glossy film coating for cover stock for protection from fingerprints, smudges, and moisture.

NAIP: National Association of Independent Publishers.

Nonfiction: fact-based book.

North American rights: the rights to sell a book in the United States and Canada.

▲

OEB: open e-book language; used to produce some e-book content.

Overs and unders: a margin over or under the number of books a printer has been commissioned to print. The industry standard is 10 percent but can be as low as 5.

Overruns: extra copies of a book's cover.

Page proofs: final, before-printing copy of a book provided by a printer for error checking.

Pantone Matching System: *see* PMS.

P-book: conventionally printed book as opposed to an electronically published book.

P-CIP: CIP made up by a publisher or its agent instead of by the Library of Congress.

PCN: Pre-assigned Card Number; what the Library of Congress calls an LCCN until the book is printed.

PDF: Portable document format.

Perfect binding: softcover bookbinding in which the cover is glued onto the book block.

Periodical: magazine or journal.

PMS: Pantone Matching System; a standard set of ink color formulas used by printers.

POD: print on demand; the process of printing a book one complete unit at a time on a digital press instead of by 16- or 32-page signatures on an offset press.

Point-of-purchase display: *see* dump.

POP: *see* point-of-purchase display.

Pre-assigned Card Number: *see* PCN.

Premium: a book or other merchandise given away by a company or organization for promotional purposes.

Print on demand: *see* POD.

Proofreader: evaluates a manuscript for correct spelling, punctuation, and grammar.

Publication date: a hypothetical book premiere date set by a publisher, generally six weeks to two months after the book is delivered by the printer; also called "pub date."

Pull quote: an interesting phrase or sentence from your text that is "pulled" and reprinted elsewhere on the page.

Recto: right-hand page.

Reprint: another printing of a book.

Request for quote: *see* RFQ.

Revised edition: another printing of a book in which significant changes have been made.

RFQ: request for quote or bid from a printer.

Running head: book or title chapter that runs across the top of each page of a book.

Saddle-stitch binding: bookbinding achieved by stapling through the center of the pages of a book.

SAN: Standard Address Number; used to identify industry entities and give billing and shipping information.

Second serial rights: rights sold after the publication date.

Serial: ongoing or frequently revised publication such as a magazine, newspaper, annual, or directory.

Sidebar: mini-articles that are one-quarter page to one-half page in length; inserted on the page to complement the text.

Signature: a huge sheet of paper used by book printers on which 16 or 32 pages are laid out and run through the press at once.

Small press: *see* independent publisher.

SPAN: Small Publishers Association of North America.

SPAWN: Small Publishers, Artists, and Writers Network.

Special Standard Mail: book rate postage; less expensive than regular postage; also referred to as "media mail."

Spiral binding: a type of wire binding.

Standard Address Number: *see* SAN.

Stock: paper.

Subhead: headline smaller than a major head that defines a subtopic within a book section.

Subsidiary rights: the rights to publish a book in various other forms.

Subsidy publisher: a company that charges money to publish an author's book; also called "vanity publisher."

Tip box: one-sentence to one-paragraph factoids that can be scattered throughout your text to add information or interest.

Trade paperback: larger or "quality" format softcover book, generally 6 inches by 9 inches to 5.5 inches by 8.5 inches.

Translation rights: the rights to translate a book into a foreign language.

Trim size: outside dimensions of a book.

Vanity publisher: *see* subsidy publisher.

Velo binding: a type of plastic binding.

Verso: left-hand page.

Work for hire: a method of payment for writing; the writer is paid a flat fee instead of royalties.

Index